Telluride Trails

Telluride Trails

Hiking Passes, Loops, and
Summits of Southwest Colorado

Covering most of the trails and
more than seventy-five summits near
Telluride in Southwest Colorado

Don J. Scarmuzzi

WESTWINDS
PRESS®

THE PRUETT SERIES

Text and photographs © 2013 by Don Scarmuzzi

Library of Congress Cataloging-in-Publication Data

Scarmuzzi, Don, author.
    Telluride trails : hiking passes, loops, and summits of southwest Colorado : covering most of the trails and more than seventy-five summits near Telluride in southwest Colorado / Don Scarmuzzi.
        pages cm. — (The Pruett series)
    Includes index.
    ISBN 978-0-87108-971-7 (pbk.)
    ISBN 978-0-87108-997-7 (e-book)
    ISBN 978-0-87108-304-3 (hardbound)
        1. Hiking —Colorado —Telluride Region —Guidebooks. 2. Telluride Region (Colorado) —Guidebooks. I. Title.
    GV199.42.C62T457 2013
    796.5109788 —dc23
                        2013022978

Designer: Vicki Knapton
Editor: Mindy Fitch

Cover photo top right: Choking on wildflowers in Waterfall Canyon above Ophir! Cover bottom: Pilot Knob, V-4, US Grant, and Island Lake from V-2

WestWinds Press®
An imprint of

GRAPHIC ARTS
BOOKS®

P.O. Box 56118
Portland, OR 97238-6118
(503) 254-5591
www.graphicartsbooks.com

Dedicated to the memory of Andy Sawyer,
who took so many to great heights in
mind, body, and spirit.

Contents

Preface

Four distinct waterfalls are visible or nearly visible from the town of Telluride, Colorado, and many more can be found near the high basins and peaks surrounding this spectacular region of the Rocky Mountains. Dozens of the 110 hikes presented in this guide begin right from downtown Telluride, while others branch out from the mountain roads nearby, and some are located closer to Durango, Silverton, Ouray, Ridgway, Montrose, Ophir, Rico, Dolores, and Cortez.

Each hike begins with essential information such as elevation, distance, duration, and difficulty level. Elevation information includes not only the highest point (or points) of a hike but also the maximum vertical gains you will experience along the trail. Difficulty levels range from "easiest" (no elevation change) to "moderate" (short hike, easy grades), "strenuous" (typical to moderate hike, hills), "very challenging" (longer hike, steeper, with varying mountain conditions), and "expert-only" (very steep, often with exposed ridge walking and loose scree, requiring climbing-type moves). Most of the hikes fall somewhere in the middle, and all hikes but those rated "very challenging" or "expert-only" will be achievable for most people. Climbing ropes, pitons, or anchor bolts are not mandatory to complete any of the hikes listed here, though that may not be the case for everyone—see difficulty levels for each hike for recommendations. You certainly won't hear me use terms like underclings, stemming, laybacks, jams, or evangelical hammerlocks!

More than half of these trails can be hiked as a loop, and I provide alternate routes (**Alt**) and optional paths (**Opt**) wherever possible. The routes described for each hike may be well-worn trails, complete bushwhacks and scrambles, or anything in between. There is something here for practically everyone, whether you would rather simply cut to the chase, as it were, and get on with something more challenging, or prefer a more leisurely stroll through the aspens, evergreens, and basins without going to a summit or having to use any climbing-type moves. You'll find detailed instructions to locating seventy-five peaks and other high points, including many mountain passes and vistas.

Many trails can be traveled by mountain bike, and others may require some four-wheel driving (4WD). You'll find 🚲 or 4WD at the beginning of each chapter. (I have even included one route—Galloping Goose Trail to Lizard

Head Pass, hike 77—that requires a bike. It is such a beautiful and classic ride, I just couldn't help myself.)

I try to keep hiking lingo simple. "Trailhead" is abbreviated as "TH." A switchback is a spot in a trail that zigzags sharply, whether once or fifty times. A shoulder is a rise or small ridge. Exposure refers to the level of risk of falling where a fall would be fatal. A trail section described as "airy" is exposed to some degree, with drop-offs. Exercise extreme caution in such areas.

Aspen line is around 11,800 feet, and tree line is around 12,200 feet in this region. I usually find that the first 20 to 30 minutes of practically any hike can be the toughest until I get into a groove with my breathing and walking. High altitude affects everybody differently, so if you feel dehydrated, headachy, or nauseous, move to a lower altitude. (Some people might even experience altitude sickness while still in Telluride, at 8745 feet.) Mountain hazards (rapidly changing weather, rock slides) and the unexpected almost always come into play, so don't count on apps from your phone to save you in the wilderness!

With so much wildlife around, don't forget to watch out for the blood burglars, including ticks and to a lesser degree mosquitoes. Luckily you probably will not run across the tiny deer ticks that cause Lyme disease, but a larger species, the Rocky Mountain wood tick, is plentiful from spring through June and should be avoided. These ticks thrive in low grass and brush in the high country—a tick check, or self-examination, during and after spring hikes is a good idea. If a tick has latched on or is slightly embedded in your skin, pull it straight out with tweezers or hold a lighter flame close until it falls away. However, tick warning aside, you would be worse off if you forgot your sunscreen or enough water on a warm bluebird day.

All right, enough talk. It's go time! You can hike the mountains in Southwest Colorado year-round if you know what you are doing and have the proper gear, but the ideal time to hike or mountain bike is late June through mid-October. All you need is a nice pair of hiking shoes, a backpack with plenty of supplies, water, phone, camera, GPS, MP3 player, pedometer, more electric junk you never used to need but now can't get by without—and the day to unfold before your very eyes, just one foot in front of the other.

Four Corners

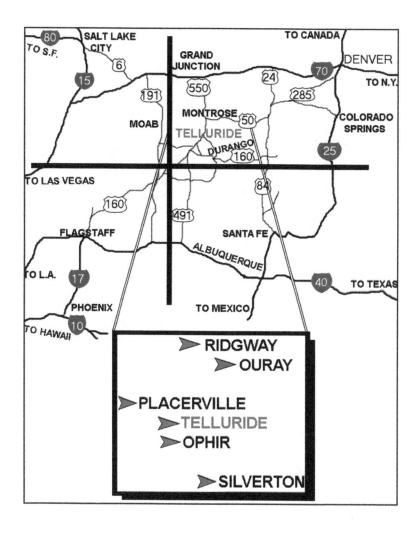

Telluride

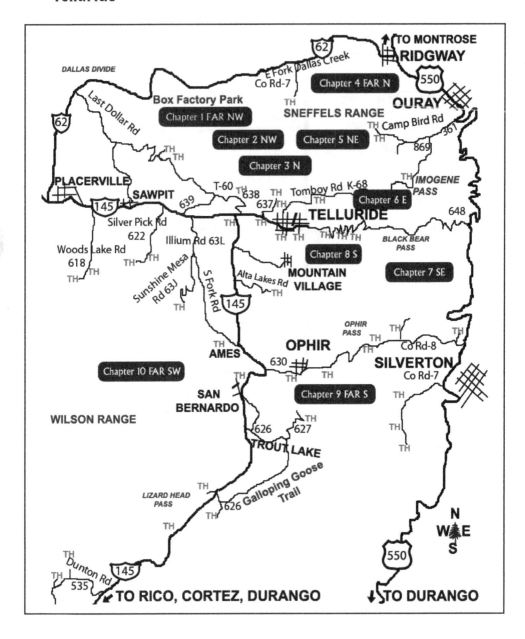

CHAPTER 1

FAR NORTHWEST TELLURIDE

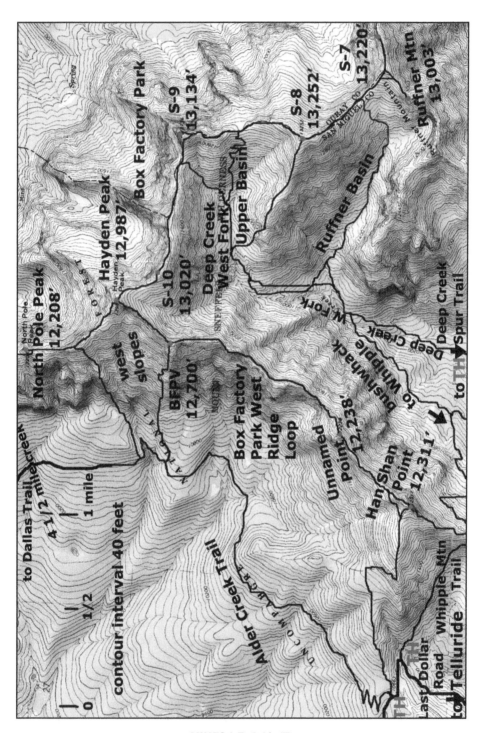

HIKES 1-5, 9-14, 17

1   Alder Creek Trail 510

Elevation: 10,663 feet at the TH, with about 300 feet loss

Distance: 4½ miles one way to the creek W of North Pole Peak,
9 miles round-trip

Duration: 2 hours each way, 4 hours round-trip

Difficulty: Strenuous. Long, easy grade. Bring the dog and kids

TRAILHEAD

There is ample parking on top of Last Dollar Road FS 638 or NE at the nearby TH following the signs.

• **Opt 1:** Drive 40 minutes and 13 miles max to the TH, including 10 minutes W down valley from Telluride on CO-145. Turn right (N) onto Deep Creek Road across from the maintenance igloo at the 75-mile marker. Go up the dirt road 2½ miles to the end and turn left (SW) onto Last Dollar Road FS 638 for almost 6 miles. Last Dollar Road FS 638 is narrow and steep, with scree at times; 2WD high-clearance vehicle needed for much of the distance, into 4WD perhaps the last mile of the road. There may also be puddles of surprisingly deep standing water.

• **Opt 2**: From Telluride, access the Airport Road/Last Dollar Road FS 638, which is less than ¼ mile E of Society Turn and 3 miles W of town on CO-145 Spur to the right (N). Go right again in 2 miles to stay on Last Dollar Road FS 638 for 8 miles more to the top ("T-60" sign) of the dirt road. Drive down N to a big curve going left (W) over a bridge, then past the intersection with Deep Creek Road on the left (S). Continue NW along a steeper section of road and possibly into 4WD to the top (10,663 feet).

Both **Opts** take you to the top of Last Dollar Road FS 638 in about the same amount of time from Telluride. People coming from down valley should take **Opt 1** (Deep Creek Road); those coming from Montrose, Ridgway, or Ouray could take Last Dollar Road FS 638 from its other end. This **Opt 3** is less than a mile W of Dallas Divide off of CO-62, 12 miles from Ridgway. It's another beautiful part of the road, not to be missed! And also could be rough for 4WD depending on the weather. Follow the signage less than 10 miles S to the top at the Alder Creek TH.

NOTES

A great trail for solitude. Drive to the top of the rough, steep Last Dollar Road and hike where few people do. The easy-sloping path drops only a few hundred

Top of Last Dollar Road to Han Shan.

feet and eventually turns into the Dallas Trail past the creek where you turn around W of North Pole Peak. Unless you are going to the high peaks or continuing down the Dallas Trail, this is most likely a one-way trip. Dallas Trail is a horse trail that shares part of the Blaine Basin Trail and goes several more miles to FS Road 851 near Ouray. Come back SSW the same way whenever you wish on the Alder Creek Trail or at the 4½-mile mark near the creek.

Fallen trees might cover part of the Alder Creek Trail along the way, and no bikes are allowed. This trail provides access to several wonderful summits known locally as Box Factory Park. Most of them can be climbed from Deep Creek Upper Basin as well.

ROUTE

From the TH in the woods near Last Dollar Road, descend gradually on the wide, effortless trail for ½ mile, encountering five switchbacks along the way. Walk NE along a straightaway and traverse well below the mountaintops on your right (E). It's less than an hour (2 miles) from the TH to the Sneffels Wilderness sign; after passing through pines, a few aspens, and lots of low flora and arnica flowers, you end up in a semi-clearing. You'll need to contend with a few downed evergreens and two to four stream crossings, depending on the runoff. At least two water crossings are close together and very near to what's left of an old cabin. Go to the right (NE) before the gravity-stricken cabin and 100 feet across the little clearing, as you stay just to the left (N) of the skunk cabbage on the faded trail near the creek.

Walk another 50 feet and go through the trees left (N) 100 feet or so and down the path to cross a 20-foot-wide rock-filled drainage gully that comes from the right (E) and above you. About ½ mile from this gully, cross a year-round creek (preceded by at least two more creeks in big runoff years) in a sizable drainage gully. The gully has a huge sheer cliff band above it (E) and rocks that line the creek above and below the trail. Hike over the rocky gully on the solid trail and continue immediately up the trail to an evergreen-covered shoulder due W of Hayden Peak and SW of North Pole Peak. (This shoulder is the TH for many of the hikes that follow this one.) Continue a mile down the main trail in the woods to another pretty creek directly W of North Pole Peak. This is the unofficial turnaround W of North Pole Peak. Return the same way back up the traverse and switchbacks to finish on top of Last Dollar Road.

TRAIL NOTES

....

....

....

....

....

....

....

Elevation: 12,208 feet, with 1850 feet vertical gain

Distance: 5 miles up, 10 miles round-trip

Duration: 4 hours up, 6 hours round-trip

Difficulty: Very challenging. Steep, long bushwhack, interesting approach, not for the average hiker unfamiliar with local terrain and climate. For most of the peak hikes it's late July or August before the snow melts and they become walk-ups, although with climate change it's earlier all the time

TRAILHEAD

Top of Last Dollar Road; see hike 1 for directions.

ROUTE

Follow Alder Creek Trail 510 about 3½ miles from the TH to the evergreen-covered, wide shoulder coming down from the right, W of and well below Hayden Peak. Welcome, finally, to the super-steep western slopes of North Pole Peak, Hayden Peak, and friends! Bushwhack to the right (E) off Alder Creek Trail 510 ¼ mile up the wide shoulder in the trees with no established trail to a good-sized clearing and small cliff band. Stay left (N) of the steep meadow, and go left of the rock band to traverse (NE) into the trees 50 feet or so. Walk across a mostly dry, narrow, rocky gully into a clearing. Turn right (E) to scramble straight up the clearing just left (N) of the gully. There may be few cairns, if any, up the super-steep, slick, rocky slope to the crux. The going is very steep and loose for a couple hundred yards to the base of the rather large cliff band and steep couloirs above. See that one couloir is up to the right (S), while one gully is directly in front of you (E), and two smaller couloirs are to the left (N) in the cliff band. Work your way up the slope, and move to the left (N) once you are at the base of the cliff band. Traverse more easily 300 feet to the farthest gully for the best up, although the closer, thinner gullies can be climbed as well with more difficulty. Climb NE up the grassy right-hand side of the highest gully to tree line and immediately to the big, WSW-facing shoulder, which is to the right (S) of the long, widening gully coming down from the high ridge.

Hike NE a couple hundred feet up the shoulder over semi-stable scree to where the grass ends. Climb far to the right (S) of the large outcrop extending W from the ridge above (N of) the shoulder and wide gully, and go directly and

Meadow near the start of the west slopes route to Box Factory Park.

very steeply to the ridge. It's about 1½ hours and only a mile from where you left the Alder Creek Trail to this high ridge at 12,360 feet. Get your bearings to remember where you reached the high ridge for the descent, and walk left (N) down the ridge ½ mile to the huge boulders that comprise the summit block of North Pole Peak.

Walk directly up to the steep wall of rock and dual summit blocks from the main ridge, and look slightly to the left (W). The rock is greenish with a center stripe of orange going to the NE straight up a long crack. From the base, look to the right for a thin ramp you must ascend 10–12 feet to a small, flat spot large enough for one person at a time. Climb from the flat spot to another flat spot about 10 feet nearly straight up the ledges. (No climbing gear or ropes are necessary.) Then work your way to the right (E) about 10 feet more on a very narrow ledge, just a foot wide. Hang on to what you can and check your holds. It looks a little tougher from afar, but the rock is actually pretty stable on both summit blocks. Just don't slip off!

Climb to the left (W) from the thin ledge where possible as the footing gets better to the top of the low summit block and down to the saddle between the two boulders. Then pick a way up the very steep-sloping but walkable rock 50 feet to the peak. Go down the same way you came up.

Elevation: 12,987 feet, with 2627 feet vertical gain

Distance: 5¼ miles to the summit, 10½ miles round-trip

Duration: 4½ hours up, 7–8 hours round-trip

Difficulty: Very challenging. Steadily steep, bushwhacking, fairly solid scree, long

TRAILHEAD

Top of Last Dollar Road; see hike 1 for directions.

NOTES

This is one of many gorgeous summits around 13,000 feet along the ridges known as Box Factory Park, which technically stretches all the way down to West Dallas Fork Creek. The park also includes North Pole Peak, S-7, S-8, S-9, S-10, Ruffner Mountain, and the other ridge and unnamed points called Box Factory Park West Ridge Loop. The Sneffels Range can be seen as well from most of the park, and the Wilsons in the San Juans are a few miles to the S. Box

Box Factory Park and the Mount Sneffels Wilderness.

Factory Park can be seen from Dallas Divide while driving, but the best views of course are from the high ridge.

ROUTE

Follow the Alder Creek Trail 510 about 3½ miles from the TH to the evergreen-covered, wide shoulder coming down from the right, W of and well below Hayden Peak. Follow directions for hike 2 to the high ridge (4½ miles from TH) and walk to the right (SE) for Hayden Peak. Go directly over a little bump in the center of the ridge. Continue up without trouble, although some careful route-finding is in order near the summit block. Stay on the narrow trail near the center of the steep upper ridge to the top, as the scree is semi-stable.

- **Bonus**: S-10 is ½ mile away from Hayden Peak to the SE.

TRAIL NOTES

....

....

....

....

....

....

....

Elevation: 12,700 feet, with 2340 feet vertical gain

Distance: 4½ miles up, 9 miles round-trip

Duration: 3½ hours up, 6–8 hours round-trip **Loop** or not

Difficulty: Very challenging. Bushwhacking, ultra-steep last sections, loose rock, scrambling, airy. A fairly difficult hike that requires some mountaineering experience, although no special gear is needed. Would be rated "expert-only" if it were any longer

TRAILHEAD

Top of Last Dollar Road; see hike 1 for directions.

NOTES

Also known as Box Factory Park View (BFPV). Expect a very steep crux climb to the high W ridge near the top. From the summit the scene is phenomenal as you view all the peaks in Box Factory Park and the large Deep Creek Upper Basin to the E.

The difficult west ridge and route of Unnamed Point 12,700 (BFPV, top left).

ROUTE

Follow the route described in hike 1 to the point of the old cabin on the creek. Go right of the dilapidated cabin (NE), staying left (N) of the creek, through the woods within ¼ mile, to a 20-foot-wide rocky drainage gully that barely crosses the trail in a clearing. This is about 1½ hours (3 miles) from the TH and is the unofficial TH for this hike.

Leave Alder Creek Trail 510, and bushwhack to the right (ESE) up the rocky gully for 75 feet before going to the left (NE) 30 feet, then E for 75 feet up a small rise next to the gully. Follow narrow trails to a larger shoulder to the left (NE). Continue E a few hundred feet up the super-steep scree directly to the base of the major crux of the climb. Hike directly under and just to the left (N) of the huge, sheer rock obstacle low on the W ridge of BFPV. It will be very steep and loose to the base of the cliff line. Ascend the rocks and scree, going to the left (N) between the outcrop for a couple hundred yards—watch your footing. Climb to the right (S) through a weakness in the cliff line when possible, and hug the right (S) side of a pretty tight, loose chute. Continue S very steeply 100 feet and 60 feet more up to the right (SW) to gain a solid chunk of the high W ridge of BFPV. Look back down the gully for the return route, and head left (E) ¼ mile up the ultra-thin ridge with steep drop-offs to the summit and high point SW of Hayden Peak.

It would be best to attempt going down this steep W ridge only after first scrambling up it, so as to have a better understanding of the descent. For this reason, climb BFPV first and come down the same route, or continue a **Loop** 10 miles long with either Hayden Peak (hike 3) or Han Shan (hike 17). See hike 5 for details.

TRAIL NOTES

....
....
....
....
....
....
....

5   Box Factory Park West Ridge Loop

Elevation: 12,987 feet, with 2627 feet vertical gain

Distance: 10 miles round-trip

Duration: 8–10 hours round-trip

Difficulty: Expert-only. Super-steep, long, semi-exposed areas, tons of scree, underrated ridge hike. Gloves come in handy on sections of sharper rock.

TRAILHEAD

Top of Last Dollar Road; see hike 1 for directions.

NOTES

Remember that there is no shelter from an incoming storm anywhere on the high ridge itself—don't get caught. Storms build up quickly in the Rockies and can be deadly at high altitudes. Your GPS and phone won't keep you safe and dry!

ROUTE

See hikes 1–3 for the description. After summiting Hayden Peak, the ridge splits into two; one route goes left (SE) to S-10, and the other route goes right (SW) for Box Factory Park West Ridge Loop. Descend an easier ridge section ½ mile to the little point at 12,700 feet (Box Factory Park View or BFPV). Farthest down to the SW you can see the final peak, the jagged Han Shan (pronounced Hawn-Shawn). From BFPV and the two other high points down the ridge, you can see all of the mountains in Box Factory Park and then some!

Continue mindfully down the ridge more than a mile to the next summit S from BFPV as the route quickly narrows to about as wide as your foot. The mountain sheers away from you on both sides, and you have some cool, short-lived exposure—pleasant, straightforward ridge walking over fairly solid terrain. Stay in the center of the ridge almost the entire way to the SW and toward Han Shan as a big hint. There is a 15-foot gully that's easy to down-climb slightly E on the ridgeline, and some interesting but not difficult hiking to a low saddle, and then up to Unnamed Point 12,238. Go SW down to the last saddle much more easily and climb steeply up to Han Shan, just N of the lower Whipple Mountain. It's only 20 minutes (½ mile) to the top from the saddle on the N side and not too tough as you go carefully up the thinning ridge, doing some minimal bouldering. From the peak, come back N to the saddle for the best descent.

Thrilling hike along Box Factory Park West Ridge Loop.

To omit Han Shan, take the bushwhack path that goes to the right (W) from the saddle, then contour down the wide, grassy, semi-rocky slope 1½ miles to Last Dollar Road and the TH. It's a steeper bushwhack the first couple hundred feet W down wide ledges to the open ridge, which soon breaks up ½ mile from the high saddle. Leave the main ridge in the flats and bushwhack steeply to the right (NE) ¼ mile and down 10 minutes or so with a steeper pitch. Go left (W) on the first well-defined trail as the pitch becomes more gradual and wider on the highest part of the nice shoulder, ending more steeply to the Alder Creek TH and saddle.

TRAIL NOTES

....

....

....

....

....

....

....

6   Deep Creek Upper Canyon

Elevation: 13,060 feet at the S-3 and S-5 high saddle; about 12,000 feet at the meadow in the upper canyon above tree line; with vertical gains of 3970 feet from the Deep Creek TH off Last Dollar Road to the high saddle, 2910 feet to the meadow in the upper canyon

Distance: 7 miles to the high saddle, 14 miles round-trip; 5½ miles to the meadow above tree line, 11 miles round-trip

Duration: 5 hours to the S-3 and S-5 saddle, 7–8 hours round-trip; 3½ hours to the meadow, 5–6 hours round-trip

Difficulty: Strenuous. Much scree, sometimes steeper, bushwhacking as the trail fades in and out, scrambling

TRAILHEAD

Drive 3 miles W of Telluride on CO-145 Spur (¼ mile E of Society Turn and CO-145 S to Lizard Head Pass/Durango), turn right (N) 2 miles up the paved Airport Road/Last Dollar Road FS 638, then right again (N) onto Last Dollar Road FS 638 (T-60 sign). Go 1 mile down the dirt road to the Deep Creek–Whipple Mountain TH. Park in the lot on the right (E).

ROUTE

Walk or bike from the parking area up a few turns in the open meadow (½ mile), then into the trees to the NE. Follow an irrigation ditch in the flats for a mile, and go left (W) at the intersection with Deep Creek Trail 418 to Whipple Mountain Trail 419 (still flat). If you biked here, park and lock your bike at the signs just before the trail narrows and continues downward. (Walking to this point, 2 miles, takes 30–40 minutes each way. Biking takes about 15 minutes up and 5 minutes down.) The trail quickly turns more to the right (NE), and you descend a straightaway ½ mile to cross the East Fork of Deep Creek over an old log bridge. After the creek crossing, exit the Deep Creek Trail for the nearby trail on the right.

Continue on dirt to the NE up Iron Mountain Road. Take the left fork in 15 minutes (more than ½ mile); it gets slightly steeper over scree and by steep terrain. Stay on the wide trail as you see several sets of small waterfalls in Deep Creek (East Fork) off to the right (S). A few cairns direct you as the main trail switches back two times around 10,800 feet in a cluster of trees (3 miles from TH). Then traverse the steep slope NE far above the creek through the giant

White rocks to Deep Creek (East Fork) Upper Canyon.

scree fields 1½ miles on the most prominent path through the rock and minimal grass. Notice good ol' Southwest Colorado loose shale and "broken pottery" as you pass what's left of a poorly insulated cabin at the base of a small tailings pile. Continue hiking the most distinct of many thin, rocky paths here in the less traveled zone of the Sneffels Wilderness Area. It is nearly 3 hours (4½ miles) to the last stand of pines from the TH.

Bushwhack more steeply a few feet to the right (E) of a wide gully filled with white rocks and boulders. Climb the hillside in the grass with the highest trees on your right and the boulder field to your left (N). Next, follow the little creek on either side to the NE and an area above tree line, and then climb left (N) of the creek steeply. The water continues under the rock-lined creek bed to a large, level meadow above. Make your way to the meadow and upper canyon at 12,000 feet. The winter snow melts into the widening creek in the meadow, and you are surrounded by small, flat rocks and grass. This makes for a beautiful reflection and an exceptional hangout in late July through September.

Return down the same way, or press on to the top of the upper canyon or the high saddle between S-3 and S-5. Bushwhack past the creek a little steeper to the right (ESE) ¼ mile up a thin, rocky drainage gully to the grassy rises above. Then follow the rises more to the left (E) and ½ mile up the middle of the canyon. The grass and paths soon end, and rock and scree are all that is left in the upper canyon. Follow the rises easily ¼ mile to the end of the canyon, where

From the S-3 and S-5 saddle.

a steep, wide gully leads ¼ mile up to the saddle on the high ridge. Climb the superthin creek bed 75 feet up the center or just to the right (S) while you are still at the bottom of the gully. (When snow is still melting above, you can hear water running under the rocks.) Go to the left (NE) once atop the little creek bed and up 50 feet very steeply with semi-loose rock to a rock rib directly above to the E. Boulder 75 feet up the right side (S) of the rib while hugging it. A tall hoodoo appears immediately on the right (S). Bushwhack up another 35 feet, then begin an ascending traverse to the right (SE) above the spire 40 feet to the nearby ridge and high saddle. Enjoy truly stunning views down the canyon you just came up to the W, or the other way toward the rather large Mount Sneffels family. (This high saddle can also be reached from hikes 31 and 32.)

TRAIL NOTES

....

....

....

....

....

....

....

Elevation: 13,360 feet, with vertical gains of 4270 feet from the bottom of Last Dollar Road at Deep Creek–Whipple Mountain TH, 4020 feet from Blue Lakes TH

Distance: 7½ miles up, 15 miles round-trip; 6 miles up, 12 miles round-trip

Duration: 5–6 hours up, 8–9 hours round-trip; 3 hours up, 5–6 hours round-trip

Difficulty: Very challenging. Long, bushwhacking, steep, much scree, easiest summit block in the neighborhood

TRAILHEAD

Deep Creek–Whipple Mountain TH; see hike 6 for directions. Or see hikes 31 and 32, and take FS 851 (East Fork Dallas Creek) off of CO-62 to Blue Lakes TH.

ROUTE

See hike 6 for the closer approach to the high saddle between S-3 and S-5 from Telluride, or climb this peak from Blue Lakes West Basin (see hike 32). From the high saddle, climb and boulder to the left (N) ¼ mile to the nearby summit. It's really steep to start as the ridge narrows, but fairly solid rock makes it quite doable for most hikers. Follow the ridge itself or go just to the right (E) from the saddle, then continue up as it widens slightly near the top.

S-3 with West Dallas Peak behind to the left from S-5.

Elevation: 13,441 feet, with vertical gains of 4350 feet from the bottom of Last Dollar Road at Deep Creek–Whipple Mountain TH, 4700 feet from Blue Lakes TH

Distance: 7 miles up, 14 miles round-trip; 6 miles up, 12 miles round-trip

Duration: 6 hours up, 10–11 hours round-trip from either TH

Difficulty: Very challenging. Route-finding, super-steep, loose scree, steep gullies, quite long

TRAILHEAD

Deep Creek–Whipple Mountain TH; see hike 6 for directions. Or see hikes 31 and 32, and take FS 851 (East Fork Dallas Creek) off of CO-62 to Blue Lakes TH.

ROUTE

See hike 6. Also see the map and hike to around 12,500 feet, leaving the last rises to the bottom of the steeps well below the S-3 and S-5 saddle. Do not attempt this summit from the connecting ridge of S-5 as it cliffs out. Begin the ascent N directly to S-6 ½ mile and 700 feet up the steep scree with no trail. The gully becomes more obvious a little higher and is angled slightly to the right (E) of the peak. The rocks are larger but loose, so mind your footing on the slog up to the very top and the ridge proper. Scramble more easily left (NW) a hundred feet to the nearby peak.

From Blue Lakes West Basin, climb to the saddle between S-3 and S-5, then descend slightly right (N) and steeply 500–600 feet (NW) into the top of Deep Creek Upper Canyon. Skirt NW over the steep slope, trying not to lose more elevation, and catch the other route S of S-6 that goes up a super-steep, wide gully to the high ridge just SE of the peak.

9   Deep Creek Upper Basin

Elevation: 11,700 feet, with 2600 feet vertical gain

Distance: 5½ miles up, 11 miles round-trip

Duration: 3 hours up, 5 hours round-trip

Difficulty: Strenuous. Some route-discovering, steeper areas

TRAILHEAD
Deep Creek–Whipple Mountain TH; see hike 6 for directions.

NOTES
It's more than 2 hours from the legal parking on Last Dollar Road to the mouth of Ruffner Basin. You climb to the N past Ruffner Basin to next big basin on the right, or Deep Creek (West Fork) Upper Basin.

ROUTE
Walk easily from the official TH on Last Dollar Road, taking the gentle trail to the left (N) up ½ mile of turns in the open meadow, before leveling out into the woods (NE) 1 mile next to a water-filled ditch to the intersection of Deep Creek Trail and Sheep Creek. Go left (W) away from Deep Creek Trail in the flats and past the sign for Whipple Mountain Trail at 2 miles from the TH. Continue down a straightaway NE ½ mile and cross Deep Creek (East Fork) over a log bridge. Pass Deep Creek (East Fork)/Iron Mountain Road on the right. Hike up to the W ½ mile from the creek, and make a sharp right turn (N) at the next intersection and sign (3 miles from the TH) onto the official trail instead of going down the "closed to public" trail. Continue across from a huge, rolling meadow and pond as you traverse the hillside (N) a mile up and down for about 25 minutes, ending in the aspens and pines near the creek. Five minutes past the Sneffels Wilderness sign, cross Deep Creek where it is safe over logs. Walk up a big switchback and through the thinning forest to a clearing. A small sign in the clearing indicates the Deep Creek Spur/Extension Trail to the right. Leave the Whipple Mountain Trail and traverse N for about 25 minutes (more than ½ mile) up and down above and left (W) of the main creek. Carefully hop over the potentially difficult water crossing at Deep Creek back to the E side, and get a look around for the return trip from here.

See S-10 straight up N at the top of the big valley. It's about 15 minutes (½ mile) more through the semi-clearing on the trail before you enter the

S-9 and Deep Creek (West Fork) Upper Basin.

aspens and pines on the right (E) side of the creek. Hike up a steeper section, and go through a small clearing with scree coming down on the right from Ruffner Mountain. Continue NNE back into the pines up the middle, perhaps noting cairns. In a few minutes the most pronounced steep path leads you to a very large meadow and clearing out of the trees at the mouth of and just below Ruffner Basin on your right (E) 4½ miles from the TH. Go N past the narrow Ruffner Basin, and bushwhack through the clearing by first going over the creek that comes down from the E. Follow the steep, wide-open, grassy slope or climb one of the rockier rises slightly to the left of the slope with little to no trails. You will be just to the right (E) of and well above Deep Creek itself. Eventually you curve up right (NE) very steeply into the high basin and your goal. It's 45–60 minutes and a mile from the small creek crossing at the mouth of Ruffner Basin to the top of tree line. There you will find more level ground at the bottom of Deep Creek Upper Basin. When you arrive you will have views of S-9 to the NE and a great panorama next to the creek coming out of the basin. Explore, watch for wildlife, and return the same way, or use this basin to get to S-8, S-9, or S-10.

10	S-7

Elevation: 13,220 feet, with 4130 feet vertical gain

Distance: 7 miles up, 14 miles round-trip

Duration: 5 hours max, 7–8 hours round-trip combined with hike 11

Difficulty: Very challenging. Long, solid to loose rock, much scree. Bouldering a bit of exposed ridge near the peak of S-7, but it's not technical

TRAILHEAD
Deep Creek–Whipple Mountain TH; see hike 6 for directions.

NOTES
If you talk to anyone about this peak or any of the S peaks, they are liable to look at you strangely and say, "Where?" At that point, simply smile! These spectacular (and less frequently hiked) peaks are part of the cluster cirque of mountains farthest W in the Mount Sneffels Range. They can be seen as far away as Grand Junction almost 100 miles north.

ROUTE
Follow the description in hike 9 to the mouth of Ruffner Basin. Instead of crossing the creek to the steep, wide-open, grassy slope at 4½ miles from the TH, hike (NE) with a decent pitch on the right side (S) of the little stream and up the most distinct trail to Ruffner Basin. You will soon be above what appears to be tree line. Go just left (N) of a very steep scree field to the high, grassy rises above. As the path levels out somewhat in the basin, cross the creek bed to the left rise in a few minutes going SE. The incline to the upper basin can be rather abrupt up the rocks and scree. See cairns and the path up the steep, grassy hill to the left of the cliffy area at the end of this lower section. A cave far above and left (E) in another cliff band is a landmark to head toward, but hike to the right well below the cave and traverse into the small midbasin. Follow the brief grassy area with ease until it ends. Then barely go to the right (ESE) and into a long, rock- and boulder-filled drainage. Climb ¼ mile straight to the top up the middle of the steep but solid gully with some cairns to help you. Up to the left (NE) from the very top of the gully in the high basin is the obvious trail. Climb steeply up the looser rock to the high saddle (NE) between S-8 and the small knob between S-7 and Ruffner Mountain. When the trail ends, bushwhack

¼ mile to the saddle by making your way up the wide, grassy areas for better footing.

The views are awesome all around and get even better momentarily. (That is, *awesome* in the original sense, before the term lost all its meaning!) Hike to the right (SE) a few hundred feet once you are on the high ridge directly to the top of the small knob. It's around 20 minutes (¼ mile) to S-7 or Ruffner Mountain from the knob. Walk to the left (E) for S-7 over semi-loose to loose rock where you will encounter a fairly exposed, fun ridge section. There you have some very workable bouldering with iron-colored rock, and this area on the ridge is quite a thrill to the peak. Mears Peak is above on the connecting ridge to the E, with Mount Sneffels in the background and the Wilsons beyond the mesas to the S.

• **Bonus:** The highest point of Ruffner Mountain is on the ridge extending SW from S-7 and the high point between them, and the going is somewhat easier from the little point down to that nearby summit. See hike 11 for more details.

TRAIL NOTES

....

....

....

....

....

....

....

Elevation: 13,003 feet, with 3913 feet vertical gain

Distance: 7 miles up, 14 miles round-trip

Duration: 5 hours up, 7–8 hours round-trip

Difficulty: Very challenging. Long scree hike, some bushwhacking, walk-up, long time above tree line

TRAILHEAD

Deep Creek–Whipple Mountain TH; see hike 6 for directions.

ROUTE

See the description for hikes 9 and 10, and get to the high saddle between S-8 and the little knob that separates S-7 and Ruffner Mountain. Once you are on the high ridge, hike to the right (SE) a few hundred feet up toward the nearby small knob. Go steeply to the top and then walk to the right and down a little more easily to the peak. Or you could take the more difficult, direct spur trail about halfway up the small knob that begins near a rock outcropping on the steeper ridge section. A very thin path may have cairns as you contour over loose scree to the right (S) 250 feet along a very steep slope to a low saddle on the ridge NE of Ruffner Mountain. From the wider ridge you will have some steep drop-offs on both sides as you scramble SW to the nearby rocky summit by staying close to the ridge crest up the rock. From the peak you will have a nice close-up of Ruffner Mountain's huge gendarmes on the continuing ridgeline SSW. (Gendarmes refer to spiked pinnacles or spires blocking a ridgeline, borrowing its meaning from medieval French soldiers standing at guard.) Return the same way or add the slightly more difficult hike 10 to spice up your day!

Large elk says "hello" before darting off.

12   S-8

Elevation: 13,252 feet, with 4172 feet vertical gain

Distance: 7 miles up, 14 miles round-trip

Duration: 5 hours up, 7–8 hours round-trip

Difficulty: Very challenging. Long, steadily steep. Great **Loop** opportunities, not terribly difficult for those acclimated to the altitude and in decent shape

TRAILHEAD

Deep Creek–Whipple Mountain TH; see hike 6 for directions.

ROUTE

Choose from three known **Opts** to this summit, the highest peak in Box Factory Park. For **Opt 1** see hike 10. Once you are on the high ridge, go to the left (NW) without difficulty ½ mile farther to the peak. Walk over a little false summit next to S-8, and reach the apex in 30 minutes from the main saddle. The scree is semi-loose over a wider ridge that narrows near the top. From S-8 you can descend by the same route, but perhaps the NW ridge of S-8 (**Opt 2**) to the high basin is grabbing your attention. It's only 30 minutes and a mile down the faintest of trails over fairly solid scree and rock to the steeps at the bottom of the ridge. Just above the super-steep area that turns into gullies at the bottom of the NW ridge, go to the right (N) and traverse a few hundred feet to the huge scree field. Bushwhack NNW down a couple hundred yards to the grass and creek in Deep Creek Upper Basin. See hike 9 for the return to the TH. For **Opt 3**, see hike 13 as the route approaches the peak from Deep Creek Upper Basin and the N ridge of S-8.

Elevation: 13,134 feet, with 4054 feet vertical gain

Distance: 7 miles up, 14 miles round-trip

Duration: 5–5½ hours up, 8 hours round-trip

Difficulty: Very challenging. Fairly steep scree scramble near the summit, very long, peaceful

TRAILHEAD

Deep Creek–Whipple Mountain TH; see hike 6 for directions.

ROUTE

See hikes 9 and 14. Once you are high in Deep Creek Upper Basin, more than 6 miles from the TH near the bottom of Last Dollar Road, hike the steep, scree-covered slopes to the E above the grassy areas between S-9 (NE) and S-8 to the right (SE). Take the most distinct steep and narrow deer trail to the E to the notch and saddle between S-8 and S-9, where the last pitch is quite steep. Hike to the left (N) ½ mile to the top, and go left (W) on the ridge proper or straight between two larger rock outcrops with some steep, loose rock to the peak. At the summit block, hug the left (N) side of a little rock rib that extends W off the ridge 50 feet S from the peak and up 30 feet or so. Then turn left (N) and walk more easily on the ridge crest to the pinnacle. Return by the same route down the

S ridge and right (W) into Deep Creek Upper Basin for the best descent. You could also stay on the high ridge another ½ mile S, where it's fairly undemanding and not too steep all the way to S-8. It's 40 minutes from S-9 to S-8 on a wide ridge withsolid scree.

Mariposa lily with a visitor.

Elevation: 13,020 feet, with vertical gains of 3940 feet from the bottom of Last Dollar Road at Deep Creek–Whipple Mountain TH, 2660 feet from Alder Creek Trail 510

Distance: 8 miles from the bottom of Last Dollar Road at Deep Creek–Whipple Mountain TH, 16 miles round-trip; 5½ miles to the peak from Alder Creek TH, 10 miles round-trip

Duration: 5–6 hours up, 9–10 hours round-trip from either TH

Difficulty: Very challenging. Hard to get to but an easy summit block, route-finding, steep scrambling

TRAILHEAD

Deep Creek–Whipple Mountain TH; see hike 6 for directions. Or top of Last Dollar Road; see hike 1 for directions.

ROUTE

See hike 9. Head left (NE) at the highest intersection of animal paths by the narrowing creek more than 6 miles from the TH. Follow the small creek to the left (NNE and left of S-9) for ½ mile up a steep gully, where snow lingers in early summer. Follow the reddish scree very steeply near the high ridge, and go left (WNW) a mile with a much easier grade to the summit. You could also hike from S-10 to S-9 (ESE) 1½ miles on a faint, steep traverse path going SE under the summit block of S-9 and ascend 100 feet E just left of the little rock rib S of the peak. See hike 13 to finish, or **Loop** back into Deep Creek Upper Basin (hike 9).

For the Alder Creek Trail route, see hike 3. From Hayden Peak it's only 20 minutes and ½ mile of comfortable walking to the left (SE) along the connecting ridge to the summit of S-10. See the obvious scree path to the right (S) of the ridgeline nearest the top and follow it up. All the basins and drainages below and to the S provide the source of Deep Creek on its West Fork.

CHAPTER 2

NORTHWEST TELLURIDE

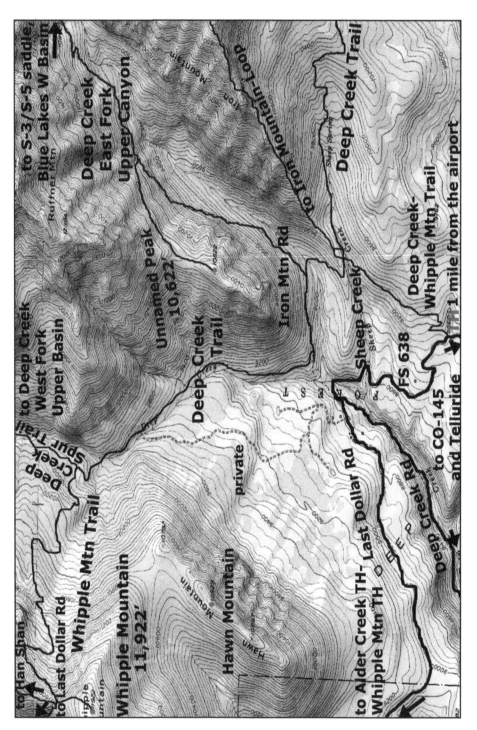

HIKES 1, 15-19, 69

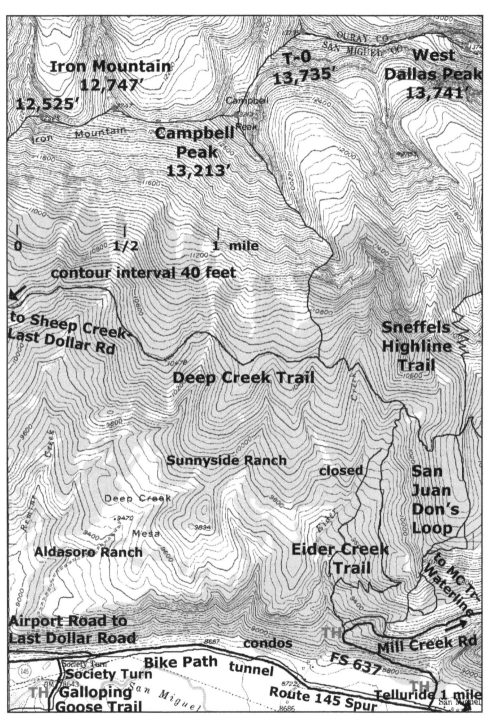

Iron Mountain 12,747'

12,525'

T-0 13,735'

West Dallas Peak 13,741'

Campbell Peak 13,213'

0   1/2   1 mile

contour interval 40 feet

to Sheep Creek-Last Dollar Rd

Sneffels Highline Trail

Deep Creek Trail

Sunnyside Ranch

closed

San Juan Don's Loop

Deep Creek

Mesa

9470

9894

Aldasoro Ranch

Eider Creek Trail

to MC Tr Waterline

Airport Road to Last Dollar Road

condos

Mill Creek Rd

145

Society Turn

Bike Path   tunnel

FS 637

Telluride 1 mile

TH Galloping Goose Trail

Route 145 Spur

TH

San Miguel

HIKES 18-25, 69, 77

Elevation: 10,620 feet, with vertical gain of 1540 feet (hiking) or 1875 feet (bike **Loop** from Telluride)

Distance: 6 miles one way on Deep Creek Trail 418 alone, plus Mill Creek Road FS 637 or Last Dollar Road and CO-145 for the short drive or bike to the THs. A couple shorter **Loops** leave Deep Creek Trail for Eider Creek Trail (hike 23, 5 miles round-trip) or San Juan Don's Loop (hike 24, 3½ miles round-trip) and will take you back to your vehicle at the water treatment plant or ½ mile below the plant at the switchback on Mill Creek Road FS 637

Duration: 3½–4 hours from the top of Mill Creek Road FS 637 to Last Dollar Road, taking the trail E to W. Have an extra car or bike shuttled to one end of the trail or the other, as Deep Creek Trail 418 only goes one way

Difficulty: Strenuous. Long walk, steeper by Mill Creek. San Juan Don's Loop (hike 24) is a more difficult bushwhack; Eider Creek Loop (hike 23) is fairly easy

TRAILHEAD

For the E side of Deep Creek Trail 418, drive 1 mile W of Telluride (past the gas station) and turn right (N) on Mill Creek Road FS 637. 2WD the dirt road, more steeply to the NW to begin, a mile up to the water treatment plant. For the W side of the trail, begin at the Deep Creek–Whipple Mountain TH; see hike 6 for directions.

NOTES

Deep Creek Trail technically goes farther E from the top of Mill Creek Trail 2 miles to Jud Wiebe Trail 432 and shares the Waterline Trail, a super-easy traverse. Start the bigger **Loop** from town if you are biking, and head to either TH. Both ends of the trail are a bit steeper.

ROUTE

From the water treatment plant, walk left (N) up the Mill Creek–Deep Creek Trail from the parking area more than ½ mile steadily to the Deep Creek Trail 418 sign and intersection. Go left (W) ½ mile steeply, including some switch-

Endless aspens on Deep Creek Trail.

backs as you hike through a big meadow and back into the trees up to the W start of the Sneffels Highline Trail. This little shoulder is also the high point on Deep Creek Trail 418. San Juan Don's Loop bushwhacks S, and Eider Creek Trail goes S ½ mile farther W on Deep Creek Trail 418. Continue along the traverse as far as you want. There are only a couple signs, and the route is obvious unless there's fresh snow on it. This marvelous path traverses 3 miles below Iron Mountain and Campbell Peak, and above Aldasoro and Sunnyside ranches through the high alpine forest and seemingly endless aspens most of the way on a fairly steady grade. It finally gets steeper down to the intersection of Sheep Creek and Whipple Mountain Trail. Go left (SW) on Deep Creek Trail 418 for 1½ miles more easily to the Last Dollar Road TH.

TRAIL NOTES

Elevation: 11,550 feet; 11,922 feet; with vertical gains of 2470 feet to the saddle, 3122 feet from the bottom of Last Dollar Road at Deep Creek–Whipple Mountain TH, 970 feet from a switchback near the top of Last Dollar Road to the saddle, 1330 feet from a switchback near the top of Last Dollar Road

Distance: 5 miles up, 10 miles round-trip; 5½ miles up, 11 miles round-trip for the summit; 3 miles round-trip including the summit from a switchback near the top of Last Dollar Road

Duration: 2½–3 hours to the saddle between Whipple Mountain and Han Shan, 4–5 hours round-trip; 1 hour round-trip from the saddle S to the summit and back; 1 hour to the saddle from a switchback near the top of Last Dollar Road, 1½ hours round-trip

Difficulty: Mix of strenuous (longer, steeper from the lower TH on Last Dollar Road) and moderate (loose and steady up but short, route-finding to the summit from either TH)

TRAILHEAD

For both THs, begin by following directions from hike 6 to arrive at Deep Creek–Whipple Mountain TH. For the lower TH, park there. For the upper TH, drive 6½ miles farther, descending N to a big curve going left (W) over a bridge, then past the intersection with Deep Creek Road on the left. Continue NW up Last Dollar Road along a steeper section, possibly requiring 4WD to the last switchback ½ mile before the top (10,663 feet). Park along the road or at the tiny signed parking area on the right (E).

ROUTE

From the lower TH on Last Dollar Road 1 mile N of the airport, take the gentle trail to the left (N) up ½ mile of turns in the open meadow, before leveling out into the woods (NE) 1 mile next to a water-filled ditch to the intersection of Deep Creek Trail and Sheep Creek. Go left (W) away from Deep Creek Trail in the flats and past the sign for Whipple Mountain Trail at 2 miles from the TH. Continue down a straightaway NE ½ mile and cross Deep Creek (East Fork) over a log bridge. Pass Deep Creek (East Fork)/Iron Mountain Road on the right. Hike up to the W ½ mile from the creek, and make a sharp right turn (N)

Sheep near Whipple Mountain Trail.

at the next intersection and sign (3 miles from the TH) onto the official trail instead of going down the "closed to public" trail. Continue across from a huge, rolling meadow and pond as you traverse the hillside (N) a mile up and down, ending in the aspens and pines near the creek. Five minutes past the Sneffels Wilderness sign, cross Deep Creek where it is safe over logs. Ascend a big switchback and go through the thinning forest to a clearing. A sign and trail posts will direct you left (NW) through the clearing to continue on Whipple Mountain Trail 419. Hike N and NW 1 mile up switchbacks on a steep, rocky hillside opposite Whipple Mountain while keeping it in your sights. This is the toughest part of the hike, walking W to the woods, high saddle, and sign below the summit.

For Whipple Mountain, turn left (S) near the middle of the wide saddle. If you started at the TH near the top of Last Dollar Road, go right (S) near the center of the main saddle. The 1-mile ascent from the Whipple Mountain TH at the highest switchback on Last Dollar Road is a leisurely stroll with many semi-loose switchbacks on a medium grade, finally coming up to the saddle SW through the woods.

From the center of the saddle, go 30 feet S into the trees and over a big downed evergreen that obscures a faint path on the other side going slightly left (SE). Follow this until it fades, and bushwhack another ¼ mile up, as you angle left steeply NE of the summit and perhaps up the little ridge. You may have to cross several downed trees along the way, fewer if you do it right. The big, grassy summit area is barely above tree line, making it totally worth the walk.

Elevation: 12,311 feet, with vertical gains of 1730 feet from Whipple Mountain TH near the top of Last Dollar Road or the very top at Alder Creek TH, 3230 feet from the bottom of Last Dollar Road at Deep Creek–Whipple Mountain TH

Distance: 2 miles up from either TH at the top of Last Dollar Road, 4 miles round-trip; 5½ miles up, 11 miles round-trip from the bottom of Last Dollar Road at Deep Creek–Whipple Mountain TH

Duration: 1½–2 hours max to the summit, 3–4 hours **Loop** or not round-trip; 3–4 hours up, 5–6 hours round-trip

Difficulty: Mix of strenuous (trail-finding, some steeps up the easier route from the high saddle/Alder Creek TH at the top of Last Dollar Road) and very challenging (super-steep bouldering on narrow S ridge)

TRAILHEAD

Bottom of Last Dollar Road at Deep Creek–Whipple Mountain TH (see hike 6 for directions) or top of Last Dollar Road (see hike 1). Begin at the lowest TH on Last Dollar Road or Whipple Mountain Trail less than ½ mile from the top of the road at the highest switchback if you are attempting the difficult S ridge of Han Shan.

NOTES

Although this mountain is officially called Unnamed Point 12,311, locals know it as Han Shan (literally "cold mountain" and the name of a legendary Chinese poet). It's the steep hill to the N of the saddle with Whipple Mountain, not to be confused with the nearby and much lower Hawn Mountain (and a newer trail with rock stairs there). Directions will be for a **Loop**, as you could start at the top of Last Dollar Road and end back at Last Dollar Road just under ½ mile down from the top of the road at Whipple Mountain TH. Go around in either direction, or hike one way and return by the same route. The Alder Creek TH at the top of the road provides easier access, and you may wish to come back by the same route and skip the difficult **Loop**. The hike from the S ridge has you boulder and then climb a very steep, short cliffy section that could be categorized as "expert-only" if it were sustained for any longer. (See the end of hike 5 for more hints.)

Han Shan and Whipple Mountain to the Wilsons in early October.

ROUTE

For the safer, more expedient route, park at the top of Last Dollar Road at Alder
Creek TH. Start up the little shoulder in the clearing on the right (E) side of the
road just to the right (S) of the trees on the solid trail as you go past the old sign
to begin. Stay in the clearing a couple feet to the right (S) of the woods when you
see private camping huts and other paths going left, and follow the main trail.
Hike into the woods more than ¼ mile. The walking is mellow for another ¼
mile and quite beautiful through the pines (E) over the crest of the shoulder.
Pass by the top of the Summit Creek drainage and its wide gully to the right (S),
immediately arriving below the main ridge and slightly left (N). Leave the main
path and bushwhack steeply past the thinning pines to the right (S) ¼ mile to get
onto the bottom of the main ridge extending W from the peak. Hike up the mellow, high ridge to the E ½ mile to the steeps on the summit block. Climb the
wide, rocky ledges with semi-loose scree E 150 feet up, where you may or may
not follow the tiny paths to the high ridge a hundred feet or so left (N) of the
summit, then make your way right (S) more easily to the top. You will be
rewarded with outstanding views of the San Miguel Range a few miles to the S
and the many jagged mountains within the nearby Sneffels Wilderness Area.
Han Shan itself looks rather formidable from most angles, and you have all of
Box Factory Park along the adjoining ridge and around the cirque!

Return the same way, or do the much more difficult **Loop** by continuing S down the ridge toward Whipple Mountain. The S ridge quickly narrows, and you have some exhilarating exposure with huge drop-offs on both sides. Climb slowly down the center of the steeper ridge to the main crux ¼ mile from the summit. A sheer rock section more than 20 feet tall impedes travel on the ridge and can be bypassed going directly to the right (W) down a short, 30-foot W-facing ramp (2–3 feet wide). The rock in the area is greenish and semisolid. Go immediately to the left (E) 25 feet back to the nearby ridge crest over a narrow ledge and green rocks to a tiny notch directly under the sheer rock face on the ridge. Or from the W-facing ramp, continue down 25 feet more (S), descend a steep 6-foot rock section to the left (SE), and take the easier grassy ledge (E) 20 feet over to the nearby notch below the sheer-rock obstacle on the ridge. The crux area isn't quite over yet. You'll need to get into the more-than-40-foot-long rocky couloir on the actual ridge two-thirds of the way down it, but first boulder 25 feet steeply down the big, flat-sloping rocks just to the right (W) of the ridgeline and couloir. The rocky gully and an opening in the outcrop will appear on your left (E) with steep-sloping rock. Carefully make your way into the gully by descending one of two steep routes around 10 feet.

If you are coming up from the Whipple Mountain saddle, it's ½ mile to the major crux section, as you go (N) up a grassy dirt path to begin. Hike slightly to the left (W), then up the center of the ridge or just left (W) to the main crux section below the summit. Take the slender, grassy runway just to the left (W) of the ridge for about 100 yards to the base of the rocky couloir and apparent obstacle. You should ascend the big boulders to the left (W) from about a third of the way up the 40-foot-long rocky gully on the ridge. Then climb the first super-steep, skinny crack about 10 feet up, or go just a couple feet farther up to free climb the steep-sloping, flatter rock and ledges. Watch all your holds as the rock is loose and crumbly.

The remainder of the ridge, from the crux area down ½ mile to the saddle between Han Shan and Whipple Mountain, is wider with better walking. Continue with some grass along the rocky ridgeline to the S, and stay near the middle or go barely right (W) of the ridge a few times. A sign at the saddle reads "Sneffels Wilderness–Uncompahgre National Forest." Go left (E) to the lowest TH on Last Dollar Road in 5 miles, or right (W) 1 mile to the TH and switchback near the top of Last Dollar Road.

Elevation: 13,213 feet, with vertical gains of 4123 feet from the bottom of Last Dollar Road at Deep Creek–Whipple Mountain TH, 4393 feet from Eider Creek TH

Distance: 12 miles round-trip **Loop**; 4½–5 miles to Campbell Peak, 10 miles round-trip no **Loop**

Duration: 9–10 hours round-trip **Loop**; 4 hours up to Campbell Peak, 6–7 hours round-trip no **Loop**

Difficulty: Mix of expert-only (super-steep down Iron Mountain's SW ridge, route-finding, very long) and very challenging (Campbell Peak alone, very steep, gullies, scrambling, bushwhacking the bottom)

TRAILHEAD

Deep Creek–Whipple Mountain TH; see hike 6 for directions. For Campbell Peak alone, see hike 23 and drive 1 mile W of Telluride on CO-145 Spur, turn right (N) on Mill Creek Road FS 637, and 2WD ¾ mile up the steep, narrow dirt road NE to a big switchback.

ROUTE

The heads-up move is to bike 10–15 minutes (2 miles) from the parking area and TH on Last Dollar Road up the turns in the meadow and along a ditch (NE) to the Whipple Mountain Trail–Deep Creek Trail intersection. Lock your bike near the sign. This will be a gracious bonus at the end of a long, exhilarating day, with only 5 minutes or so to bike back to the TH. To do the **Loop** in a counterclockwise direction, start by warming up on Deep Creek Trail 418. Hike about 2 hours (3 miles) to the right (E) from Sheep Creek and the sign for Deep Creek Trail 418. Ascend steeply to begin, as the trail undulates through high aspens and evergreens under Iron Mountain and Campbell Peak. The TH is unmarked and easy to miss. Look for it on a small corner in the evergreens beside a large fallen pine that has had a sizable section removed. Deep Creek Trail 418 continues immediately down two switchbacks and crosses Eider Creek. From the top (N) end of Eider Creek Trail (1 hour, 2½ miles), turn left (W) on Deep Creek Trail 418 for 1 mile, cross Eider Creek's W drainage, and hike up two switchbacks directly to a small corner to begin. Bushwhack from the high corner above the switchbacks, and head to the left (N) off of Deep Creek Trail 418 (right if you came up Eider Creek Trail) as you stay high on the little shoulder. Stay to the right (E) of most of the fallen pines to a steeper area on the rise. This can be a little tricky, but remember to stay nearest the rise itself when it flattens a bit (¼ mile from Deep Creek Trail 418) to avoid having to go over too many large, fallen trees. Then climb NE ¼ mile through a clearing below giant rock spires on the lowest part of Campbell Peak's SE ridge. Aspens are to your left, and there's a small clearing to the right (E) from the actual base of the ridge. You may or may not see the faint path that becomes clearer on the solid ridge a few hundred feet up.

Climb the grass and scree very steeply (NW) 150 feet up the treeless slope, and go to the left (N) of the bigger spire and cliff, and right (W) of a smaller spire. Notice a baby spire at the bottom of and between the larger spires; you must ascend 75 feet to get past the baby spire on either side, though the right (E) side will probably work best. Continue about 35 feet more (NW) very steeply up the widening gully, and turn right (E) to climb the grass and rock another 25 feet and grab a solid piece of the main SE ridge. When you are on top with better footing, get a good look around and study the area in case you are descending by this route. Follow the obvious ridge very steeply to the NW (1 mile to summit) above tree line, through scree fields, and directly in the middle for the best way up to the main crux and large rock obstacle ¼ mile SE of Campbell Peak.

From the base of the huge boulder on the ridge, go 8–10 feet NW up the first little steep, narrow part without difficulty, then slowly climb fairly steeply 50–60 feet and a few feet to the right (N), as you actually follow cairns up the boulder and top it out. (Happily, it's not nearly as difficult as it appears from lower on the ridge.) Finish the last section of ridge over larger, looser scree a couple hundred yards NW to the peak—a section that turns out to be more fun than most of Campbell's SE ridge. It's at least 4–5 hours and 5 miles to Campbell Peak from the TH and parking area off of Last Dollar Road if you take the **Loop** counterclockwise. From the pinnacle and highest point, return the same way, or continue the more difficult **Loop** down Campbell's W ridge almost a mile to the dual peaks of Iron Mountain. Hike directly on or just to the left (S) of the steep ridge on the trail over more flat, loose scree. Go from Iron Mountain's summit to its lower peak SW in about 30 minutes (½ mile) with an easier grade but with steep drop-offs.

It's 3 difficult miles more down to Deep Creek Trail 418. Walk down from the reddish rock and scree-covered summit block to the SW as the going quickly becomes steep. Boulder down a short section (SW) 50–60 feet over loose rock and scree by staying on or close to the wide ridge crest itself to an easier section below. Pass by a rock and scree cave someone built in the middle of the ridge to a cliffy section, but go hard to the right (W) for 50 feet or so

Big Brave Dave gracefully makes his way up to the ridge proper on Campbell Mountain.

before it gets too steep on the ridge, and head SW to a small opening in the rock band. Descend the narrow rock gully 12–15 feet steeply, and walk directly to the left (E) under the greenish cliff band for about 40 feet to the main ridge again. Move SW down the center of the ridge to the next immediate obstacle: a jagged, slick boulder cone. Go to the right (W) of the cone and down loose, rocky shelves a few feet. Traverse a couple hundred yards max 50 feet below the ridge crest to the W over a very steep slope, on the very thin path as it meets the ridge again.

Follow the ridge briefly to the next major outcropping and blockage. You must escape to the left (SSW) now, and leave the main ridge for ½ mile to avoid the areas ahead that cliff out. The path goes very steeply through the woods and scree, as you will begin to contour 100 feet or so below the huge spires on the ridgeline. This part is a little awkward and very narrow, with brush and small aspens on or near the path, so move slowly and make your way back to the ridge proper past the outcropping and spires. Continue on the more solid path steeply ½ mile to the lower ridge, where you may have to go just left (SW) of the ridgeline a couple times. Hike through scrub oak near the bottom, and follow the ridge to the end. Or bushwhack to the left (S) a few hundred feet before the end of the ridge to the nearby, visible Deep Creek Trail 418 and culmination of the **Loop**. It's less than 2 miles SW to the TH, going by the long ditch and finally down the last turns in the meadow to the parking on Last Dollar Road.

19   Iron Mountain

Elevation: 12,525 feet; 12,747 feet; with 3667 feet vertical gain

Distance: 3 miles up, 6 miles round-trip

Duration: 4 hours up, 7 hours round-trip (less than 1 mile per hour on average round-trip!)

Difficulty: Expert-only. Grueling ridge up to the dual summits, scrambling, faded path, no traffic

TRAILHEAD

Deep Creek–Whipple Mountain TH; see hike 6 for directions.

ROUTE

Walk 30 minutes or bike 10–15 minutes (2 miles) from the parking area and TH on Last Dollar Road up the turns in the meadow and along a ditch (NE) to the Whipple Mountain Trail–Deep Creek Trail intersection. Lock your bike up near the sign, and walk to the right (E) up Deep Creek Trail 418 only a couple hundred yards before you leave the trail to bushwhack left (N) and straight up 100 feet to Iron Mountain's SW ridge. Or you could start at the creek and intersection. Either way, head up through the scrub oak to the NE of the bulk of it and to the obvious trails on the low ridge. Climb the steep hill and ridge, and go over what you can and just to the right (SE) of what you can't. Try to hug the ridge when possible, but you have no choice over ½ mile from Deep Creek Trail 418, as you drop well off the ridge crest to the right (ENE) around two huge spires from the steep woods. A narrow path (if any) is barely apparent most of the mid to upper ridge, including ½ mile around the outcropping and spires, where you must climb very steeply N back to the main ridge. It's easy to get cut up by trees, bushes, and rocks from here on, so go slowly and perhaps use gloves. (This is most people's least favorite part of the climb, up or down.)

Just a few more obstacles to pass, so hang in there. Climb the steep, narrow ridge (NE) again for a moment. Next is a jagged boulder cone that breaks up and would be very difficult to go over. Go left (NNE) to bushwhack a couple hundred yards about 50 feet below the top of the cone to the W. Hike around the cone and climb the loose, rocky shelves back a few feet to the ridgeline. A greenish-and-orange rock band 100 feet above blocks the ridge. Hike up to the cliff from the ridge, and walk about 40 feet left (NNW), hugging the rock band until you find a weakness and the steep, loose route up 12–15 feet to the right

Iron Mountain from Last Dollar Road.

(NE). Look for cairns here and on the rest of the ridge, as you pass a rock cave in the middle of the scree-filled ridge. The last super-steep section requires some bouldering with loose scree up 50–60 feet. Stay on or near the ridge itself. The route gets much easier near the top as you approach the iron-rock-covered low summit of the horseshoe. The ½-mile walk over the connecting ridge is okay but narrow on solid scree. Hope you left any fear of heights back at Deep Creek!

TRAIL NOTES

....
....
....
....
....
....
....

20　T-0

Elevation: 13,735 feet, with 4915-plus feet vertical gain
Distance: 6 miles up, 12 miles round-trip
Duration: 4½–5 hours up, 7–8 hours round-trip
Difficulty: Very challenging. Quite long and steep, much scree. Campbell Peak climbed first

TRAILHEAD

Drive 1 mile W of Telluride on CO-145 Spur, turn right (N) on Mill Creek Road FS 637, and 2WD ¾ mile up the steep, narrow dirt road NE to a big switchback.

ROUTE

See hike 18 and continue NE 1 mile on the connecting ridge to T-0 up steeper but fairly stable scree. It's only 45 minutes to the top from Campbell, including an ascent of about 735 feet more from the low saddle between summits, and hundreds more going SW back to Campbell Peak.

21　West Dallas Peak

Elevation: 13,741 feet, with 5513-plus feet vertical gain
Distance: 7½–8 miles up, 15–16 miles round-trip
Duration: 6 hours up, 9–10 hours round-trip
Difficulty: Expert-only. Exceptionally long, route-discovering, no storm shelter possibilities for hours back to tree line, three peaks mandatory

TRAILHEAD

See hike 20 for directions.

ROUTE

See hikes 18, 20, and 23 for the description. Continue from T-0 down and E for 1½ miles on the long, intimidating connecting ridge. Descend to the left (NE) at the end of the little notch within the first ¼ mile, then up and over the top of the very next one. A cairn on top may help, as you stay in the center of the ridge when possible. Loose, rotten scree and a narrow ridge make it harder. Go left (N) again for any other boulders you can't climb over. Finish ESE for an easier hike than the nearly 1-hour ridge walk from T-0. Most of the hikes through chapter 8 are visible from this peak, T-0, or Gilpin Peak! Nearby Dallas Peak towers to the E.

22 Mill Creek Trail to Waterline Trail

Elevation: 9760 feet, with 1015 feet vertical gain

Distance: Almost 3 miles from N Aspen Street and the start of Jud Wiebe Trail 432 to the bridge over Mill Creek, 6 miles round-trip; 6 miles bike **Loop** from Telluride

Duration: 1½ hours from town on Jud Wiebe Trail 432 to the bridge (high point) and end of the Waterline Trail, where it continues as Deep Creek Trail 418 going W (6 miles) or Mill Creek Trail going S (¾ mile), 3 hours round-trip; 30 minutes max walking up Mill Creek Trail, 1 hour round-trip; 1½ hours biking round-trip **Loop**.

Difficulty: Moderate. Steady climbing (hiking or biking). Waterline Trail is an easy traverse along the hillside above the Telluride valley

TRAILHEAD

Jud Wiebe Trail 432; see hike 29 for directions. Or take Mill Creek Road FS 637 1 mile W of Telluride on CO-145 Spur, turn right (N) up the steeper dirt road (requires 2WD high-clearance), and follow it to the end, 1½ miles, at the water treatment plant.

ROUTE

Great bike **Loop** W to E if you take the Bike Path 1 mile W of Telluride to Mill Creek Road FS 637 and go N (1½ miles) up to the Mill Creek–Deep Creek TH at the water treatment plant. From the water treatment plant, it's steeper up the fairly straight trail N (¾ mile) to the bridge on the right (E) over Mill Creek. Watch for lingering snow in late spring. The walk is a simple 20- to 30-minute uphill climb to the bridge overlooking the beautiful creek. Return the same way, or continue SSE from the bridge for the **Loop** on the Waterline Trail if you are biking. Contour under a cliff 2 miles to Sneffels Highline Trail going E. Stay on the main trail to cross Butcher Creek immediately, then go SE a few

Blanket of autumn gold on the Waterline Trail.

hundred feet to Jud Wiebe Trail 432, where you go right (SW, then SE) a mile to Telluride.

From Telluride, walk NW (1 mile) steeply up the W side of Jud Wiebe Trail 432 from N Aspen Street to the Deep Creek Trail 418 sign at the first intersection. Go left (NW), cross the bridge at Butcher Creek, and continue 2 miles past the sign for Sneffels Highline Trail 434. The jaunt to the bridge over Mill Creek is fairly level on the Waterline Trail from Butcher Creek as it turns (SWW) to come out and traverse a cliff band for a ways. Enjoy the view, because the trail turns NE and N into the woods up to the Mill Creek bridge.

TRAIL NOTES

....

....

....

....

....

....

....

Elevation: 10,260 feet, with 1130 feet vertical gain

Distance: 2½ miles up, 5 miles round-trip, 6½ miles round-trip **Loop** with Deep Creek Trail 418 to Mill Creek Trail and FS 637

Duration: 55–65 minutes up, 2–3 hours round-trip, 3–4 hours round-trip **Loop**

Difficulty: Moderate. Steeper up first official part, solid trails, slightly longer **Loop**

TRAILHEAD

See hike 20 for directions.

ROUTE

Walk left (NW) from the sign and gate at the only switchback up Mill Creek Road FS 637 to the rocky trail, as opposed to going straight (NNE) at the gate, which is the return of San Juan Don's Loop. The narrow trail soon climbs steeply up switchbacks. Move up the little shoulder E and turn back sharply left (N) at about 9700 feet (less than 1 mile), remembering to step off the trail when you see mountain bikers coming down. This trail is longer than "old" Eider Creek Trail, but it's enjoyable through a sizable aspen grove as it winds around private property. It meets the old trail high in a meadow and continues more steeply N ½ mile up to Deep Creek Trail 418 and signs.

Up Eider Creek Trail in the spring.

Proceed down the same route, or try this clockwise **Loop**. Go right (SE) a mile on Deep Creek Trail 418 through two meadows divided by a creek, and hike steadily (E) up to Sneffels Highline Trail 434 sign going N. Walk 1 mile (E) down steeply, turn right (S) on Mill Creek Trail before the Mill Creek bridge, and continue ¾ mile to Mill Creek Road FS 637, where you walk the road easily about a mile down to the switchback and parking. (Snowshoe these routes in winter. Some route-finding will be necessary with snow coverage.)

24   San Juan Don's Loop

Elevation: 10,620 feet, with 1500 feet vertical gain

Distance: 3½ miles to the high point, 5 miles round-trip **Loop**

Duration: 2 hours up, 2½–3 hours round-trip **Loop**

Difficulty: Strenuous. Animal trails, steady up and down with a couple of short, steeper areas, bushwhacking

TRAILHEAD

See hike 20 for directions.

ROUTE

See hike 23 to get to the Sneffels Highline Trail sign and high point. The **Loop** will be easier in a clockwise direction because of route-finding in the trees S from Sneffels Highline Trail 434. Go right (S) at the signs or 50 feet W of the signs to bushwhack down the wide shoulder off of Deep Creek Trail 418. Walk just to the left (E) of the pines on the wide shoulder extending (S) and close to the aspens on animal trails for about 10 minutes (¼ mile) to where the pines end and the aspens take over. Stay on the faded path and rise, and walk S ¼ mile into the next set of pines with a few aspens dispersed over flatter ground. Again try to walk barely left (E) of the thick trees to start, then go more to the middle and right near the end of the evergreens. Look for elk and deer to the end of the hike.

Bushwhack ¼ mile SW down through aspens as the terrain widens, staying slightly to the right (W) on the highest areas of the shoulder. It's slightly disorienting, and if you veer to the left (S) you will get to the top of a decent cliff band in a couple hundred yards with great views and flat spots for hanging out. No worries. A solid trail you cross near the cliff band takes you to the right (SW) a few hundred feet back to the crest of the main shoulder. The path becomes more obvious again as the main shoulder narrows and becomes slightly steeper SSW for ¼ mile. See rutting marks from the elk on the aspens, and follow the dirt trail more steeply as the shoulder changes shape again. It's ¼ mile of fun hiking (SW) down past the boulders, ancient pines, and scrub brush, as you stay on or just left (E) of the narrow, steep shoulder to the end of the trees. This is also the end of the shoulder. Get a look around for the remaining route. This hike has a good feel, like so many others in the mountains around Telluride, and the perceptual experience is sumptuous!

At the end of the shoulder you will see before you a huge patch of scrub brush and oak. Go fairly steeply to the left (SE) over 150 feet down off the end of

Oh hey, y'all!

the shoulder and left of the bushes to a flatter meadow below, with little to no trail. Follow the meadow (S) a few feet to the right (W) of another, smaller shoulder that continues S. You can follow the meadow or that small shoulder down ½ mile. Both ways lead into an aspen-filled gully and the faded trail just to the right (SW) of the wide gully. The faint path becomes more solid on the right side of the lively gully ¼ mile down to a tiny meadow, then a few hundred feet SW to an old road that parallels Mill Creek Road FS 637. From the old road, Mill Creek Road is 100 feet to the left (S), but I recommend heading to the right (SW) and down the less steep trail for a prettier, less dusty walk off the main road. It's ½ mile to the TH and parking on the switchback of Mill Creek Road FS 637.

TRAIL NOTES

....

....

....

....

....

....

....

CHAPTER 3

NORTH TELLURIDE

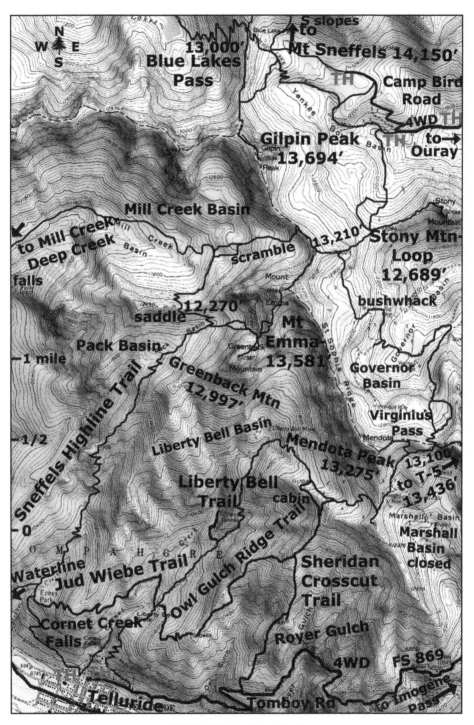

HIKES 25-30, 38, 40-44

Elevation: 12,270 feet, with 3450 feet vertical gain

Distance: 6½ miles up W side (Mill Creek Basin), 13 miles round-trip; 5½ miles up E side (Pack Basin), 11 miles round-trip, 14½ miles round-trip **Loop** including almost 2 miles of the Waterline Trail, which connects both ends of Sneffels Highline Trail 434

Duration: 3–4 hours up W side, 5–6 hours round-trip; 3 hours up E side, 4–5 hours round-trip; 6–8 hours round-trip **Loop** from Telluride

Difficulty: Strenuous. Lengthy, steeper, popular, solid trail

TRAILHEAD

Both routes will be for one way to the high saddle (12,270 feet) between Mill Creek and Pack Basins.

• **Opt 1:** For the Mill Creek Basin (W) side, take Mill Creek Road FS 637 1 mile W of Telluride on CO-145 Spur, turn right (N) up the steeper dirt road (requires 2WD high-clearance), and follow it to the end, 1½ miles, at the water treatment plant.

• **Opt 2:** For the Pack Basin (E) side, start on the W side of Jud Wiebe Trail 432; see hike 29 for directions.

ROUTE

For the W side of the trail from the water treatment plant (**Opt 1**), take Mill Creek Trail more steeply and fairly straight going N ¾ mile to the end. Hike left (W) on Deep Creek Trail 418 steeply more than a mile to the Sneffels Highline Trail 434 sign on the shoulder. Go right (N) through the trees up the little shoulder to climb again in the partial clearing. After about a mile, ascend several switchbacks and gain elevation quickly over 2 miles. The trail will head right (NE) for a while around the little ridge and into Mill Creek Basin under Dallas Peak. It's more gradual from here and the last 2 miles (NE, then SE) up to the high saddle between basins. The upper falls would be hard to miss on the right (E) halfway up Mill Creek Basin. Then follow the trail over low grass by wooden post markers. The route turns to the S at the top of the basin under Mount Emma, as you go past the giant cairns to the right, across a little shelf, and finally up more steeply to the main saddle at 12,270 feet.

For the E side of Sneffels Highline Trail 434 (**Opt 2**), hike steeply up Jud Wiebe Trail 432 1 mile to the first fork, go left (NW) on Deep Creek Trail 418 a couple hundred feet to cross the bridge over Butcher Creek, and walk up immediately to Sneffels Highline Trail 434 on the right. Take the narrow trail N just W of Butcher Creek gradually up through the forest the first mile through a few switchbacks. It's steep and rocky near the creek, as switchbacks lead N to upper Butcher Creek for another mile. At the big, narrow picnic rock off the trail to the right, head left (NW, then NE) and continue ½ mile up a little shoulder past the "portal" into Mill Creek Basin. Step off the trail 10 feet to the left (W), and get a

good first look from here. If snow lingers in the portal itself into late spring, Pack Basin above will also have snow and may not be reachable. This is a good rule of thumb. Climb up the ridge and more switchbacks (1 mile from the portal), then continue about ½ mile steeply NE to a sharp left turn (NNE) on the trail that leaves that ridge. Traverse next to a huge cliff band on the right (E) for ½ mile. The trail is super-narrow here and surrounded by steep yet beautiful terrain. Ice and snow often block

A curious red-tailed hawk was not afraid of people yet!

the trail into mid-June. The path ascends slowly as you get back into the thicker, high evergreens. Turn right of the old cabin on the hill and up a couple more switchbacks to leave the trees and gain the low basin ½ mile from the cabin foundation.

Extra-large cairns mark the trail through Pack Basin, as huge boulders and rocks blanket the unsurpassed, wildflower-covered, treeless meadow. Continue NE more than ½ mile through the basin more easily to the end, and go left (NW) a bit more steeply ½ mile up to the high saddle between Pack and Mill Creek Basins. Both basins are grand in very different ways. Connect the basins for a stupendous **Loop** (slightly easier going counterclockwise up to Pack Basin first) using Waterline Trail at the bottom to finish, as you would begin and end the **Loop** in Telluride. From the bottom of the Highline Trail on its W side, go left (E) down Deep Creek Trail 418 just over 1 mile steeply and cross Mill Creek over the bridge, then continue 2 miles (SE, then NE) along the Waterline Trail. Walk past the E side start of the Highline Trail to cross Butcher Creek immediately, and go a couple hundred feet to the Jud Wiebe Trail, where you head right (SSE) a mile steeply down to N Aspen Street.

Elevation: 12,997 feet, with 4117 feet vertical gain

Distance: 5½ miles up, 11 miles round-trip

Duration: 3½–4 hours up, 5½–7 hours round-trip

Difficulty: Very challenging. Steep, route-determining from Pack Basin, scree, longer

TRAILHEAD

Jud Wiebe Trail 432; see hike 29 for directions.

ROUTE

See hike 25, **Opt 2**. From the top of Pack Basin almost 5 miles from the start, leave the trail at nearly 12,000 feet, when it switches back to go NW up to the saddle between Pack and Mill Creek Basins. Bushwhack right (E) off the trail a couple hundred feet and up the ultra-steep, grassy slope 75 feet to the right (S) of a 60-foot-narrow, rocky gully that extends in the same direction. Scramble very steeply ¼ mile up the center of the scree-filled wider gully that extends E to the saddle between Mount Emma and Greenback Mountain on a faint path. Catch your breath at the saddle (12,700 feet) between Pack and Liberty Bell Basins.

Greenback Mountain has two ways up from the main saddle. Adventurous hikers climb 20–25 feet straight up fairly solid rock holds to the high ridge through one of the super-narrow, steep chutes directly in the center of the ridge (SE) to begin. Most hikers, however, follow a faint trail just left (SSE) of the ridge that contours around a huge boulder 30 feet below it. On the other side of this boulder, scramble (W) 30 feet up a steep but wide gully to the ridge crest. Large boulders along the ridgeline (SW) make the route more difficult the last ¼ mile. If it helps, angle to the right (W) near the very top, leaving the ridgetop for a moment to go through a rock doorway 15 feet W of the summit.

Mount Emma

Elevation: 13,518 feet, with vertical gains of 4836 feet from Telluride, 2180 feet from Yankee Boy Basin above Ouray

Distance: 6 miles up, 12 miles round-trip; 3 miles up from the main TH in Yankee Boy Basin, 6 miles round-trip

Duration: 4 hours up, 6 hours round-trip; 2 hours up, 4–5 hours round-trip from the main TH in Yankee Boy Basin

Difficulty: Expert-only. Extremely steep and loose, difficult route-finding, tight couloirs from Pack Basin, crack climb near the peak on the NE ridge from Yankee Boy Basin

TRAILHEAD

Jud Wiebe Trail 432; see hike 29 for directions. Or Yankee Boy Basin; see hike 37 for directions.

ROUTE

For the more difficult route, from Telluride, see hike 26 and go left (NE) from the saddle (12,700 feet) between Mount Emma and Greenback Mountain up Mount Emma's hugely steep S ridge on a faint, sometimes nonexistent trail. Start a few feet to the right (E) of the ridge crest, ascend the path ¼ mile, and traverse 200 feet left (N) of the first huge obstacles on the ridge: two very steep, narrow, Pack Basin–facing couloirs more than 100 feet long. It is possible to go a few feet left (NNE) of the actual ridge and climb one of the couloirs, but it's much easier to hug the rock band and couloirs to the left (N) to a small weakness 200 feet from the ridgeline. Climb up the loose rock and dirt easily 10 feet (E), then make your way 200 feet ENE on an ascending traverse back to the ridge crest for about ¼ mile more of steep hiking.

Now it gets fun! The couloirs on the ridge itself to the nearby peak are much steeper and might require ropes, but less difficult couloirs to the right (E) on the Liberty Bell Basin side will be better to ascend and descend without climbing gear, as there are several **Opts**. If you get dead-ended going up or coming down, backtrack and find a more suitable gully to climb.

At the next crux and cliffy area, **Opt 1** is to traverse about 50 feet E around the ridge on the Liberty Bell Basin side, where you can clearly see the jagged Saint Sophia Ridge extending SE from Mount Emma. Ascend a skinny, short

Yankee Boy Basin from Mount Emma.

gully 20–25 feet to the NW. At the top of it, go left (SW), cross another 10-foot-wide, thin couloir immediately to the other side, and turn sharply to the right (N) up big rocks to the next set of gullies while still on the E side of the ridge proper. A few well-placed cairns help; please leave these to assist others.

• **Opt 2** from the cliffy area on the ridge near the summit is to stay on or near the ridgeline up to a huge, round boulder (10 feet across) lodged in the ridge within a steep gully surrounded by rock walls that rise up 50 feet or so. Carefully climb under the boulder up the chute. Contour right (NE) on the Liberty Bell Basin side in the direction of the distinct Saint Sophia Ridge around the cliffs to meet **Opt 1**, and scramble 30 feet up (NW) the first climbable steep, loose gully back to the ridge. Contour more level ground 75 feet to the right (E) of the ridge and summit again; crossing loose scree past narrow gullies on your left (W), you'll come to a wider gully that is super-steep but doable, with okay holds for about 25–30 feet up. Traverse left (SW) 50 feet, turn right (N) up a short (about 30-foot), steep, thin gully that widens near the top, and walk more easily to the right 30 feet more (NE) over flatter rock to Mount Emma's awe-inspiring peak.

From Yankee Boy Basin, see Stony Mountain (hike 38) to the high, grassy saddle (12,300 feet) between Stony Mountain and the high point SW on the connecting ridge to Mount Emma. Hike right (SW) up the main ridge very steeply less than ½ mile over a tiny outcropping to a knob (13,210 feet) on the high ridge between Mount Emma (SW), Gilpin Peak (NW), and Stony Mountain (ENE). For Mount Emma's NE ridge just more than ¼ mile to the peak, walk to the left (SSW), and go to the left (E), right (W), and left (E) of obstacles on the ridgeline, in that order, fairly easily. Work your way a few feet right (W) and climb up a W-facing, steep, tight gully 10–12 feet back to the ridge proper. Continue up and left (E) a few feet around tall rock blocks back to the main ridge without difficulty. Just below the summit (ENE) on the ridge is a decent crux. Large, black, cracked boulders, known as the Block Tops, surround and obstruct easier travel on the ridge; they go all the way to Dallas Peak. Some people go to the left (SE) below the boulders and traverse a thin ledge 50 feet or so to find a steep, rocky, narrow couloir; unless snow or ice are present, from here you can go to the right (W) 30 feet back up to the ridge to a small notch.

It is more fun, however, to try the difficult, interesting, short free climb straight up the ridge through the cracks and directly over the huge boulders (rope belay not mandatory). There is some brief exposure here and up to the notch just NE of the peak. Pick your boulders and climb the crux area 50–60 feet, and then go over the notch immediately. Finish more easily the final few feet over flat rocks to the wonderful, wider-than-expected summit. You really get to experience firsthand the raw, powerful, intangible beauty of these tremendous mountains.

TRAIL NOTES

....

....

....

....

....

....

....

Elevation: 9200 feet, with 300 feet vertical gain

Distance: ¼ mile up, ½ mile round-trip

Duration: 20–30 minutes up, 1 hour round-trip

Difficulty: Moderate. Narrow, surprisingly steep, icy in winter, muddy when wet

TRAILHEAD

Jud Wiebe Trail 432; see hike 29 for directions.

ROUTE

Go straight up (NNE) past the sign and stay on the right side (E) of Cornet Creek the whole way. National Forest rangers fix the trail constantly because of

its location along a steep slide path. The hike ends for most people at the base of the beautiful, year-round, thin, 80-foot waterfall. The frozen falls are barely accessible many times throughout winter. The curious few hike much more steeply another ¼ mile and a few hundred feet over loose rock and scree to the right (NE) of the water, up to a small bridge near the top of the falls.

Cornet Creek Falls in its winter glory.

Elevation: 10,090 feet, with 1190 feet vertical gain

Distance: 1½ miles up the W side, 3 miles round-trip; 2 miles up the E side, 4 miles round-trip; 3½ miles round-trip **Loop**

Duration: 45 minutes up the W side, 1½–2 hours round-trip; 1 hour up the E side, 2–3 hours round-trip; 1½–2 hours round-trip **Loop**

Difficulty: Moderate. Steeper in a few spots; pretty popular, wide, obvious trail

TRAILHEAD

Jud Wiebe Trail 432 at the top of N Aspen Street in Telluride. To avoid the frustration of trying to park legally next to the THs (2-hour limit, free Sundays and holidays), park at the free lot on the SW end of Telluride (Mahoney Drive, first right at the traffic circle coming into town), or nearby off of Mahoney Drive on W Pacific Avenue to Carhenge parking lot just E of Lift 7. Walk up to a mile to the THs on the N side of town, or grab the free bus that comes every 10–20 minutes most times of the year and get off on Colorado Avenue or the street you want (hint: this might take longer for hikes on the N side of town).

Snowshoe on Jud Wiebe Trail.

NOTES

Both routes are for uphill only to the high traverse and small wooden bench overlooking the valley. The trail is steeper and slightly longer on the (E) side, but it still makes an excellent **Loop** in either direction. You can hike or snow-shoe this trail year-round!

ROUTE

If you start on the W side of Jud Wiebe Trail 432, walk left (W) over the bridge and Cornet Creek. The route rises more steeply to the NW for about 20 minutes, including a couple of switchbacks. Around the corner now going E (1 mile from the TH), see a sign indicating a trail left (W) to Mill Creek, Deep Creek, and Sneffels Highline Trail 434. Continue up the trail immediately by the "no horses" sign to the right (E) and 200 feet over the little ridge known as Epees Park. After some steeper switchbacks, you gain the high traverse and come up to the bench seat and high point in the clearing. You will have postcard views of the whole valley, including Bridal Veil and Ingram Falls, and many high basins and peaks. Walk down the same route, or do a **Loop** ending on Tomboy Road a couple blocks E from the other start.

For the E side of the trail, walk to the right (E) at the top of N Oak Street onto Tomboy Road FS 869 and go left (NW) at the first road, switchback, and gate, barely ¼ mile up the dirt road. Continue up steep, rocky switchbacks beyond the water storage tanks and into the wonderful aspen grove on a straightaway. Hike up a small hill on the trail (1 mile from the TH) and down a few feet directly to Liberty Bell Flats in the aspens. Going straight (NE) will take you up Liberty Bell Trail; going right (E) will take you on the faint Owl Gulch Ridge Trail 420. To the left is Jud Wiebe Trail 432. Go left (NW) down ¼ mile into the "enchanted" forest and over the wooden bridge crossing the

creek. Snow lingers late into spring here. Hike steeply into the aspens and follow the trail as it gradually winds (SW) up to the high traverse and bench out of the woods. Hike down the same way, or better yet continue the **Loop**, which will be easier and shorter in this counterclockwise direction.

Bridge to the enchanted forest on Jud Wiebe Trail.

Elevation: 10,420 feet at the Stillwell Tunnel; 11,890 feet at the tiny old shed; 12,500 feet at the high saddle E of Liberty Bell Basin; with verticals gains of 1540 feet, 3010 feet, 3620 feet

Distance: 1½ miles up, 3 miles round-trip; 3 miles up, 6 miles round-trip; 4 miles up, 8 miles round-trip; 6 miles round-trip **Loop** with Sheridan Crosscut or Owl Gulch Ridge Trails to the same TH

Duration: 1½ hours to the Stillwell Tunnel, 3 hours round-trip; 2½ hours to the tiny old shed, 4–5 hours round-trip; 3–3½ hours to the high saddle E of Liberty Bell Basin, 5 hours round-trip

Difficulty: Strenuous. Consistently steep, semi-loose rocks near the high saddle

TRAILHEAD

Jud Wiebe Trail 432; see hike 29 for directions.

ROUTE

See hike 29 for the description on the E side of the trail to Liberty Bell Flats 1 mile from the TH. Go straight (NE) at the forks on the wide, flat trail instead of continuing left (W) down on Jud Wiebe Trail 432. Cross a couple seasonal creeks with ¼ mile of easier walking, then hike much more steeply a couple hundred yards (NE) to a fork where you head left (NW) if your goal is to hike to the flatter Stillwell Tunnel area. The trail levels the last ¼ mile or so to the tunnel site in the side of the cliff band. It is locked up for safety reasons but blows a cool breeze out full-time and might feel nice on a hot summer day!

The fork and route to Liberty Bell Basin goes to the right (NNE) up more steeply past old miners' cabins compacted and reclaimed by the forest. Above them and two switchbacks is the even steeper trail and a little rock ridge to the left (N). Take the super-steep trail NE to another switchback, and you will soon get to the lower basin while still in the trees (2 miles from the TH). It's easy to get lost as the trail turns back sharply a few times (¼ mile) going up (SE). Also you finally realize why you worked so hard to get up here, as you break out of the thick trees and gaze at the superb beauty of the basin, Saint Sophia Ridge, and the peaks of Greenback, Emma, and Mendota.

Keep going SE, left (N) about 100 yards or so of a little ridge. Stay on the

Virginius Pass and T-5 from the top of Liberty Bell Basin.

trail as it makes a sharp right (SSW) to the little ridge. Also on that turn is a faint path that goes up the grassy slope, at first, to the high saddle at the top of the basin (1 mile away). Hike up ESE or follow the main trail SW to the little ridge, then SE into the high evergreens on the widening trail. This goes ¼ mile over to the tiny old shed, which is also the top of hikes 40 and 41. From there you can still proceed up to the high saddle that separates Liberty Bell Basin from Marshall Basin. Find the trail that angles to the left (NW) above the shed from the right (E) of it over to the little ridge. Bushwhack up to a faint path that goes NE into the high basin to meet Liberty Bell Trail going E in a few hundred feet.

If you are going to the high saddle from the meadow ¼ mile below the old shed, hike the faint path more steeply up the right (S) side of the basin, center, then left (NE) side with some easier route-finding almost 1½ miles to the high saddle. It's much steeper and more loose, rocky, and narrow up the left side (NE) of the back of Liberty Bell Basin going (SE) ¼ mile to the high saddle. Return down Liberty Bell Trail, or **Loop** with hike 40 or 41.

Hike and snowshoe these trails in late fall or spring, although route-finding becomes difficult near the basin if you are coming up Liberty Bell Trail. Use the little ridge over to the tiny shed as a guide, and stay away from avalanche-prone areas.

CHAPTER 4

FAR NORTH TELLURIDE
(RIDGWAY–OURAY–MONTROSE)

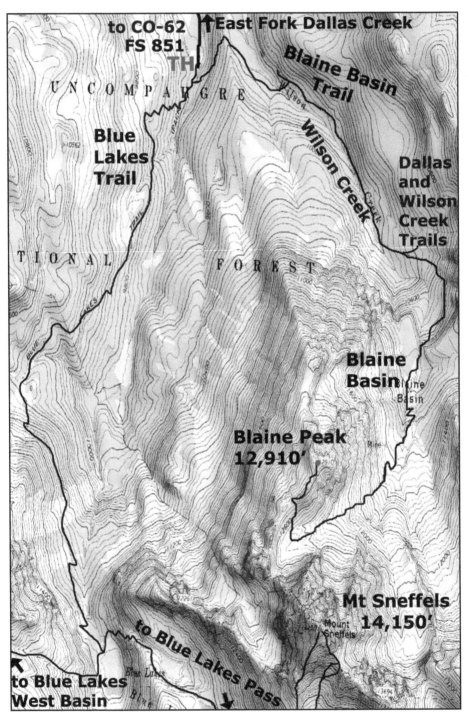

to CO-62
FS 851
TH

↑East Fork Dallas Creek

Blaine Basin Trail

UNCOMPAHGRE

Blue Lakes Trail

Wilson Creek

Dallas and Wilson Creek Trails

TIONAL

FOREST

Blaine Basin

Blaine Peak 12,910'

Blaine Basin

Mt Sneffels 14,150'

Mount Sneffels

to Blue Lakes Pass

↑
to Blue Lakes West Basin

↓

HIKES 31, 32, 35, 36, 39

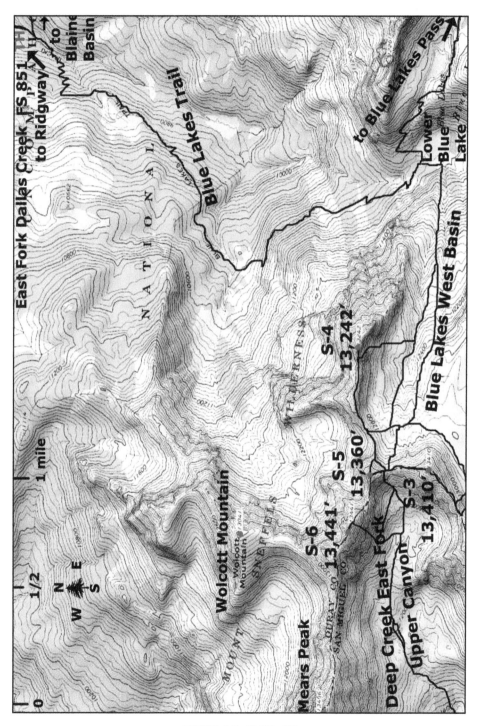

HIKES 6-8, 31-34, 39

31 Blue Lakes Trail 201 to Blue Lakes Pass

Elevation: 11,000 feet; 13,000 feet; with vertical gains of 1660 feet to Lower Blue Lake, 3660 feet to Blue Lakes Pass

Distance: 3⅓ miles to Lower Blue Lake, 7 miles round-trip; 5⅔ miles to Blue Lakes Pass, 12 miles round-trip

Duration: 1½ hours to Lower Blue Lake, 3–4 hours round-trip; 3½–4 hours to Blue Lakes Pass, 6 hours round-trip

Difficulty: Mix of moderate (steady, steep with some breaks, horse trail) and strenuous (steep above tree line, loose scree, many switchbacks)

TRAILHEAD

From Montrose, drive 25 miles S on US-550 to Ridgway, then 5 miles toward Dallas Divide and Telluride on CO-62 W to Dallas Creek/Ouray Co-7 Road, which goes left (S). From Telluride, drive 16 miles down valley on CO-145 W, then 19 miles on CO-62 E to E Dallas Creek/Ouray Co-7 on the right near the bottom of Dallas Divide. A sign on CO-62 says "Forest Service Access; Dallas Creek." Stay on the main 2WD dirt road FS 851 going S for 40 minutes max (nearly 9 miles from CO-62), following the signs, and cross a total of seven cattle guards. At the last one, 7 miles from CO-62, you enter the Uncompahgre National Forest. The road is not steep but is bumpy in places. Cross the creek over the bridge at 8 miles from CO-62, drive by a camping area, and pass the little three-way intersection to the nearby TH and sign. There is a portable restroom and plenty of parking.

ROUTE

Walk up the trail from the signs and come almost immediately to a fork. Blaine Basin Trail goes to the left (E). Hike SW up steeper turns and in a few minutes begin a series of eight switchbacks. About 1½ miles from the TH, you will ascend two more switchbacks before it levels out to the Sneffels Wilderness sign. You will be above the aspen line in the evergreens as you contour easily for a bit before going S down slightly and briefly to cross a western arm of East Fork Dallas Creek in a clearing. Hike up again (SE) into the trees and up two switchbacks before traversing SE ½ mile or so around the mountain. Walk (1 mile to

Another great Southwest Colorado sunset.

last switchbacks) over the little log bridge covering wetlands in the flats, and go past the first little cascading falls while you are still in the trees just before a semi-clearing. The second cascading waterfall is visible to the left (E) as you hike up two more quick switchbacks in the clearing. Contour into the pines on an easier grade ¼ mile to Lower Blue Lake. See the sign and fork in the woods before the lake.

It's about 2½ miles (SE) more to Blue Lakes Pass. To the right (S) are lake-viewing trails and the bushwhack to Blue Lakes West Basin and peaks S-3 through S-6. Spend some quality time at this exquisitely colorful setting, and return by the same route. To go to the two upper lakes or Blue Lakes Pass, walk to the left at the sign before and NW of the lake, and continue up the trail and steeper switchbacks. Go by grass and wildflowers above the big, bright blue, lower lake. Ascend about 500 feet (SE) before you level out some. Walk to the right (S) of the next lake, which is much smaller than Lower Blue Lake. The trail will take you up more easily to the mouth of the last deep blue lake, where you go to the left (N) of it and debate making the long, steep climb to the pass. Then again, you can't enjoy views of Yankee Boy Basin unless you climb the nearly twenty pesky switchbacks (E).

Elevation: 12,800 feet, with 3460 feet vertical gain

Distance: 5-plus miles up, 11 miles round-trip

Duration: 2½–3 hours up, 5–6 hours round-trip

Difficulty: Strenuous. Thin path to bushwhacking only above Lower Blue Lake

TRAILHEAD

See hike 31 for directions.

ROUTE

Walk ¼ mile to the right (W) of Lower Blue Lake from the sign before the lake. There are many paths, but take the most pronounced one as you go by a small rock fire pit while you are still in the trees. Leave the lake and go right (W) to follow the first of two streams coming out of Blue Lakes West Basin. The faint trail starts on the near side (N) of the closer stream. You will be lined up with the center of the big lake and low basin. Hike steeply in the trees to start as the trail fades out. Stay on the right (N) side of the creek into the clearing, then cross to the left (S) ¼ mile from the lake as the route will become much steeper. Follow the grassy rise ¼ mile steeply up to the W.

Lower Blue Lake from Blue Lakes West Basin.

A smaller creek begins to appear on the left (S), with a decent stream farther left (S) in the basin coming out of the mountain under the imposing Dallas Peak. Stay on the steep rise, as you will hike by a multitude of wildflowers near the bottom of the basin. Go to a steeper, rockier area straight up the rise or bailout in the grass to the right (NNW), but still left (S) of the main creek. If you take the lower, slightly easier bushwhack, angle back to the left (W) and toward higher areas in a couple hundred yards. This will be moments after you see the creek (W) going up much more steeply ahead in the rock band. A thin path may be present. If you stayed on the highest bushwhack past the rockier area in the grass, stay near the middle of the rise, and go left (SW) 50 feet around or through the last of the pine bushes to the midbasin. Stroll over nicer terrain and a tad to the left (W) ¼ mile up to the next rise in the grassier areas. Then walk through the boulder-laden meadow ¼ mile to the high basin. You will have to climb up a wide, rocky, steeper area just below the high basin.

Choose from many options from this beautiful basin. **Opt 1** is the simplest: go down by the same route you came up. **Opt 2**: Continue to the left (SW) in the middle of the high basin, and go ½ mile to the highest areas and back of the magnificent basin under T-0 (N of Campbell Peak, S of S-3). **Opt 3**: Continue with a steep scramble NW ¼ mile up to the saddle between T-0 and S-3. **Opt 4**: Climb WNW ¼ mile to the wide saddle between S-3 and S-5 (slightly to the right from the top of Blue Lakes West Basin; may be the best choice of saddles to visit). **Opt 5**: Go N ¼ mile to the saddle between S-5 and S-4 from the top of the basin. The last few options will be more difficult, but as always in Colorado, the higher you get, the better the views!

TRAIL NOTES

....

....

....

....

....

....

....

Elevation: 13,410 feet, with vertical gains of 4070 feet from Blue Lakes TH, 4300 feet from the bottom of Last Dollar Road at Deep Creek–Whipple Mountain TH

Distance: 6½ miles up, 13 miles round-trip; 7¼ miles up, 15 miles round-trip

Duration: 3½–4½ hours up, 6–7 hours round-trip **Loop**; 5½ hours up, 8 hours round-trip

Difficulty: Very challenging. Tedious hike, exposed N ridge, super-steep

TRAILHEAD

See hike 31 for directions. Or Deep Creek–Whipple Mountain TH; see hike 6 for directions.

ROUTE

See hike 32, **Opt 4**, to the saddle N of S-3 (shortest route), and reverse the directions below from the saddle. Walk left (SW) ½ mile to the low areas in the middle of the highest basin to hike a clockwise **Loop** around S-3 from Blue Lakes West Basin and avoid sidestepping a long section of scree coming down from the right and S-3's SE face. Continue with a very steep scramble NW ¼ mile up the rocks to the saddle between T-0 (SW) and S-3 (NE) by going a few feet to the left (S) of the rock ribs extending down from the saddle. A slightly shorter **Alt** route: ascend a scree rise to the right and NE of the saddle a few hundred yards before you get to the base of the saddle; and traverse the super-steep slope NW ¼ mile through the scree to the nearby high ridge 100 feet NW of the saddle.

Hike up the ridge (NE) carefully ¼ mile to the peak, as the going is narrow and semi-exposed with huge drop-offs on both sides. The scree is loose and crumbling with every step. The walk up the last part of the summit block is wider as you steeply climb the yellow and reddish flat rock on or just to the left (W) of the actual ridge. The ridge section to the N to the main saddle between S-3 and S-5 is not as tough as it looks from most angles but does require your utmost attention.

Return the same way down the SW ridge, or for a slightly more challenging descent, hike a **Loop** around the peak: From the peak, descend the N ridge ¼ mile to the saddle over many small impediments, spires, and much loose

From the southwest ridge of S-3.

rock. Climb and boulder straight over most of the knobs on the ridgeline closer to the summit. A really steep, loose spire directly above the saddle will force you to go to the right (E) 30–40 feet off the ridge crest and contour 200 feet or so through the rocks just below the super-steep section; then hike directly back to the ridge near the bottom of the N ridge. Hike down from the saddle to the right (ESE) steeply and loosely into Blue Lakes West Basin, staying high and to the right (SE). For the easiest descent, head down the center of the big basin (E).

Elevation: 13,242 feet, with 3900 feet vertical gain

Distance: 6 miles up, 12 miles round-trip

Duration: 3½–4 hours up either of two routes, 6 hours round-trip

Difficulty: Mix of expert-only (from S-4 and S-5 saddle on a clock-wise **Loop** around the peak, narrow, exposed ridge, gripping crux W of the smaller summit, steep-sloping boulders) and very challeng-ing (up and back down the big S-facing couloir just W of the peak, extremely steep and loose, steep-sloping boulders)

TRAILHEAD

See hike 31 for directions.

ROUTE

See hike 32 for the description. From the high basin under the E shoulder of S-3, walk to the right (N) and traverse 1/4 mile to the long, rocky saddle between S-5 and S-4 fairly easily. Go right (NE), and stay a few feet right (S) of the actual ridge or on it to the major crux and headwall a few hundred feet away. The headwall on the ridge W of the lower summit goes about 20–25 feet nearly straight up NE to the main ridge. The best way is to climb the sheer rock wall only a few feet to the right (S) of the ridge center. There are solid hand- and footholds, but take your time. About 10 feet farther to the right of the ridge, the climb would be looser and more difficult. And about 30 feet or so right (S) of the ridge proper and down is a difficult crack climb. Just below that (S) is a thin, S-facing, narrow, rock-filled gully that folks can slowly ascend N 50 feet and go left (NNW) 30 feet more to the ridge crest for better footing.

Hike NE directly to a small high point (lower summit) on the narrow, exposed ridge. Enjoy the magnificent views while you are stationary, and watch where you plant your feet for the rest of the route to be safe. Walk a few feet E to the base of the true summit block and boulder up. It's fairly difficult in one more little spot with large, flat, steep-sloping boulders to go over (only 10–12 feet max), so proceed mindfully one at a time. Climb the short, rock-filled gully just to the right (S) on the ridge to the nearby scree-covered peak.

Return the same way if you want, but it's easier to descend directly S into Blue Lakes West Basin. Boulder down (W) from the summit back to a low spot in the high ridge E of the lower summit and major crux section. Work your way

S-4 ridge including the major crux from S-3.

to the long, S-facing couloir in the wide outcrop (with slightly reddish rock) to the left (SE) 50 feet or so on a traverse above tight couloirs to the widest one from the high ridge between the dual summits. Hint: you can easily see the route, couloirs, and spires from Blue Lakes West Basin to the N. The super-loose, steep talus and rock can be ascended as well by this route if you wish to avoid the 20- to 25-foot rock wall climb at the crux (climbing gear is not mandatory, but climbing attitude is). Ski the scree and scramble 600 feet straight down S, hugging the rib on your right (W). The rocks get bigger near the bottom of the couloirs, where you slow down and bushwhack another 100 feet to the lowest areas in the grass near the creek. Follow the creek bed down a mile to Lower Blue Lake, or head toward the grassy area down a bit lower (½ mile) and just to the right (S) of the creek. Cross the creek again to the left (N) near tree line, and follow the more solid trail to Lower Blue Lake.

Elevation: 10,800 feet in the lower basin; 12,000 feet in the upper basin; with vertical gains of 1460 feet, 2660 feet

Distance: 3 miles one way, 6½ miles round-trip; 4 miles one way, 8 miles round-trip

Duration: 1½ hours to the low basin, 3 hours round-trip; 2 hours to the upper basin, 4–5 hours round-trip

Difficulty: Strenuous. River crossings could be difficult during high water in spring, some steeper areas

TRAILHEAD

See hike 31 for directions.

ROUTE

See the big sign for Blue Lakes TH at the end of the parking lot, and follow the trail for only a minute to the main intersection and more signs. Blaine Basin Trail shares the next 2⅓ miles with the Dallas and Wilson Creek trails. Go to the left (E) over the wooden bridge immediately and cross East Fork Dallas Creek. The wide trail gains little elevation in the aspens and evergreens for the first mile on the traverse NE, then SE to the first crossing of Wilson Creek. The ATV (all-terrain vehicle) trail crosses the stream; ignore it and continue up the right (W) side of the creek on the thin path 100 feet before you cross to the left (E) over the logs. The ATV trail continues to the left (NW) at the fork on the other side of the creek, and Blaine Basin is to the right (SE) on the fat trail. The next water negotiation in ½ mile is okay. When the ATV trail runs into the creek again, skip it and continue very briefly on the left (E) side of the water for two more chances and more suitable log crossings. When you are on the other side of the water again, follow the stream on its right (W) side for another ½ mile to yet another crossing of Wilson Creek. Go 20 feet up from where the trail runs into the water again, and across to the left (E) over two logs tied together. Look far up valley (S) to see waterfalls coming through a crack in the pine-covered cliff band. Walk on the left (E) side of the creek briefly, and go to the left (SE) up slightly more steeply at a sign indicating that Blaine Basin is 1 mile away and a different thin trail continues along the water. Get to another convergence of paths in a hundred feet. The sign says the Dallas Trail (horse trail) goes 7½ miles

From beautiful Blaine Basin.

to FS 852 near Ouray. Wilson Creek Trail uses part of the Dallas Trail; it would make a good **Alt** day hike, taking the same amount of time as the Blaine Basin hike. For the Wilson Creek Trail, you would go steadily and more steeply about 1½ miles NNE to the high point of the trail above the trees; here you'll enjoy delightful views of Blaine Basin, Mount Sneffels, and the summits of Box Factory Park (and on a clear day, the La Sal Mountains of Utah).

Staying en route to Blaine Basin, follow the narrowing trail to the right (SE) at the signage, and immediately cross a thin, rocky drainage. Continue much more steeply to the bottom of a semi-clearing, traveling over fairly loose rock. Thankfully you only ascend very steeply for 5 minutes here before traversing to the right (S) well under the cliffs. Back into the pines, it is steep at first, then easier as you cross two more thin, rocky drainages on the trail. Contour along a steep, rocky little clearing, and then hike more steeply for a minute back into the trees before descending slightly. Continue up more easily SW on the solid trail to the bottom of the lower basin, which is in a big clearing and meadow. Grasses, wildflowers, skunk cabbage, creek feeds, and good picnic spots are abundant in this great little basin.

Return by the same route, or press on to the middle or upper basins. To get to better views above, quickly cross two little creek feeds in the flats of the lower left-hand (E) side of the basin. Take the solid trail up somewhat more steeply ¼ mile to the small midbasin. The main creek is on the right (W), and cascading falls are to the left. Behind you a sign announces "Blaine Basin."

Walk over the brief flat area to the steeper switchbacks (S), and hike to the nearby boulder-filled high basin, where you are greeted with remarkable views of several high thirteeners and one fourteener. A huge scree field lies ahead and left (SSE) under Mount Sneffels and Cirque Mountain. Large boulders lie in front of you, with steep, grassy slopes of Blaine Peak to the right (W). A fork is on the knoll at the top of the upper basin in which the left-hand **Alt** takes you on a traverse to the E around the N ridge of Cirque Mountain and into East Blaine Basin. That would make for yet another great day hike. The route to the right continues to the trail visible ahead on the steep, grassy hillside E of Blaine Peak and goes to that summit. Return the same way.

TRAIL NOTES

....

....

....

....

....

....

....

36   Blaine Peak

Elevation: 12,910 feet, with 3570 feet vertical gain

Distance: 5½ miles up, 11 miles round-trip

Duration: 3–4 hours up, 7–8 hours round-trip

Difficulty: Very challenging. Longer than it looks, route-discovering, steep scrambling, slight exposure

TRAILHEAD

See hike 31 for directions.

ROUTE

See hike 35 to the upper basin, and follow the trail to the right (SW) on the steep, grassy slope ESE of Blaine Peak (out of sight). To begin, immediately cross two small creeks to the right (W) of the boulder field in the flats. Easily follow the cairned path and ascend a steeper section to the right (W) for about 150 yards on the less-than-obvious trail. Then traverse to the left (S) a moment on the more pronounced path above tree line. Climb the steep switchbacks. The hiking is not too difficult across the slope, but everything changes as the trail abruptly ends at a creek and creek bed crossing. Bushwhack and boulder up the super-steep rise on the left (S) side of the creek. Then climb a shorter, easier stretch as you follow the cairned route SW over the fairly solid boulders and rocks to the left (S) of a little low spot in the scree and over to the nearby grassier areas. Remember this section for the return trip, as you will go to the right (S) of the sunken area in the scree field and down (NE) the steep, rocky rise. You will leave the rise before it ends and head to the left (N) across the creek, seeing the obvious trail on the other side to descend the steep hillside NE to upper Blaine Basin.

Golden eagle on Blaine Peak!

Hike up the big, grassy rise in the center of the rocky, high saddle SW of Blaine Basin a few hundred feet toward (W) the gendarmes made of huge, rock towers on the ridge that connects Mount Sneffels and Blaine Peak until the rise splits into two. The grassier way goes to the left (SW); the rockier way goes to the right (N). Scramble to the right, and leave the rocky rise and otherworldly basin almost right away, climbing the super-steep, scree-covered hillside to the N ¼ mile to the ridge proper. Look up in the scree and perhaps see cairns as you climb a couple of easier turns in the semisolid rock field. Then go steeply up to a little grassy area below a line of rocks on the right (E) below the ridgeline. Hike to the left (W) through a weakness in the little rock band. There is some looser rock and grass around, but you will reach the high ridge quickly. You will arrive at a small saddle to the right (NE) of two little bumps and the huge spires on the connecting ridge. Finally see Blaine Peak on the ridge to the NE.

Getting to the high ridge is not hard but is more time consuming than you might suspect. As an **Alt** you could bypass all of the obstacles on the first section of ridge by skirting them down to the left (W) more than ¼ mile, then gaining the ridge high in the grass again. But the ridge walk is far more interesting and picturesque. Walk up the ridge crest in the middle where it's easy at first, and pass grassy, moss-covered rock. Notice steep drop-offs as you boulder to the first would-be crux. See the small spire on the ridge directly in front of you and the larger outcropping on the ridge beyond a small saddle. Pick your way down the super-steep rock on the ridge proper, or go just to the left (W) or right slightly and down short rock ramps that each go a few feet back to the actual ridge. Immediately go just to the right (E) of the small spire blocking the ridge through a convenient crack in the rock. Walk more easily to the right (E) of the outcropping ahead through the scree to the grassy, wider section of ridge that meets the bypass route.

Do not hike to the top of the bump in the center of the ridge just S of the peak, but proceed to the left (NW) in the grass by boulders to a low saddle below the summit block. From there, and with no more grass, pick a path up the boulders and rock, as you go just to the left or right of the actual ridge, which seems plenty wide enough for the moment. It's not difficult, but check your hand- and footholds up the semisolid, steep rock, as there is a little exposure near the peak. The summit looks very steep from most angles, and indeed it is; but it has the dubious distinction of hanging in the shadows of the colossal Mount Sneffels, which towers almost 1250 feet above Blaine Peak to the S. The other peaks to the left of Mount Sneffels are Kismet, Cirque Mountain, Mount Ridgway (directly E), and Whitehouse Mountain.

37   Gilpin Peak

Elevation: 13,694 feet, with vertical gains of 1894 feet from Wrights Lake TH, 2294 feet from where most people park (in the flats near the outhouse, below the steep section ½ mile E of Wrights Lake TH)

Distance: 2 miles up, 4 miles round-trip

Duration: 2 hours up, 3 hours round-trip, 5 hours max round-trip clockwise **Loop** including the Blue Lakes Pass ridge between Gilpin Peak and Mount Sneffels

Difficulty: Mix of strenuous (steep scree trail, bushwhacking) and very challenging (with the Blue Lakes Pass ridge, exposure, scrambling)

TRAILHEAD

Yankee Boy Basin. Drive 35 miles from Telluride to Ridgway (CO-145 W, then CO-62 E), turn right (S) on US-550, and go 9 miles more through the alluring Box Canyon town of Ouray. After the first big switchback S of town, turn right (SSW) onto Camp Bird Road FS 361. It's about an hour from Telluride to Camp Bird Road (20 minutes and 23 miles from Silverton, 1½ hours and 70 miles from Durango on US-550 N) and another hour to the high parking at Wrights Lake TH. Drive up the dirt road 4 miles (SW) as it gets rougher for 2WD vehicles. Park if you question your vehicle's clearance. At 5 miles from US-550, the road gets rockier below the overhanging mountain. The turnoff for Imogene Pass Road FS 869 appears at nearly 6 miles and 30 minutes up the road. Continue to the right (W) at the fork with Governor Basin, and 4WD to the right of the green "Ouray-26 County" sign. About 7 miles from US-550, the terrain flattens out some near a decent outhouse on your left. Most people park around this general area in Yankee Boy Basin and hike from there. It's about a 20-minute walk to the Wrights Lake TH. Or you can 4WD ½ mile steeply up to a very sharp switchback and TH. There are only a couple of spots at the TH, but you can also park at the next turn or down the road a hundred feet or so. The 4WD is expert-only the last mile past the Wrights Lake TH and the switchback to the end of the road at Mount Sneffels TH.

ROUTE

Walk up the steep road ½ mile W or drive to the TH and sign that says "Wrights Lake .5, Blue Lakes Pass 1.6." The trail (W) is well defined through grass and rocks above tree line. Continue around the small lake easily and briefly on a dirt road, observing a nice reflection of Gilpin Peak. Go NW up steeper switchbacks beyond Wrights Lake on the main trail for ½ mile, and leave it before the sign for Blue Lakes Pass or Mount Sneffels to bushwhack to the left (SW) to the low saddle of Gilpin Peak. Blue Lakes Pass and the connecting ridge from Mount Sneffels are great for a semi-difficult side trip, but are not necessary for ascending Gilpin Peak in a timely fashion. Bushwhack ¼ mile on an ascending traverse S through the grass to the steep scree coming down from Gilpin's NW ridge connecting with Mount Sneffels. Climb 200 feet up the left (S) side of a rock rib extending down E from the low saddle on the main ridge just N of the steeps on the ridge itself. The rock is bigger and stable, but pretty steep, and there is no concrete trail. Contour to the left (SW) just below the actual ridge en route to the small saddle.

Hike up the ridge S on the faint rock path, and go to the left (E) of the two major obstacles (rock fins) ahead, barely getting back to the ridge proper between them. Gloves come in handy on the steep, loose, rocky path. Stay close to the second obstacle and spires up the steep ridge section by climbing just left (E) of the ridge and to the right of a lingering snow field, then make your way back to the ridge crest. The walking is better on top of the steeps, as you go to the left (SE) for the last ½ mile to the peak. There is some fun bouldering and semi-loose rock, and you go straight over or around the sub-summit to the right (W) on the wide ridge. The traverse trail around the knob thins out as you sneak up to the nearby peak.

From the low saddle below the steepest part of the NW ridge, you can hug the rock rib steeply E and NNE down to the top of Yankee Boy Basin and catch the trail E down to Wrights Lake as in the ascent route. Or continue the ridge walk for less than 45 minutes and ½ mile N to Blue Lakes Pass so you can savor the spectacular views of both huge basins a while longer on a **Loop** back to Yankee Boy Basin. With some judicious route-finding, this section of ridge is still more difficult than the entire rest of the ridge connecting Gilpin Peak and Mount Sneffels! From the low saddle NW of Gilpin Peak, continue to follow the ultra-thin ridge N, with certain exposure directly over the first bump to the next problem. Go to the right (E) just a few feet and up a short, super-steep, fairly narrow chute back to the ridge crest. The rock is more stable than on Gilpin's summit block, but definitely check all hand- and footholds; again, wearing gloves will help deal with the sharp rock. The walking is a little better near Blue Lakes Pass but is razor thin at times and makes you wonder if you are doing the right thing! Stay directly in the center of the ridge as long as possible. It's about 45 minutes and more than 1½ miles down SE to the TH from Blue Lakes Pass, as you go on either trail past Wrights Lake or the Mount Sneffels TH on the popular trails.

Elevation: 12,698 feet on Stony Mountain; 13,210 feet on the high ridge between Mill Creek and Yankee Boy Basins; with vertical gains of 900 feet from the official Wrights Lake TH and tiny parking area in Yankee Boy Basin, 1300 feet from the big meadow ½ mile below the steep road to Wrights Lake TH for the most popular TH, 4500 feet from downtown Telluride

Distance: 2½ miles up, 5 miles round-trip from the big meadow; 7½ miles up, 15 miles round-trip from Telluride

Duration: 2 hours up, 3–4 hours round-trip; 6 hours up, 10–12 hours round-trip

Difficulty: Mix of strenuous (from Yankee Boy Basin, thin path fades to bushwhacking, drop-offs, loose rock) and expert-only (from Telluride, really long, punishing, super-steep ups and downs, some exposure, route-locating, scrambling, much scree)

TRAILHEAD

Yankee Boy Basin; see hike 37 for directions. Or see hike 29 for the difficult route from Telluride.

ROUTE

Start on the trail W from the official Wrights Lake TH. Immediately leave the main trail for one of two paths to the left (S) that quickly take you past a little rock pile, then across a small meadow to cross Sneffels Creek. You can see Stony Mountain to the SE on the other side of the sizable basin S of Yankee Boy Basin, which you must ascend. When you are safely over the water, climb up steeply and briefly, then traverse the thin trail to the left (SE), and around and S into the basin W of the peak. In July and August you will pass incredible numbers of wildflowers here and all the way (1 mile more) up to the high ridge SW of Stony Mountain. From the main path, cross a much smaller creek in the center of the large side basin, and bushwhack up S to two solid paths. The steeper one to the left (SE) works, and so does the easier traverse on the right (SW). From the traverse, head up more steeply to the left (SE) and go left again (S) on a pretty simple contour to the main ridge. There are no discernible trails high in the basin, but then again you can see the summit from the whole hike if you start in

Yankee Boy Basin. It's only 45 minutes from the TH proper to the high ridge and grassy saddle between Stony Mountain and a high point on the connecting ridge with Mount Emma.

Boulder left (NE) up the thin, loose, rocky main ridge with no trail, as it gets slightly steeper a mile (30 minutes) to the peak. Go NE, then slightly E, to a high point on the ridge, but cut to the right (S) about 30 feet before the top, and carefully traverse E around to a large saddle. You can also go straight over the small high point, then down 50 feet E to the nearby saddle. The challenging climb up the ridge proper from the large saddle goes ESE up and down over bumps ¼ mile to the peak with much loose rock. By skipping the high ridge with that large spire in the middle of another notch, you can hike up grassy ledges and ramps S of the peak with great footing instead. From the saddle, traverse over 100 feet about 50–75 feet below the ridgeline S of the peak, but first ascend a thin, short gully directly on the ridge and only a few feet to the right (S). Traverse over 100 feet across and down (SE) a grassy ramp to a rockier area. Begin to climb (NE) up another fairly short, steep, narrow gully directly across from a longer gully coming down from the notch just W of the peak. Hike to the left (N) and up the steep, obvious, grassy ledges to the semi-grassy peak.

From Telluride, see hike 25's Pack Basin (E) side, and go to the high saddle (12,270 feet) between Mill Creek and Pack Basins. From the saddle, see the route in the highest parts of upper Mill Creek Basin to the high ridge between Gilpin Peak and Mount Emma. Take your eyes to the NE from the saddle and as far to the right as possible along the high ridge, before the nearby rough ridge of Mount Emma blocks your view of the rest of the other ridge. On that far, high ridge to the right (NE), observe a craggy section and three very large rock spires directly below it on the left side of the upper basin. You will eventually be ascending after the second spire from the left (most W) and before the third spire (most E). You will climb to the high ridge just to the left (W) of the craggy ridge section. First hike down the main trail and switchbacks N into Mill Creek Basin, and drop nearly 300 feet from the high saddle, as you contour (½ mile from saddle) easily W of Mount Emma. Just before the first big switchback leading W down the basin, hike past a giant cairn in the grass and leave the solid trail. Bushwhack to the right (E) off of the main trail onto a faint trail (if any), and go left (N) of a tiny pond in the flats to a rocky drainage. The scree on the left of the gully is lighter than the scree and boulders on the right (S). Hike up the center of the drainage for about 200 feet to where the light scree meets the dark rock; then go to the left (N) and follow a steep path for a hundred feet. Curve to the right (E) in the center of the upper basin, and hike ½ mile up more steeply to the base of the spires. The scree to the left (W) of the first large spire is

Ridge to Stony Mountain.

reddish. Avoid it for a better climb, which is just to the right (E) of the second wide rock spire. Hug the spire for the more solid rock up the super-steep scree field, and make your way N up its right (E) side. From the upper basin you see that the third spire on the right (most E) is part of a longer outcrop. The scree is loose and the going is super-steep, but use the more solid rock near the second spire to hoist yourself up N 75 feet. Once you are on top of the spires and out-crop, stay on a NW ascending traverse as you go 30 feet or so straight up the little rise above the spires (or rock fins); then turn to the left (NW) for 40 feet through loose scree to the high ridge. It's about 1½–2 hours (1½ miles) from the saddle between Mill Creek and Pack Basins to the high ridge (13,100 feet) between Mill Creek and Yankee Boy Basins.

You can see a lot more from the ridge as Yankee Boy Basin and Wrights Lake come into view (N), with Mount Sneffels and the gang of high thirteeners sud-denly surrounding you. This is also your first glimpse of Stony Mountain down the connecting ridge to the NE. Barely down the ridge to the NW toward Gilpin Peak is a tiny bump. Use this as a landmark, and do not go past it on your way to the ultra-steep downhill hike back into upper Mill Creek Basin for the return. You will leave the ridgetop and go left (SE) down to the two obvious spires in upper Mill Creek Basin. From there, go to the left of the second large spire and hug its left (E) side, as you descend to the scree fields in upper Mill Creek Basin.

Now hike right (SE) ¼ mile to the little high point at 13,210 feet NNE of Mount Emma. There are drop-offs along the craggy ridge section, so take heed, though no climbing moves are necessary. As you continue to the high point on the ridge connecting Gilpin Peak, Mount Emma, and Stony Mountain, hike to the left or right of the first two obstacles. Go directly up to the first rock obstacle, and contour 20 feet to the left (N) around it, or go just right (S) of the ridge and up a 4-foot-wide crack in the rock and immediately back to the ridge. The next outcrop is directly in front of you. It might be easier to go barely to the left 10 feet (N) of the outcrop blocking the ridge crest on a traverse for about 30–40 feet and directly back to the ridge (only in the absence of snow). Hiking to the right (S) works well too, as you descend steeply and slowly about 35 feet from the ridge and then contour to the left (SE) around the obstacle over very loose rock and talus. Hike 40 feet over more level terrain and back up to the ridge somewhat more easily on an ascending traverse. A few more blockages can be passed on either side, as the going gets easier to the high point (13,210 feet) on the ridge. See the faded bailout trail to the left 40 feet below the top of the high point. Follow this ENE to the SW ridge of Stony Mountain, or scramble up to the high point. Return the same way, or go NE down and up over a mile to Stony Mountain by first going over a little outcropping close to the high point en route to the low saddle on the ridge. Follow directions from Yankee Boy Basin to finish.

TRAIL NOTES

....

....

....

....

....

....

....

Elevation: 14,150 feet, with vertical gains of 1730 feet from the highest 4WD parking in Yankee Boy Basin at the official TH, 2750 feet from the big meadow in Yankee Boy Basin, 4800 feet from Blue Lakes TH

Distance: 1½ miles up, 3 miles round-trip from the official TH; 3 miles up, 6 miles round-trip from the big meadow in Yankee Boy Basin; 6 miles round-trip clockwise **Loop** to Blue Lakes Pass, up the SW ridge and down Scree Col from the big meadow in Yankee Boy Basin; 7 miles up, 14 miles round-trip from Blue Lakes TH

Duration: 2 hours up max, 4 hours round-trip **Loop** or not from Yankee Boy Basin; 5 hours up, 7–8 hours round-trip from Blue Lakes TH

Difficulty: Mix of strenuous (very steep, loose scree—some wear a helmet because of falling rock potential) and very challenging (long and steep from Blue Lakes, scrambling, route-finding)

TRAILHEAD

See hike 31 or 37 for directions.

NOTES

Welcome to one of Colorado's preeminent summits! It is among the most widely photographed and climbed peaks in the state, mostly because of its relative ease to peak out for a fourteener. Of the many routes up the summit, most people go up and down from Scree Col on the S slope, but the SW ridge from Blue Lakes Pass is greatly underrated. Do a fantastic **Loop** in either direction. Both routes are for one way to the top. The longer trek from Blue Lakes TH is more than twice as long, high, and difficult, but it has the advantage of a much easier, shorter drive from Telluride, plus you get to visit all three Blue Lakes.

ROUTE

From Wrights Lake TH in Yankee Boy Basin, take that trail W slightly longer; it provides better walking than the rough road to the official TH, as you go by Wrights Lake in ½ mile, then another ½ mile NW to the main route after switchbacks. If you parked in the flats below the Wrights Lake TH like most folks, it's about an hour's walk NW (1½ miles) up the 4WD road or Wrights

Mount Sneffels to Yankee Boy Basin and Wrights Lake.

Lake Trail to the giant couloir at the base of Mount Sneffels. If you parked at the official TH, it's only a 10- to 15-minute stroll NW (½ mile) to the huge couloir and popular S slope route.

Scramble the gigantic gully with loose scree N almost a mile and 800 vertical feet to the top (known as Scree Col or Lavender Col) by going slightly right (E) of the center up whatever solid rocks you can. The other path goes up left (W) of the super-steep, slick center and is steeper than the right (E) side of the gully. Respectfully avoid starting any rockslides, and call out to warn people if any rocks do come down. Once you are at the top, head left (NW) and hike up a long (few hundred yards), steep, narrow slot with some bigger rocks, instead of going right (SE) toward Kismet. Climb this to near the top like most people do, and turn left (WNW) to finish the summit block. You can also leave the narrow gully about a third of the way up (100 feet) to go left (W) and scramble some broken ledges (NW). Or walk over to the bottom of the narrow gully and immediately climb steeply up the left (W) to gain the broken ledges. Here you will be able to hike with better footing than in the narrow gully. The first part of this is the hardest, however, with cairns to follow. Whichever option you choose, hike close to (just S of), and then back to, the main ridge going W near the very top.

Hike Blue Lakes Trail 201 or Wrights Lake Trail to the top of Blue Lakes Pass at 13,000 feet, and start N up the SW ridge a mile to the peak. Hike by the pinnacles low on the ridge to the left (W) of them (only in the absence of snow). Go between a couple of spires hugging the right (E) side, then climb to the big notch above the sharp pinnacles. Walk right (E) immediately at the cairn, and scramble briefly up the S-facing gully, then directly back to the ridge proper. Hike straight up the high ridge NNE or just to the right (E if needed) to the nearby peak. It's a bit steeper and more exposed close to the top, but the holds are surprisingly solid for Southwest Colorado.

TRAIL NOTES

....

....

....

....

....

....

....

NORTHEAST TELLURIDE

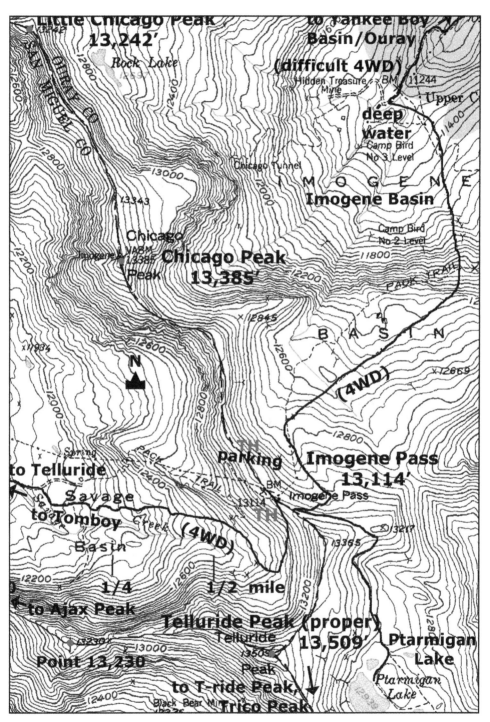

Little Chicago Peak
13,242'
Rock Lake

to Yankee Boy
Basin/Ouray
(difficult 4WD)

Hidden Treasure
Mine

BM 11244

Upper C

deep
water

Camp Bird
No 3 Level

Chicago Tunnel

IMOGENE

Imogene Basin

Camp Bird
No 2 Level

X3343

Chicago
Peak

VABM
13385

Chicago Peak
13,385'

PACK TRAIL

BASIN

(4WD)

N

Spring

Parking

Imogene Pass
13,114'

to Telluride

Savage

to Tomboy

Basin

PACK
TRAIL

BM
13114

Imogene Pass

(4WD)

1/4

1/2 mile

to Ajax Peak

Telluride Peak (proper)
13,509'

Telluride
Peak

Ptarmigan
Lake

Point 13,230

to T-ride Peak,
Trico Peak

Ptarmigan
Lake

Black Bear Mine

HIKES 44, 45, 47-49

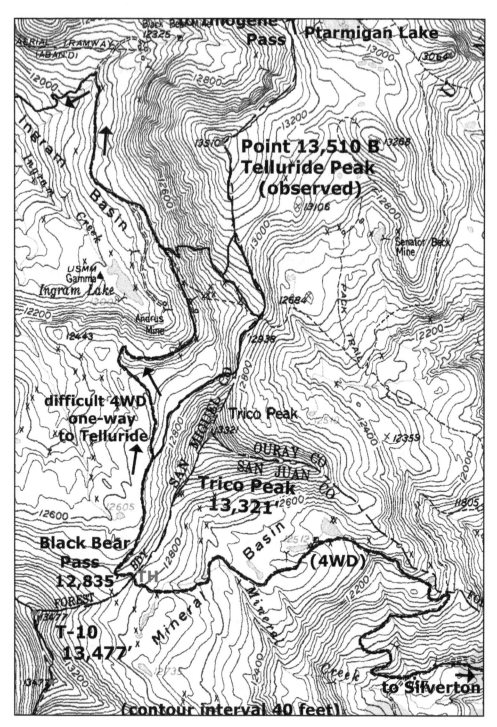

HIKES 49-51

40   Sheridan Crosscut Trail

Elevation: 11,890 feet at the tiny old shed; 12,500 feet at the high
saddle E of Liberty Bell Basin; with vertical gains of 3010 feet,
3620 feet

Distance: 3½ miles up, 7 miles round-trip **Loop** or not; 5 miles up,
10 miles round-trip to the saddle

Duration: 2½ hours up, 4 hours round-trip **Loop** or not; 3 hours up,
5 hours round-trip to the saddle

Difficulty: Strenuous. Steadily steep, faint path

TRAILHEAD
Jud Wiebe Trail 432 (E side); see hike 29 for directions.

ROUTE
Walk about 35–45 minutes (more than 1 mile) up Tomboy Road FS 869 past
two big switchbacks. Go a few hundred feet to a clearing that opens up on the
left (N). The trail is on the left (N) off of Tomboy Road FS 869 just before you
would continue into the aspens. It switches back sharply and goes 100 feet NW
up to a small rock outcropping. Take the narrow path NNE through the trees
briefly, and go to the right (E) to cross the clearing again. Walk N through more
aspens a few hundred feet to an intersection, then hike more steeply directly up
to the left (NW) 30 feet to avoid private property and gain the low ridge. Hike
NE up the center fairly steeply 300 feet, then go to the left (W) of the first major
rock obstacle, right (E) of the second, and left (W) of the third, while staying on
the obvious trail. Many flat rocks up the ridge provide great picnic spots and
360-degree views about a mile from Tomboy Road FS 869. Hike on the most
distinct ridge trail ¼ mile up through the woods to a really steep fork under a
big rock (30 feet high from the bottom). To the right (E) of the rock, the route is
not as steep. To the left (W) is a solid trail that's only super-steep to start. Both
paths go 75 feet around the rock to the clearing above the aspens. Bushwhack a
few hundred feet N up the little shoulder in the high grass to the pine trees at
about 11,500 feet. Get a good look at the rock below that marks the trail. It's left
(E) of those larger, jagged rocks that are more toward Owl Gulch. This spot at
11,500 feet also marks the approximate **Loop** with Owl Gulch Ridge Trail 420
(or an easier route up 150 feet N higher). Stay on the ridge crest NNE, ignoring
animal trails going to the left (W) until you are near tree line and the last ever-

Bridal Veil Falls and Basin from Sheridan Crosscut Trail.

greens on the ridge. See any elk or deer yet? Now go left (NW) off the ridge and down 25–35 feet on the most worn trail on a descending traverse a couple hundred yards to an old mine shaft, steel rails, and a tiny old shed. A tree has fallen on the shed, but it seems like a sufficiently safe, dry spot for anyone in a pinch with bad weather.

Return the same way, or **Loop** with Liberty Bell Trail or Owl Gulch Ridge Trail to the same TH. You can also proceed up to the high saddle that separates Liberty Bell Basin from Marshall Basin. Find the trail that angles to the left (NW) above the shed from the right (E) of it over to the little ridge. Bushwhack up to a faint path that goes NE into the high basin to meet Liberty Bell Trail going E in a few hundred feet. Hike the distinct trail up a mile more to the saddle. Over halfway up, you climb steeply from the grass and scree to the ultranarrow, rocky traverse trail at the back left (NE) side of the basin ¼ mile to the saddle.

41   Owl Gulch Ridge Trail 420

Elevation: 11,890 feet, with 3010 feet vertical gain

Distance: 3½ miles to the tiny old shed at the top, 7 miles round-trip **Loop** or not

Duration: 3 hours up, 5 hours round-trip **Loop** or not

Difficulty: Strenuous. Steeper, some route-determining, loose rock

TRAILHEAD

Jud Wiebe Trail 432 (E side); see hike 29 for directions.

ROUTE

See hike 29's E side to Liberty Bell Flats; find the obscure trail going E, opposite the sign for Jud Wiebe Trail and 10 feet farther NE, while Liberty Bell Trail continues NE through the flats. Take the faint path E at first 150 feet up and past an old teepee frame in a little clearing, then traverse S on the more pronounced trail a few hundred yards. Head E up four steep but short switchbacks. Before (W of) a small clearing, see the maintained steeper trail and fifth switchback that briefly takes you (NE) up a small rise. Then traverse 100 feet to the right (E) to another shoulder. Here you either go left (NNE) steeply straight up the shoulder a few hundred yards to the main ridge and the grassy knoll at 10,464 feet, or stay on the traverse trail through the aspens another 100 feet or so to the short cliff band, where you climb left (W) of it going 150 feet NE steeply up to the main ridge and knoll at 10,464 feet. It takes more than an hour (2 miles) from the TH to get to the bottom of the ridge, where you can see the old trestle and mining debris ¼ mile NE up the ridgeline. Pass a small rock outcropping easily on the left (W) halfway to the old trestle. Immediately bypass the next obstacle on the thin trail to the left (W) or straight over the flatter boulders on the ridge crest 50 feet to the end without difficulty. The old wooden trestle comes down S to the right (E) from the ridge. Mining refuse blocks the ridgeline above the trestle, and you must leave the ridge for about ¼ mile by going carefully NE on the thin, loose, rocky path traversing under the trestle, then immediately very steeply NW up rocky shelves back to the ridge with a few cairns to help. Hike with better footing very steeply NE without any more obstacles ½ mile more into the woods and ENE up to where the steep ridge meets the main ridge coming from Sheridan Crosscut Trail. Go S down that trail or continue NNE ¼ mile up to the last of the trees on the ridge. Then go NW on the traverse down

Route from the bottom of Owl Gulch Ridge.

25–35 feet and a couple hundred yards over to the tiny old shed. Return the same way, or ascend Liberty Bell Basin and go down by that route, or Sheridan Crosscut Trail for easier **Loops**.

42   Mendota Peak

Elevation: 13,275 feet, with 4475 feet vertical gain

Distance: 5½ miles up, 11 miles round-trip

Duration: 4 hours up, 6–7 hours round-trip

Difficulty: Very challenging. Longer than most, steep off main trail

TRAILHEAD

Jud Wiebe Trail 432 (E side); see hike 29 for directions.

ROUTE

See hike 30 to the high saddle E of Liberty Bell Basin. It's at least 3 hours (4 miles) to this saddle. Go left (N) into Marshall Basin, gradually traversing NNE down a few hundred yards, then ½ mile steeper NNE up to the marker and the Mendota Peak Trail to the left (W). If you continue NE on the scree trail, you will end up at Virginius Pass in more than ¼ mile. Scramble NW up the thin trail over a super-steep, semi-loose hillside a few hundred yards to Mendota's high ridge NE of the summit. Turn left at the wooden markers to easily walk SW 200 feet.

TRAIL NOTES

....

....

....

....

....

....

....

43   T-5

Elevation: 13,436 feet, with 4636 feet vertical gain

Distance: 6 miles up, 12 miles round-trip

Duration: 5 hours up, 8 hours round-trip

Difficulty: Very challenging. Long, easy scrambling, extra little
  summit, walk-up

TRAILHEAD

Jud Wiebe Trail 432 (E side); see hike 29 for directions.

ROUTE

See hikes 30 and 42. Continue NE more than ¼ mile on the main path past the
Mendota Peak Trail turnoff (going NW) in Marshall Basin. It is steeper up
the last pitch over the loose scree and rocky trail, but the route is obvious to the
saddle known as Virginius Pass at 13,100 feet. It's 30 minutes to the pass from
the lower saddle and no more than an hour and a mile to the summit. There are
great views of the Sneffels Range through Governor Basin and the Telluride
mountains from windy Virginius Pass. Bushwhack with no solid trail right (E)
from the pass and immediately up and around a large outcropping on your left
(N). Climb 30–40 feet going left (NE) steeply at the cairn through the loose
rocks, perhaps just to the left (W) of the smaller outcropping, and scramble to
the nearby high ridge. Follow it E directly through the next couple of small
rock outcrops easily up to the fake summit at 13,337 feet. Walk SE down the
wide ridge slightly, and continue up to T-5 without difficulty, picking up the
only trail near the summit.

Elevation: 13,114 feet, with vertical gains of 1324 feet to Royer Gulch, 2629 feet to town of Tomboy, 4238 feet to Imogene Pass

Distance: 2 miles up, 4 miles round-trip; 5 miles up, 10 miles round-trip; 6½ miles up, 13 miles round-trip

Duration: More than 1 hour up, 2–3 hours round-trip; 2 hours up, 3–4 hours round-trip; 3 hours up, 5 hours round-trip; less than 1 hour up a semi-difficult 4WD to Imogene Pass

Difficulty: Mix of moderate (steady incline) and strenuous (longer, rocky section; very long, steep, solid road to Imogene Pass)

TRAILHEAD

Jud Wiebe Trail 432 (E side); see hike 29 for directions.

ROUTE

Tomboy Road FS 869 is very popular with 4WD vehicles from July through September. The first incredible area is Royer Gulch. Walk, bike, or drive up N Oak Street, and turn right (E) at the top onto Tomboy Road FS 869 (sign on the dirt road says "County Road K-68"). It's smooth for the first ½ mile and not

too steep until Owl Gulch. Falls flow in this cove part of the year. The route gets a little steeper and rockier beyond the cove. Get to the first switchback opposite the big tailings pond across the valley (S) in less than ¼ mile. Hike steeply a few hundred yards to the next switchback, and then go E ¼ mile through the aspens on the wide road. At the corner and scenic overlook, turn left (NNE) into Royer Gulch while still in the trees. Go ¼ mile up to the bend on an easier grade to enjoy

Royer Gulch Falls at full steam.

Mining remnants near the town of Tomboy.

the cascading twin waterfalls (best in late spring). Watch for frequent rock slides in this general area, as you catch your breath and enjoy the views.

Hike ½ mile up the rest of the horseshoe in Royer Gulch steeply over solid rock, and pass through the short rock tunnel at the top. Walk more easily for a mile up to the Tomboy ruins as you go by old buildings while staying on the main road; more than 6000 people once lived there. Return to town the same way, or proceed to Imogene Pass by hiking the steepest part of the road yet a mile up to Savage Basin directly below Imogene Pass. No worries: it's plenty rocky and loose too! Go left (E) or right (SE, which is steeper) at the first part past Tomboy, and stay right (S) of a fork on top of that. Turn sharply left (N) at the end of the basin, and slog steadily and steeply ¼ mile up to Imogene Pass. At the top, find plenty of parking and an outhouse. Hike or snowshoe as far as Royer Gulch in the winter. Return the same way if hiking or continue by an expert-only 4WD to Ouray.

• **Bonus:** Ptarmigan Lake makes a great side visit from the pass. Go into the Imogene Basin side a few feet, and head right (E and S) at the fork. Walk the trail ½ mile down to the lakes easily, losing only a couple hundred feet in elevation.

Elevation: 13,385 feet, with 270-plus feet vertical gain

Distance: 1 mile one way, 2¼ miles round-trip; 2 miles one way, 4 miles round-trip

Duration: 1 hour one way, 2 hours round-trip; 1½ hours one way, 3 hours round-trip

Difficulty: Strenuous. Some route-finding, steep drop-offs, big payoff for little effort

TRAILHEAD

Imogene Pass; Jud Wiebe Trail 432 (E side); see hike 29 for directions.

ROUTE

Continue NW from the expansive parking area at the top of the pass to immediately walk Chicago Peak's long ridge. The trail is clear at first. When in doubt ¼ mile from the TH, go right (E) easily around the small spires blocking the ridgeline. About ¼ mile farther at one big cairn on the ridge, head right (E) again and around and down an easier route, or go a couple feet right (E) of the big cairn and 12–15 feet down a very steep, short gully. Hug the huge rock outcropping on the right (E) directly back to the ridge again. Hike more leisurely ½ mile up Chicago Peak's S ridge to the top, where you can see Ouray and Telluride at the same time.

Brilliant wildflower near the ridge to Chicago Peak.

• **Bonus:** Walk the euphoric ridge N to Little Chicago Peak (Point 13,242), as you descend very briefly from Chicago Peak and over flat, mossy rock without a solid trail. Head NNW over another rocky but very doable section ¼ mile from the top, and go just to the right (E) where the route is obvious. Then work back to the nearby ridge crest and up to the summit. Views of the Sneffels Range and Rock and Thorne Lakes are mind-blowing!

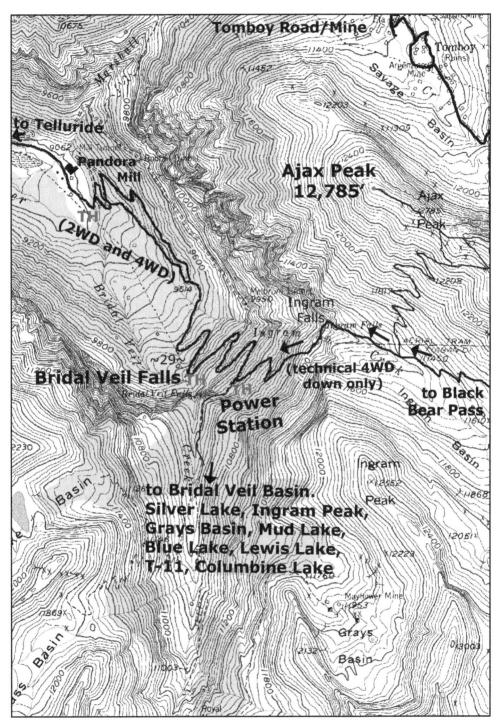

Tomboy Road/Mine

Ajax Peak
12,785'

to Telluride

Pandora
Mill

TH
(2WD and 4WD)

Ingram
Falls

~29~

Bridal Veil Falls TH

TH
Power
Station

(technical 4WD
down only)

to Black
Bear Pass

to Bridal Veil Basin,
Silver Lake, Ingram Peak,
Grays Basin, Mud Lake,
Blue Lake, Lewis Lake,
T-11, Columbine Lake

Grays
Basin

HIKES 46, 48-51

Elevation: 9850 feet; 10,120 feet; with vertical gains of 1100 feet to the falls, 1375 feet to the power plant from the bottom

Distance: 1½ miles up, 3 miles round-trip; 2 miles up, 4 miles round-trip; 4 miles from Telluride, 8 miles round-trip

Duration: 45–60 minutes up, 2 hours round-trip; 1½ hours up, 3 hours round-trip; 20- to 25-minute 4WD to the falls and 5 minutes more to the power plant with limited parking

Difficulty: Moderate. Steady grade to falls, steeper above, dusty, much traffic

TRAILHEAD

Two miles E of Telluride where CO-145 turns into dirt road FS 636 right of the Pandora Mill to the nearby large parking area on the corner, or at Bridal Veil Falls, or above the falls to the power station.

ROUTE

This is a popular road for a walk, bike ride, 2WD high-clearance route, or 4WD down-only route (Black Bear Pass from Silverton), and provides access to several trails and summits. It's only open late May through October, depending on the avalanche danger. Take the dirt road left (N) immediately from the corner at the bottom. Go right (SW) at the first nearby turn more steeply, and proceed around the switchback to the left, watching for downhill traffic even though uphill has the right-of-way. It immediately gets a little confusing. The next two right turns are steeper with no switchbacks ½ mile to the road above. The first is much shorter, rockier, and a more burly 4WD or hiking route when passable. That road also crosses the main one you're on and goes down toward Pandora too. Follow the main road FS 636 steadily up switchbacks, then proceed (SE) straighter for a mile as you pass the steeper route coming up on your right (S). Go ½ mile up two steeper, rockier switchbacks to Bridal Veil Falls and a parking area. At 365 feet, this is the longest free-falling waterfall in the state.

Continue more than ½ mile up three more moderately steep switchbacks to the power station. Park appropriately at the top so that other vehicles can fit, and do not block the gate and private driveway to the still-inhabited, operational power station or the very difficult one-way road coming down from

Colorado's highest waterfall at the east end of Telluride.

Black Bear Pass. You could also park down the road or at Bridal Veil Falls and walk up the road 20–25 minutes to the power station. (When this station was built in 1890 it became the first commercial alternating-current plant in the US. The first noncommercial AC plant was built in nearby Ames, below Ophir.)

TRAIL NOTES

....
....
....
....
....
....
....

Elevation: 13,509 feet, with 400 feet vertical gain (plus 200 feet if you add Point 13,510B)

Distance: ½ mile up, 1 mile round-trip; 1½ miles up, 3 miles round-trip

Duration: ½ hour up, 1 hour round-trip; 1 hour up, 2–3 hours round-trip

Difficulty: Mix of moderate (undemanding but steep drop-offs) and strenuous (extra summit, bushwhack, scramble)

TRAILHEAD

Imogene Pass; see hike 44 for directions.

ROUTE

From the large parking area on Imogene Pass, Telluride Peak is visible to the S. Hike directly up the ridge SE on a thin trail across the road from Imogene Pass, where the path turns SSW and continues as a relaxed walk to the summit. Telluride Peak is not visible from Telluride and vice versa, except from the far W end of the valley.

• **Bonus:** Follow Telluride Peak's adequately wide SE ridge ½ mile and turn right (SW) ½ mile to Point 13,510B (the real Telluride Peak to locals—see also hike 49). Stay near the ridge as you approach the summit on fairly solid scree. Early in the summer, snow might linger. Head to the left (S) of the snowfield and around and up (W) if needed, but either way the faint trails are steeper near the top.

Indian paintbrush comes in many delicious colors.

48   Ajax Peak

Elevation: 12,785 feet, with 2665 feet vertical gain
Distance: 2½ miles up, 5 miles round-trip
Duration: 2 hours up, 3–3½ hours round-trip
Difficulty: Strenuous. Steady grade, well-traveled trail

TRAILHEAD

See hike 46 for directions.

ROUTE

Walk steeply left (NE) up the one-way road past the tight switchbacks to cross Ingram Creek in 25–30 minutes max (almost 1 mile). Ascend the last switchback immediately, and hike very steeply 200 feet up the rocky steps into Ingram Basin. Watch the expression on the faces of four-wheel drivers contemplating their lives as they come down! A hundred yards or so above this very steep part at the bottom of the basin, and still close to the creek, is the TH off to the left (N). The route begins up a small clearing, and tailings pile as you catch the more solid trail on the right (E). The going is steep a few hundred feet to a little shelf where you go left (NW) to walk on top. Follow the nice trail, zigzagging up the hillside a mile above tree line, and finally to the high saddle SE of the peak. It's ¼ mile over, down, and up, while you are slightly left (S) of the high ridge to the astonishingly vast and grassy summit.

• **Bonus:** Hike to Point 13,230 by following the ridge SE up ½ mile from Ajax Peak. It's much steeper and rockier than the rest of the trail but affords exceptional

views. The trail leaves the ridgeline about 50–60 feet below and for a hundred yards or more to the right (S), and you regain it at the very top.

Looking up the ridge from Ajax Peak.

49   Telluride Peak (Observed)

Elevation: 13,510 feet, with 3400 feet vertical gain

Distance: 4 miles up, 8 miles round-trip; 6 miles up the **Alt**, 12 miles round-trip

Duration: 3 hours minimum to the peak, 5–6 hours round-trip

Difficulty: Very challenging. Really steep and loose above main 4WD road, scrambling, scree

TRAILHEAD

See hike 46 for directions.

NOTES

Locals also call this peak No Name. It's official title is Point 13,510B.

ROUTE

Walk steeply left (NE) up the one-way dirt road past the tight switchbacks to cross Ingram Creek in 25–30 minutes max (almost 1 mile). Turn right up the last switchback immediately, and hike very steeply 200 feet up the rocky steps into Ingram Basin. Continue 2 miles generally SE, crossing a NE fork of Ingram Creek halfway up to the scramble off FS 648. About 1½ hours from the power station, exit the main dirt road for the shortcut, and go left (E) across from and just past Ingram Lake. Get permission for the shortcut if possible, or see the **Alt** below to avoid private property. For the shortcut you'll be heading for the miners' debris 150 feet straight above, but first look for a faint trail above the main road that goes in the same direction as the road. The first 10–15 feet of the path are missing, so it's a little tricky; it gets more prominent and turns back to the left (N) in 200 feet to catch an old road 300 feet over to the miners' old conveyor and remnants. Be mindful here as nails, steep

Sky pilot flowers close to Telluride Peak.

Telluride Peak and the route in Ingram Basin to Black Bear Pass.

scree, and open mines all pose dangers for ¼ mile and the hardest part of the climb. Go left (N) of the miners' conveyor (a steep-sloping trough) up a very steep hillside. Then cross the trough over to the right (S), almost immediately picking up a faint, pretty steep, rocky trail. Do not go near or into any mine entrances near Telluride, as many begin horizontally but drop vertically without warning. Continue up and look to the right (SE) for a small cairn and the wider trail you follow up directly to the high grassy meadow. Bushwhack more steeply a few hundred yards N up to the high ridge to bypass a little bump on the ridge crest, or continue SE a bit more easily a few hundred yards to the high ridge and go left (N). Once you are on the fat, high ridge, stay in the middle or a little to the left (W) the whole way NNW (more than ¼ mile farther), finally catching a rock trail near the top of the large summit block with a bird's-eye view up the Telluride valley.

The **Alt** is simpler and 2 miles longer. Follow the main 4WD road S of Ingram Lake almost another mile to the clear trail that goes to the left (NNE) ½ mile on a shelf hundreds of feet under Trico Peak (E). It gets steeper and rockier up to the saddle between Telluride Peak (observed) and Trico Peak. Hike N for 1 mile up the scree-filled ridge, go to the right (E) a few feet of the large outcropping easily, and head NNW ¼ mile steeply.

Elevation: 12,835 feet; 13,321 feet; with vertical gains of 2715 feet to Black Bear Pass, 3200 feet to Trico Peak

Distance: 4 miles up, 8 miles round-trip; 4½ miles up, 9 miles round-trip

Duration: 2 hours up, 3½ hours round-trip; 2½–3 hours up, 5 hours round-trip

Difficulty: Strenuous. Rocky, steeper into steady grade, obvious road, not demanding

TRAILHEAD

See hike 46 for directions.

ROUTE

Walk steeply left (NE) up the one-way road past the tight switchbacks to cross Ingram Creek in 25–30 minutes max (almost 1 mile) from the power station. Turn right up the last switchback, and immediately hike very steeply 200 feet up the rocky steps into Ingram Basin. (And that's putting it nicely!) Enter picturesque Ingram Basin, and stay on the main rocky dirt road (3 miles to the pass) SE past Ingram Lake and S finally up to Black Bear Pass. This is the most difficult route of the three possible 4WD roads to Telluride from the E or S; all are technically open to off-highway vehicles (OHVs or ORVs) until you get to city streets. Go left (NE) on the wide ridge section to Trico Peak from Black Bear Pass. Go left (W) around the super-steep areas ½ mile up from the road and saddle. Then catch the trail again straight up over fairly stable scree to the peak.

Telluride Peak, Trico Peak and Black Bear Pass from T-10.

Elevation: 13,477 feet, with 3357 feet vertical gain

Distance: 4½ miles to the twin peak S of T-10, 9 miles round-trip

Duration: 3 hours up, 5½ hours round-trip

Difficulty: Very challenging. Really steep, semi-loose. T-10's S twin is even steeper to get to by this route

TRAILHEAD

See hike 46 for directions.

ROUTE

See hike 50 and walk right (WSW) from Black Bear Pass a few hundred yards up the thin 4WD road directly to the steepest part of T-10's E ridge. The trail actually continues ¼ mile up the center of the boulder-filled ridge, and a few cairns help. When you descend, remember to go toward Black Bear Pass down the rocky, boulder-filled, steep E ridge. Traverse S to the twin peak over the ridge 200 feet (more fun), and go left (E) where permissible, or go left (E) of the spires from the N peak on a descending traverse 40–50 feet below the ridgeline. Either way, stay just E of the larger spires and perhaps see the cairns down and over 250 feet S on the traverse to the super-steep, rocky stairs and ledges back up to the ridge. Climb 100 feet directly W to the high ridge up super-steep ledges. Finish a hundred feet or so more easily on the high ridge S to the top. Many lakes can be seen below in every direction from the S peak. It's ½ mile round-trip from its northern twin and back.

Steep ridge between summits of T-10.

CHAPTER 7

SOUTHEAST TELLURIDE

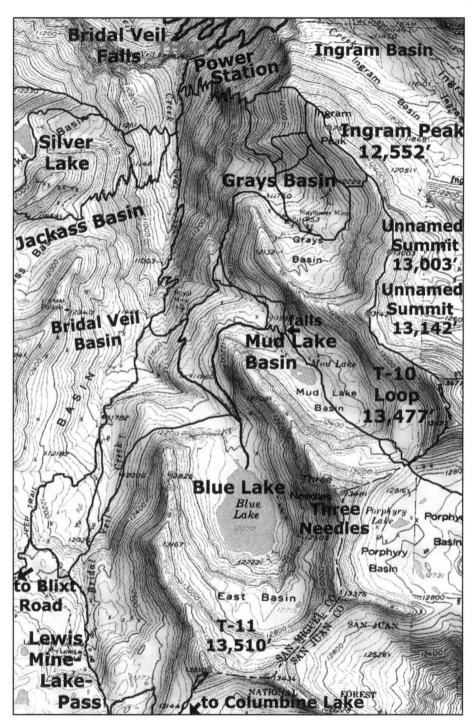

Bridal Veil Falls
Power Station
Ingram Basin
Silver Lake
Jackass Basin
Ingram Peak 12,552'
Grays Basin
Unnamed Summit 13,003'
Unnamed Summit 13,142'
Bridal Veil Basin
Falls
Mud Lake Basin
T-10 Loop 13,477'
Blue Lake
Three Needles
Porphyry Basin
to Blixt Road
East Basin
Lewis Mine Lake Pass
T-11 13,510'
to Columbine Lake

HIKES 51-59, 63, 64, 66, 68

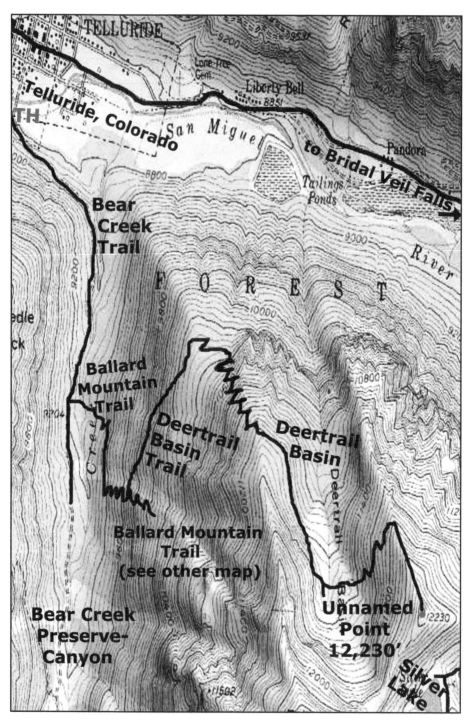

TELLURIDE

Lone Tree
Gem

Liberty Bell
8851

Telluride, Colorado

San Miguel

Pandora

TH

to Bridal Veil Falls

8800

Tailings
Ponds

Bear
Creek
Trail

9300

River

F O R E S T

10000

10800

Ballard
Mountain
Trail

Deertrail
Basin
Trail

Deertrail
Basin

Ballard Mountain
Trail
(see other map)

Bear Creek
Preserve-
Canyon

Unnamed
Point
12,230'

12230

Silver
Lake

12000

11502

HIKES 60, 61

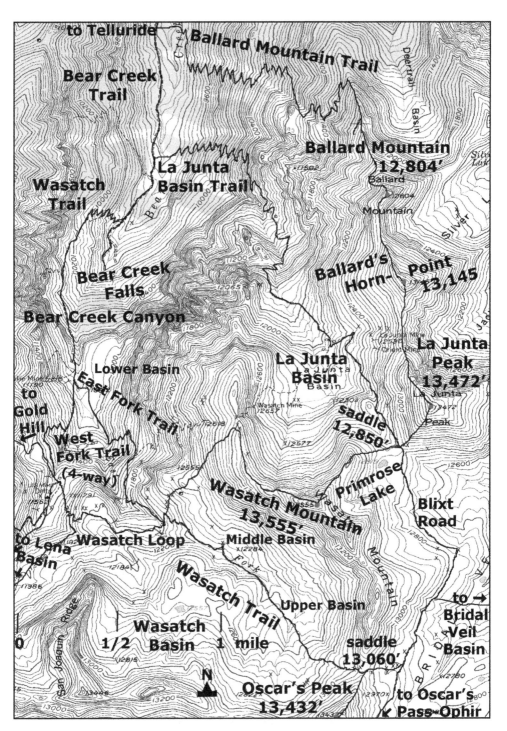

HIKES 60-68, 70, 71

Elevation: 12,000 feet, with 1880 feet vertical gain

Distance: 2 miles up, 4 miles round-trip; 5 miles round-trip **Loop** to Mud Lake

Duration: 2 hours up, 3–4 hours round-trip

Difficulty: Strenuous. Some route-finding, steep switchbacks

TRAILHEAD

See hike 46 for directions.

NOTES

Hikes 52–59 can be done separately or with a **Bonus** basin or lake and **Loop** back to the same TH.

ROUTE

Walk ¼ mile past the steel gate and power station S to Bridal Veil Basin before turning left (E) onto the trail, which is easy to miss and rough to begin. If you can see the triangular peak S up the trail at the top of the basin, you've gone 20–25 feet too far. It starts directly across from the grassy ledges on the other side (W) of the creek. The narrow, steep trail switches back and turns a total of twenty times, going E if you include the turn from the main trail at Bridal Veil Creek. Well under the cliff band and at about 30 minutes (¾ mile) of hiking from the power station, head right (S) and follow the pipeline over a hundred yards to a small clearing. Don't go to the end and the last clearing, where the pipeline goes up steeply, but hike by old pipes, piles of wood and rock, and a big cairn left (E) of the pipeline. Walk left (NE) from the pipeline through the trees to catch the trail going up again. Stay on it ¼ mile as you climb the final few switchbacks to the cliff band, and follow it right (S). Notice the wooden tower across from a narrow, rocky creek bed. Turn left (E) to climb the creek bed a couple hundred feet to a small pond and level ground at the bottom of Grays Basin. Hike left (N) of the small pond on a faint path that stays to the left (N) in the basin a few hundred feet more and goes SSE through shrubs and high grasses before dissipating. Bushwhack ¼ mile to the right (S) through the meadow and up a bit steeper to the Mayflower Mine, where there are a few sites. Be careful around the highest mining shaft, which is very deep.

Go down the same way, or **Loop** 1 mile to the main trail near Bridal Veil

Creek (and 1 mile N to the TH), or **Loop** 1 mile up to Mud Lake (and 2 miles to the TH). For both **Loops**, exit Grays Basin from the S side at the far left (W) in the scree going ½ mile to an old tin-roofed cabin on the creek at the bottom of Mud Lake Basin. Head around the ridge near tree line from Grays Basin, and contour to the S, staying high on a faint trail. To **Loop** down, traverse the well-defined path S under ¼ mile past the old cabin on the creek to a rusty gate on a big switchback on the main trail (up to Blue Lake). Walk right (W) 100 yards on the wider but steeper and rockier trail to Bridal Veil Creek and down N 1 mile to the TH, including some switchbacks. To **Loop** to Mud Lake, stay on a high traverse, leaving the path down to the old tin-roofed cabin (or go down to and up the creek SE from the cabin), and bushwhack ½ mile mostly SE to the high meadow. Hike ½ mile steeply up switchbacks below waterfalls, then scramble left (N) of the falls on a thin trail (if there is one) up to Mud Lake. See hike 54 for more details and descent options.

Tower at the mouth of Grays Basin.

53   Ingram Peak Loop

Elevation: 12,552 feet; 13,477 feet; with vertical gains of 2232 feet, 3357 feet for a counterclockwise **Loop** with T-10

Distance: 3 miles up, 6 miles round-trip, 9 miles round-trip **Loop** with T-10

Duration: 3 hours up max, 4–5 hours round-trip, 6–7 hours round-trip **Loop** with T-10

Difficulty: Mix of strenuous (route-finding, some steeps) and very challenging (long **Loop,** scrambling, five summits)

TRAILHEAD

See hike 46 for directions.

ROUTE

See hike 52 for Ingram Peak alone. From above the Mayflower Mine far to the SE in Grays Basin, continue a few hundred feet up to the E (with a tiny lake on the right, S), and go to the left (N) ¼ mile on an ascending traverse up the grassy, wildflower-covered hillside to the right (SE) side of Ingram's high ridge with little to no trail. Once you are on the grassy ridge, follow it ¼ mile NW over or left (W) of a couple of bumps easily to the nearby summit. Return the same way or from a steeper, shorter **Opt** down a small shoulder that extends W from Ingram Peak into Grays Basin. Start down the ridge NW (toward Telluride) for a few hundred feet from the summit, and traverse left (S) on the faint path 200 feet around to the W shoulder. Descend the shoulder W steeply a few hundred feet straight through or just left (S) of the flora, and go left (SE, then SW) above the cliffy area 200 feet steeply to the main path in Grays Basin, where you go right (NW) to exit the basin. You could also continue the traverse 75 feet from the W shoulder (SW of Ingram Peak) to a smaller rise and descend it steeply SW ¼ mile into Grays Basin to meet the main trail in the high grass and shrubs and go NW.

For the long **Loop** with T-10, see hike 54 and hike to Mud Lake Basin from the hydroelectric plant E of Telluride. Continue (1 mile to high saddle) walking more easily SE through the high basin, past lakes and over grassy landscape with some bigger boulders and no distinct trail. In July and August you'll encounter endless wildflowers including Indian paintbrush. Bushwhack to the back of the basin to the SE to the scree-covered, steep slope and rocky creek bed. Aim for the right (S) side of the creek bed, where water flows under the rocks part of the way up, and hike over grass at first. Follow the creek bed very steeply 100 feet or so up the ultra-loose rock. It feels like the mountain is coming down with your every step, as you hug the rock ribs to the right (S) for better footing. Follow the thinnest of trails to the right (S) on a traverse just above the rock ribs for a few feet to a large, rocky, flat shelf. Walk to the right (S) on the flat shelf 100 feet around the huge scree pile to the steeper, bigger rocks that lead you 200 feet more ESE up to the high ridge. It's around 2½ hours to the high ridge and saddle that separates Mud Lake and Porphyry Basins from the power station by this route.

Hike up the steep ridge to the left (NE) to ascend T-10's S twin with the exact same elevation. It's less than 30 minutes and under ½ mile to the top from the saddle on the thinning ridge, as you hike over loose but flat and manageable rock. From the S peak, enjoy the surroundings and lakes of Porphyry and Bullion King to the S, Mud Lake to the NW, and the ponds of Mineral Basin to the ENE. Continue 100 feet on the ridge N toward the N T-10 summit, but down-climb to the right (E) before it gets too steep. The ridge proper is very difficult for most hikers to free climb. Descend carefully to the right (E) 40–50 feet below the ridge crest and down super-steep rock shelves. Traverse about 250 feet to the left (N) around a small rock rib. Then either go steeply W back to the ridge proper to boulder a more interesting route with some exposure and semi-loose rock N to the other peak, or continue on an ascending traverse to meet the high ridge 200 feet S of the N summit. From the top you will be about 3½–4 hours from the start of the counterclockwise **Loop** and at the highest point of the hike—again! The 360-degree views from T-10 are crazy-cool. Black Bear Pass lies to the E, with Trico Peak beyond that to the NE. Three Needles is the spire-covered summit to the SW. You also have the first look at the rest of the hike and the connecting ridge down to Ingram Peak and Grays Basin to the NNW.

It's 20 minutes and ½ mile NW down to the next little summit at 13,142 feet over the wide ridge with more solid rock than previous. Some grass appears too, and you go just left (W) of a small bump on the ridge. Continue ¼ mile to the next high point, Unnamed Summit 13,003, by following the rocky ridge to the N leisurely, with the route becoming grassier near the top. The hike quickly becomes more attention grabbing from the unnamed summit, more than ½ mile to Ingram Peak. Boulder and hike down the ridge center to the first would-be obstacle. Descend a wide, short (30-foot), not-so-steep, rocky gully on the ridge itself, and momentarily head to the next dilemma. Carefully hike straight over the fairly solid rock in the very center of the short, thin ridge section to easier ground below. The scree gets smaller and the walking gets easier as the ridge widens and turns to solid grass the last ¼ mile to Ingram Peak. Go over or just to the left (W) of the last two minuscule bumps to the final peak of the day.

54   Mud Lake

Elevation: 12,260 feet, with 2140 feet vertical gain

Distance: 3½ miles up , 7 miles round-trip

Duration: 2 hours up, 3 hours round-trip

Difficulty: Strenuous. Some route-finding, steeper areas

TRAILHEAD

See hike 46 for directions.

ROUTE

Walk through the gate and past the power station immediately into the amazing Bridal Veil Basin. Continue S almost a mile up the easy, main, wildflower-surrounded trail (in July and August), ascending a couple switchbacks opposite cascading waterfalls in the creek, and ¼ mile farther S to four steeper, rockier switchbacks E. Continue a couple hundred yards S, go left (E) at the fork, and

Three Needles into Mud Lake.

take the steeper way another 100 yards toward Blue Lake to an old, rusty yellow gate and the TH on a big switchback. Traverse to the left (NE) under ¼ mile over to the old, tin-roofed cabin on the narrow path. Hike much more steeply up the left (N) side of the creek, going E above the old cabin. The path also goes N from the cabin to Grays Basin by following the pipeline until it starts going down, then catching the high traverse ½ mile to that basin. Or you could walk a bit more easily by taking that path another 150 feet or so N past the cabin to the traverse trail right (SSE) to Mud Lake Basin, and meet the steeper path in the creek above a small tarn pond. Hike ¼ mile E up past the small tarn pond to the high meadow, and either stay on the path a couple hundred yards SSE to the switchbacks below the base of the little waterfall, scrambling steeply up the rocky way on the left (N) of the falls, or aim for the weakness on the left (N) side of the short cliff band that extends ESE a few hundred yards to the top of the falls. Hike 25–30 feet steeply up the grass and loose scree E to gain the cliff band most easily; then contour effortlessly to the right (E and S) to the top of the falls on a wide shelf above the cliff band. Meet the scramble route, and go to the left (SE) near the end of the shelf before the falls. Hike briefly and fairly steeply a few hundred feet to the next large, grassy meadow and basin more easily again directly to the picturesque lakes.

Return the same way, or **Loop** W and S toward Blue Lake for an easier, slightly longer descent by following the rock-covered pipeline leading to Mud Lake ½ mile out of Mud Lake Basin to the left (NNW). A big telephone pole is a marker at the head and W of the basin, where you continue S ¼ mile on the path and leave the high traverse at the end for the main trail (going sharp right, NW) immediately unless you plan on going ¼ mile S up to Blue Lake. Meet the Mud Lake trail at the gate on the switchback in ½ mile going down NW and N, and finish W to Bridal Veil Creek and over a mile N to the power plant.

55	Blue Lake

Elevation: 12,200 feet, with 2080 feet vertical gain
Distance: 2½ miles up, 5 miles round-trip
Duration: 1½ hours up, 3 hours round-trip
Difficulty: Moderate. Steady, some steeps, rocky, obvious, wide trail

TRAILHEAD

See hike 46 for directions.

ROUTE

Walk through the gate and past the power station immediately into the overwhelming Bridal Veil Basin. Continue S almost a mile up the easy, main, wildflower-surrounded trail, ascending a couple switchbacks opposite cascading waterfalls in the creek, and ¼ mile farther S to four steeper, rockier switchbacks E. Continue a couple hundred yards S, and go left (E) at the fork (1 mile more total) up the steeper way. The flatter trail continues S to Lewis Lake. Hike SE up a few switchbacks, then S steadily to the striking Blue Lake, passing an old shack and house to the right (W), as the main road turns to a path at the end.

Elevation: 12,450 feet at Lewis Mine; 12,700 feet at Lewis Lake; 13,058 feet at Lewis Lake Pass; with vertical gains of 2330 feet, 2580 feet, 2938 feet

Distance: 3½ miles up, 7 miles round-trip; 4 miles up, 8 miles round-trip; 4½ miles up, 9 miles round-trip

Duration: 2 hours up; 3 hours round-trip; 2½–3 hours up, 4–5 hours round-trip; 3½ hours up, 5–6 hours round-trip

Difficulty: Strenuous. Steeper, some route-discovering, scree, possible glissades

TRAILHEAD

See hike 46 for directions.

ROUTE

See hike 55 for the description. About an hour (1¼ miles) S from the power station, go right (S) at the fork opposite the steep trail to Blue or Mud Lakes, and hike ½ mile up to the next fork at 11,800 feet. Stay to the right ½ mile (SSW, then SE) on the main trail, following the old road up to some small ponds. A couple hundred feet before the ponds (NW), a post marks the path SW up to the Blixt Road and a great **Loop** into Bear Creek for another time. Walk between the ponds, and go S ¼ mile up Bridal Veil Creek to the mill and the decent little shelter above Lewis Mine. (Please be respectful.)

To continue to Lewis Lake, climb the steep drainage gully to the left (E) from the little shelter and right (W) of the creek, going S a couple hundred yards up the solid scree trail if snow isn't covering it. The trail ends at the dammed end of the largest of ten other high alpine lakes

Locals cross the old bridge up to Lewis Lake.

An avid hiker takes a well-deserved break at Lewis Lake.

and ponds in this pristine area. It might be best not to go into the lakes themselves, as you will turn hypothermic more quickly than you thought possible! Hike 30 minutes and ½ mile more to the saddle S (Lewis Lake Pass, 13,058 feet) to see Columbine Lake (hike 80) and more of the San Juans. Simply walk SSE past Lewis Lake through the rock meadow to the end of the basin, turn left (NE) a few hundred feet, and go right (S) on the switchback up the visible, solid rock path ¼ mile to the pass.

TRAIL NOTES

....

....

....

....

....

....

....

Elevation: 13,510 feet, with 3400 feet vertical gain

Distance: 5 miles up, 10 miles round-trip

Duration: 4 hours up, 7 hours round-trip

Difficulty: Strenuous. Long but not hard, scree fields

TRAILHEAD

See hike 46 for directions.

ROUTE

See hike 56. Hike to the left (NE) from Lewis Lake Pass up the wide ridge ½ mile to the peak over a narrow, semisolid rock path. Climb easily directly over the first immediate bump on the high ridge to the large, wide, grassy meadow on the ridgeline. See the trail up the left (N) side of the ridge, and follow it from there. You can also stay on the ridge proper for a slightly more difficult, looser route up and down the summit block. Spoiler alert: from the top you are greeted with a magnificent sight, as three huge, bright blue, high alpine lakes become visible—Columbine Lake, Blue Lake, and Lewis Lake.

Blue Lake from T-11.

58   Jackass Basin

Elevation: 12,200 feet, with 2080 feet vertical gain
Distance: 2 miles up, 4 miles round-trip **Loop** or not
Duration: 1½–2 hours up, 3–4 hours round-trip **Loop** or not
Difficulty: Strenuous. Route-locating, steep into the basin

TRAILHEAD

See hike 46 for directions.

ROUTE

Go past the steel gate to Bridal Veil Creek, and walk only 10 minutes (½ mile) S on the main trail to the trail and creek crossing on the right (W). You might get wet if the big boulder in the water to the right is covered. Walk over it or cross the stream. Head up the trail with the route to Silver Lake, immediately going straight up and right (W) at the intersection, while you take the path to the left (SSW). One slightly easier **Opt** would be to take the Silver Lake Trail up ½ mile to a left-hand fork and traverse (S) from the base of the long, black-rock-covered cliff band about 500 feet over toward Jackass Basin, where you pick up the steep switchbacks and faded path going WSW.

Another cabin loses the battle of time at the bottom of Jackass Basin.

From the main trail near Bridal Veil Creek, continue left (SSW) when the trail splits on a traverse 80–100 feet above the creek 500 feet through bushes and loose rocks. Catch faint animal trails heading SW ½ mile to the mouth of Jackass Basin, as you ascend and hug the big rocks on the right (N) side of the steep slope, making your way up grassy ledges. After the switchbacks you level off, coming up to the cabin (with a decent-sized sunroof) from the far right (N) side of the basin. The old cabin is off the trail to the left (S) near the creek at the mouth of Jackass Basin. To get to the saddle between basins, walk to the right (W) from the cabin or last switchback ½ mile on an ascending traverse high above the meadow on a faint trail up to a notch in the rock band. There are terrific views of both vastly different basins.

Loop to Silver Lake from the saddle by going steeply N down semi-loose scree around 300 feet on the thin trail that contours N over to the center of the meadow high in Silver Lake Basin. Bushwhack down NE ¼ mile through this, and catch the solid trail on the right (S) side of the creek closer to the lake. This basin is on fire with Indian paintbrush in July. Walk more easily around the S side of the lake, and follow the fairly steep trail down a mile to Bridal Veil Creek.

TRAIL NOTES

....
....
....
....
....
....
....

Elevation: 11,780 feet, with 1660 feet vertical gain

Distance: 1½ miles up, 3 miles round-trip; 4 miles round-trip **Loop**

Duration: 1½ hours up, 2–3 hours round-trip; 3–4 hours **Loop**

Difficulty: Strenuous. Short but steep, overgrown trail, loose rocks

TRAILHEAD

See hike 46 for directions.

ROUTE

Walk through the gate, and go ½ mile S up to the trail at Bridal Veil Creek. Cross the water to the W over that big boulder just to the right if needed. Start up the trail, and climb to the right (W) when a faint trail continues to the left (SW) up to Jackass Basin. The trail gets much steeper and narrower, and lots of high bushes surround you. It's a little workout to get to the big clearing below the lake almost 1 mile from Bridal Veil Creek.

The trail levels out a bit, but not for long, as you go to the right (N) of the mini-falls on the trail the last ¼ mile up to the nearby lake, which indeed looks quite silver from Ajax, Telluride, or Ingram Peaks. Cruise around, check out the high meadow and basin, and return down the same way, or **Loop** with Jackass Basin by bushwhacking a few hundred yards up the center of the basin SSW through the wildflowers. Look up for the little notch to the left (S) with scree coming down, and then traverse more steeply over 300 feet to it and see Jackass Basin.

Good-sized rainbow trrout in Silver Lake.

60   Bear Creek Trail

Elevation: 9800 feet, with 1000 feet vertical gain

Distance: 2¼ miles up, 4½ miles round-trip

Duration: 1–1½ hours up, 2–3 hours round-trip

Difficulty: Moderate. Cliffy area near mouth of Bear Creek, rocky, wide, steady grade, very popular

TRAILHEAD

S Pine Street in Telluride at the gate for the Bear Creek Preserve. To avoid the frustration of trying to park legally next to the THs (2-hour limit, free Sundays and holidays), park at the free lot on the SW end of Telluride (Mahoney Drive, first right at the traffic circle coming into town), or nearby off of Mahoney Drive on W Pacific Avenue to Carhenge parking lot just E of Lift 7. Walk several blocks E, then S, or grab the free bus that comes every 10–20 minutes most times of the year and get off at Oak Street or Pine Street.

NOTES

Bring the kids and dogs. This is one of the easiest walks in the area, with close-up views of the rugged landscape, as the steep mountains rise 4000 feet to the peaks above. Walk, jog, bike, snowshoe, or cross-country ski this trail, Jud Wiebe Trail, San Miguel River Trail, Idarado Trail, and a few others year-round depending on conditions.

ROUTE

Walk or bike up the steep (old jeep) trail from the sign and gate E above Town Park in the aspens. The path to the right (W) 200 feet from the TH goes more steeply to 9200 feet on the lower portion of Camel's Garden Trail. It goes to the ski area (½ mile) and down to the right (N) ½ mile for a short **Loop** back to town, or follows the Telluride Trail 2 miles very steeply up to the gondola.

Hike E to the kiosk more than ½ mile from the TH up the steep, rocky trail, and go S into Bear Creek Basin and canyon. Stay on the main trail for a some-what easier stretch another mile to the Wasatch TH on the right (W), which will be just as you can finally see Bear Creek Falls up the valley. Continue less than ½ mile S on Bear Creek Trail to the huge boulder and flat area a couple hundred yards below the falls. A steeper single track goes to the base of the 100-foot cascading falls and rock band if you're up for it, whether or not snow and ice are present.

Elevation: 11,400 feet, with vertical gains of 2600 feet, 3430 feet to Unnamed Point 12,230

Distance: 4½ miles up, 9 miles round-trip; 5 miles up, 10 miles round-trip to Unnamed Point 12,230

Duration: 3 hours up, 5 hours round-trip; 4 hours up, 6 hours round-trip

Difficulty: Strenuous. Steep switchbacks, solid trail to the basin

TRAILHEAD

See hike 60 for directions.

ROUTE

Walk steeply E up Bear Creek Trail for ½ mile, turn S into the basin from the kiosk on a slight corner, and walk more easily into the greater Bear Creek Canyon and Preserve. Go ½ mile up to the first big clearing on your left (E), and leave Bear Creek Trail to go left (E) down the clearing on another trail 150 feet to Bear Creek. Cross the 5-foot-wide creek section over the narrow log bridge, and begin to climb the Ballard Mountain Trail, which shares the bottom with the Deertrail Basin hike. There are no signs for either here, but solid trails exist the whole way. Continue E steeply 250 feet through the trees and a little clear-

Deertrail Basin sign on Ballard Mountain Trail.

ing, where you hike to the right (S) on the trail for an easier stretch. It's a hundred yards to the first two switchbacks up, which occur just before you cross a tiny creek and fresh water feed. Walk through the thinning trees S past the remains of an old cabin to a clearing made by a slide path. Follow the thin trail S across the clearing, and go back into the woods (½ mile from Bear Creek) where you begin to hike very steeply for 1 mile and eight more switchbacks. Take some comfort—this is the easiest part of Ballard Mountain Trail!

On the tenth switchback from Bear Creek, the Deertrail Basin path breaks off from the Ballard Mountain Trail at a steel sign posted on a tree indicating the Deertrail Basin hike. The latter goes to the left (NNE), while the Ballard Mountain Trail is to the right (SE). Cross a narrow gully immediately, and walk ½ mile more easily on a long traverse that gains only a small amount of elevation before you get to the first of two short but steep switchbacks now heading SE. Continue a bit more easily a few hundred feet up the small shoulder. Then go slightly left (E) and much more steeply up thirteen more switchbacks going SE (1 mile), as you finally hike above the aspen line. Contour ¼ mile along a very steep slope in the beautiful evergreens along a gentle grade—by far the most effortless part of the hike to the lowest parts of Deertrail Basin. Hike steeply through the thinning pines on the thickest trail SSE up the basin (¼ mile more total). Ascend the very steep trail to the left (E) of the fixer-upper log cabin, and go to the end of the forest and open meadow, which (in this rare case for Southwest Colorado) runs almost to the top of the basin, limiting your views. Cruise around, as wildflowers abound in summertime, and deer and elk can be as elusive as fellow hikers. Remember to return on the proper trail, which is at the top of the trees that are farthest W in the basin.

To get to Unnamed Point 12,230, walk left (E) through the bottom of the high meadow directly over the next rise. Stay on the path (¼ mile to the ridge) NE into the woods; you will steeply ascend two switchbacks, then hike two further switchbacks close to the ridgeline, where there is some scattered mining debris. Climb to the right (SE) ¼ mile up the grassy ridge to the nearby grassy, rock-covered summit. Silver Lake is right there to the S, and Ballard Mountain is above on the connecting ridge to the SW. Ingram Falls and Ingram Basin are to the NE, and Telluride is visible to the NW. If you return by the same route, it's 1 hour and 15 minutes from the summit down to Ballard Mountain Trail.

62 Ballard Mountain

Elevation: 12,804 feet, with 4054 feet vertical gain

Distance: 4 miles up, 8 miles round-trip

Duration: 3–4 hours up, 6–8 hours round-trip

Difficulty: Very challenging. Super-steep, numerous switchbacks, scrambling, route-finding

TRAILHEAD

See hike 60 for directions.

ROUTE

See hike 61. Continue up from the tenth switchback (1½ miles) from Bear Creek at the Deertrail Basin intersection, and get to at least forty-one switchbacks total. If you are counting switchbacks, not S-turns, then number twenty-six (or thirteen if coming down) goes on a long straightaway (SSW) ½ mile up to a rocky, grassy meadow. A massive spire at the base of the meadow is a good reference point from here up to the alpine meadow. It's at least 1½ hours (3 miles) to the meadow from the TH and 2 hours more to the peak. Hike E up the middle of the meadow in the low grass about 100 yards steeply, catching the trail as you go to the left (N) through a few little evergreens, around the rocky corner, and up from the meadow. Do not be fooled by the first couple of lefts that go around the rocky corner and then go down while you are in the meadow.

Telluride from the top of Ballard Mountain.

From the top of Ballard Mountain looking south.

From the high ridge near tree line (¼ mile after you first reached the ridge-line), the summit trail breaks off from the Boardinghouse Trail (traversing SW and ends in ¼ mile) and stays on the ridge crest. Follow it steeply SE through scree under Ballard, staying on the high ridge over 300 feet, then contouring to the right (SW) a couple hundred yards on the most prominent path through the loose, steep scree, and up to the wide, rocky, W-facing gully NW of the summit. Try to stay left (N) in the gully, scrambling up more solid rock about 250 feet E to the widening top. It's just 5 minutes and a few hundred feet more of steeper hiking S to the grass-covered, large summit.

TRAIL NOTES

63 Ballard's Horn

Elevation: 13,145 feet, with vertical gains of 4345 feet from Ballard Mountain, 4672 feet from La Junta Peak, 3352 feet from La Junta Peak and the power station

Distance: 5 miles up, 10 miles round-trip from all routes

Duration: 5 hours up, 8–9 hours round-trip from all routes

Difficulty: Mix of expert-only (very long, steeper, sheer from Ballard Mountain) and very challenging (from Bridal Veil Basin or La Junta Basin, steadily steep, long, drop-offs, scree)

TRAILHEAD

See hikes 46 or 60 for directions.

ROUTE

See hikes 62 and 64 for the description. From Ballard's summit, walk easily down S 100 yards or so on the connecting ridge and up a few hundred yards on the ridge, as it gets extremely steep to the base of the huge rock band. You can climb the super-steep rock band SE directly on the ridge with good holds 20–25 feet nearly straight up the obstacle and S to the summit a few feet away. Or traverse around Ballard's Horn (as locals call it, though the technical name is Point 13,145) slightly more easily to the right (W) next to an extremely steep hillside. Hug Ballard's Horn carefully 75 feet over to its S ridge on the thin ledge, and go 50 feet left (N) more easily to the elusive summit.

From La Junta Peak, the route to Ballard's Horn and Ballard Mountain is more apparent down the center of the ridge. Good to keep in mind if you attempt a **Loop** involving these three peaks. It's ½ mile to Ballard's Horn over loose scree, steeper NW and N down the ridge from La Junta Peak to a saddle, and then somewhat better the last half N to the top.

For the route from the power station TH, see hikes 55 and 56, and walk about an hour (1¼ miles) S from the power station, right (S) at the fork opposite the steep trail to Blue or Mud Lakes ½ mile up to the next fork at 11,800 feet. Go right ½ mile (SSW, then SE) on the main trail, following the old road up to some small ponds. A couple hundred feet before the ponds (NW) is a post marking the path up to Blixt Road. Hike right (SW) semi-steeply ¼ mile, right on Blixt Road (opposite the way to Oscar's Pass or the Wasatch Trail) on an easy traverse NNW more than ½ mile, and past (E of) Primrose Lake directly to the saddle between La Junta Peak and Wasatch Mountain. Then make your way NE steeply up to La Junta Peak.

64 La Junta Peak

Elevation: 13,472 feet, with vertical gains of 4672 feet from Bear Creek, 3352 feet from the power station

Distance: 4½ miles up, 9–10 miles round-trip from either route

Duration: 4½–5 hours up, 7–8 hours round-trip from either route

Difficulty: Very challenging. Steeper than most, loose scree

TRAILHEAD

See hikes 46 or 60 for directions.

ROUTE

See hike 65 and climb to the high saddle between La Junta Peak and Wasatch Mountain. Scramble left (NE) from the saddle very steeply up a well-traveled path on La Junta's wide ridge. Gain more than 500 feet up semi-loose scree to the colossal summit marker. See the end of hike 63 for the more easygoing route from the power station.

• **Bonus:** Hike down to Ballard's Horn and Ballard Mountain to reach three peaks on a very difficult, 10-mile, counterclockwise **Loop** back to Bear Creek.

TRAIL NOTES

....

....

....

....

....

....

....

65   La Junta Basin

Elevation: 12,850 feet, with 4050 feet vertical gain

Distance: 4 miles up, 8 miles round-trip

Duration: 3½–4 hours up, 6 hours round-trip

Difficulty: Very challenging. Consistently steep, loose, some route-finding

TRAILHEAD

See hike 60 for directions.

ROUTE

See hike 60 and walk 30 minutes (1½ miles) up the trail to the second big, open meadow in the canyon on the left (E). There are big, flat rocks and fallen trees to walk over next to the main trail you exit; carefully cross Bear Creek there. It is slightly disorienting with no precise trail to start, but look for the huge boulder on the other side of the creek (E) and down 50 feet or so. The trail is above the boulder from the creek. A small scree field and smaller creek bed (and creek with falls when running) come down from La Junta Basin (farther E) W to the big boulder. This is the start of the steep uphill climb to the basin, and already

Short but very sweet wildflower season in the mountains.

you begin to understand why this hike is rated "very challenging." Go left (N) across the scree and up 100 feet to catch the rocky trail. Walk to the left (ENE) into the woods, then steeply up a total of thirty-seven switchbacks SSE to the high saddle above the basin. When you are finally out of the thick trees, notice the sheer black rock wall at the mouth of La Junta Basin (1½ miles from Bear Creek). It's nice when water runs down the wall and Bear Creek Falls is visible far below. Climb S up to the mining ruins in a hundred feet or so, and go a couple hundred yards straight over and SSW up to the scree field on the narrow path. Remember how you came up, as it's easy to get a little confused here. When you are going down, the trail is slightly to the left (W) in the rubble. Bushwhack up 200 feet steeply and find the trail slightly to the right (S) through low brush and bushes. Up a couple hundred feet more, cross the little creek to the left (E) and continue SE up ¼ mile to meet an old road that crosses the basin in the semi-flats. Catch the trail going left (E) a few hundred yards to the last switchback before you traverse SE ½ mile straight up to the high saddle at 12,850 feet.

Go down the same route, or **Loop** clockwise with hike 67 by taking Blixt Road easily 1 mile S from the saddle to the other saddle (John McCarron Junction at 13,060 feet) at the top of Wasatch Trail 508. Then go 5 miles steeply down Wasatch Trail 508 through Bear Creek Basin to Telluride.

TRAIL NOTES

....

....

....

....

....

....

....

66   Wasatch Mountain

Elevation: 13,555 feet, with vertical gains of 3435 feet from the power station, 4755 feet from Bear Creek

Distance: 5 miles up, 10 miles round-trip from either route

Duration: 3–4 hours up, 5–6 hours round-trip from either route

Difficulty: Very challenging. Steeper from town, loose scree, route-finding, long

TRAILHEAD

See hike 46 or 60 for directions.

ROUTE

For the route from the power station TH, see hikes 55 and 56, and go about an hour (1¼ miles) S from the power station, right (S) at the fork opposite the steep trail to Blue or Mud Lakes ½ mile up to the next fork at 11,800 feet. Hike right ½ mile (SSW, then SE) on the main trail, following the old road up to some small ponds. A couple hundred feet before the ponds (NW) is a post marking the path up to the Blixt Road. Go right (SW) semi-steeply ¼ mile, right on Blixt Road (opposite the way to Oscar's Pass or the Wasatch Trail) on an easy traverse NNW more than ½ mile, and then E of Primrose Lake directly to the saddle between La Junta Peak and Wasatch Mountain.

Go left (WSW) from the high saddle at 12,850 feet, and scramble very steeply to start a few hundred yards up over a rock trail. Keep going ¼ mile up the more defined ridge SW over large, stable rocks and scree to the summit with little to no trail near the top. See La Junta Basin from Bear Creek Trail and follow from the high saddle.

TRAIL NOTES

....
....
....
....
....
....
....

Elevation: 13,060 feet, with 4260 feet vertical gain

Distance: 5 miles up, 10 miles round-trip

Duration: 4 hours up, 6 hours round-trip

Difficulty: Strenuous. Very long, steep, long time above tree line

TRAILHEAD

See hike 60 for directions.

ROUTE

Walk or bike up the steep (old jeep) trail from the sign and gate E above Town Park in the aspens to the kiosk more than ½ mile up the rocky trail, and head S into Bear Creek Basin and canyon. Stay on the main trail (which is somewhat easier) another mile to the Wasatch TH on the right (W), which will be just as you can finally see Bear Creek Falls up the valley. Follow the single track from the sign steeply up nearly a mile and around fourteen switchbacks, not including back-to-back S-turns. Some cairns help at the small creek you cross several times. There are a total of forty-four switchbacks to John McCarron Junction and the apex of the hike, but who's counting? On top of the first fourteen or so switchbacks, the trail levels out somewhat ½ mile S up the creek. It gets steeper, rockier, looser, and narrower to the aging wooden bridge crossing and up to the nearby Nellie Mine ruins another 150 feet up on the right (W). It's an easier walk a couple hundred yards to the bottom of the big Lower Basin, where you will arrive about 1 hour from Bear Creek Trail.

Many options open up from this strikingly large basin. **Opt 1**: Continue on Wasatch Trail 508 (sign says "East Fork 513") to the left (SE) across the meadow, and **Loop** clockwise higher on West Fork Trail (more than 1 mile away), or go to the high point and saddle at 13,060 feet (2 miles away). **Opt 2**: Go right (SSW) up the rocky West Fork Trail to get to Gold Hill, Lena Basin, or do a counterclockwise **Loop Alt** with Wasatch Trail 508 from West Fork Trail at the creek (four-way intersection), and continue back down without going to the high saddle. For this, go right (SSW) in the Lower Basin less than ¼ mile up the steeper, rockier trail, then up six switchbacks (W) before heading S a couple hundred yards and down to the creek bed. Cross the creek bed to the E side at the sign ("Wasatch Trail–Telluride Ski Area") and four-way intersection for the **Loop Alt** or Lena Basin, and go left (SE) on Wasatch Trail (West Fork) up more

Sign on the west fork of the Wasatch Trail.

steeply for a couple hundred feet. Then go ¼ mile E easily over the hill and down to meet the main East Fork Trail at the creek where you go left (NW) and down.

For **Opt 1**, walk up the creek from the sign and intersection N in the Lower Basin. Carefully cross the creek almost immediately, and catch the trail 350 feet to the other side of the meadow to the main creek feed. Hike switchbacks 250 feet up much more steeply E, then contour S about ½ mile over to meet the West Fork Trail at the creek. The trail is narrow and loose for a short time. **Loop** here if you wish to go back down to the Lower Basin by taking that faint trail W over the grassy hill and NW to the creek bed and four-way intersection. From there you go down to the right (N) at that intersection on the trail closest to the creek.

To continue on Wasatch Trail 508 to Oscar's Pass or John McCarron Junction and the high saddle, however, hike up from the creek (SE) to the smaller Middle Basin and high meadow ¼ mile away. Indian paintbrush owns this damp meadow during wildflower season. Try to stay on the trail here and through the Upper Basin, as the landscape changes dramatically for the last ¾ mile. Keep looking ahead on this one and you should be able to observe the faint path above. It's a little steeper at the end and the final switchbacks near the high saddle. Go down the same route, or do a **Loop** with La Junta Basin via the Blixt Road (1 mile N easily).

Elevation: 13,432 feet, with vertical gains of 4632 feet from Bear Creek, 3312 feet from the power station

Distance: 5 ½ miles, 11 miles round-trip from either route

Duration: 5 hours up, 8 hours round-trip from Bear Creek; 3 hours up, 5 hours round-trip from the power station

Difficulty: Mix of very challenging (quite long, steadily steep) and strenuous (long, scree, harder drive)

TRAILHEAD

See hike 46 or 60 for directions.

ROUTE

See hike 67 for the Bear Creek route or hike 66 for the power station route. For the latter, go left (SW) once you are on the Blixt Road high in Bridal Veil Basin for ½ mile, including the right turn (W) away from the trail to Oscar's Pass (SW) to the nearby saddle. Climb left (SW) from the high saddle, also called John McCarron Junction, and leave the trail to hike a rocky path up the ridge or 20 feet to the right (W). Oscar's Peak (officially Point 13,432) is a cinch, which is nice if you came the long way from Bear Creek. The views of Lookout Peak and Ophir Pass are magnificent.

Upper Wasatch Basin to Oscar's Peak from Gold Hill.

CHAPTER 8

TOWN AND SOUTH TELLURIDE

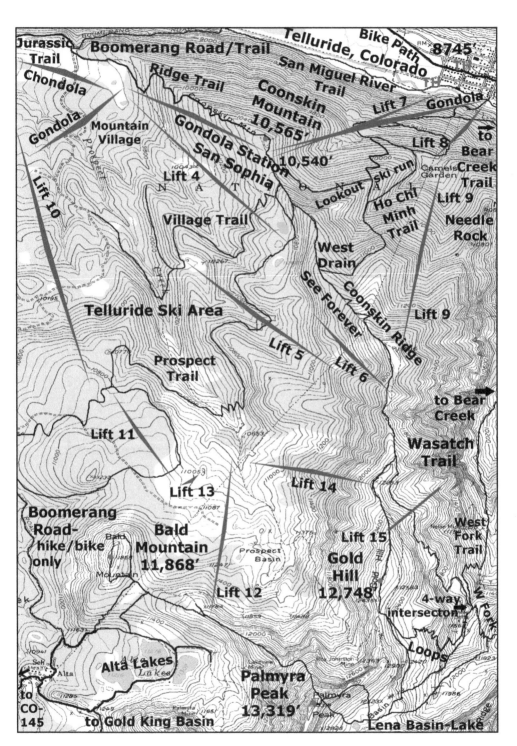

HIKES 69-75

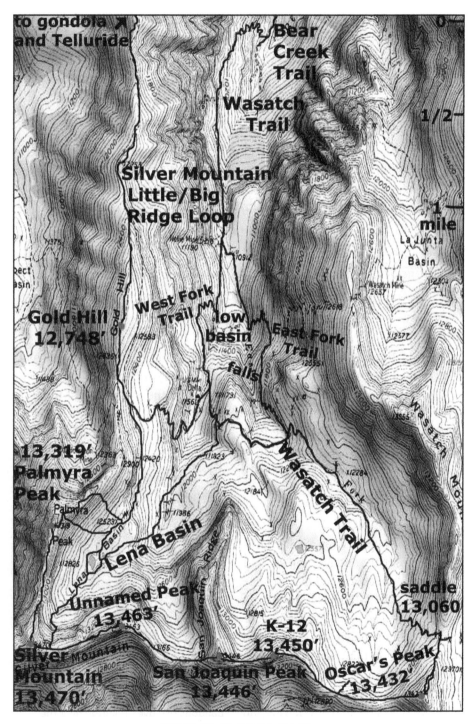

to gondola
and Telluride

Bear
Creek
Trail

Wasatch
Trail

0

1/2

1
mile

Silver Mountain
Little/Big
Ridge Loop

La Junta
Basin

Wasatch Mine
12657

Gold Hill
12,748'

West Fork
Trail

low
basin

East Fork
Trail

falls

Wasatch Mou.

13,319'
Palmyra
Peak

Palmyra
Peak

Wasatch Trail

Lena Basin

saddle
13,060

Unnamed Peak
13,463'

K-12
13,450'

Oscar's Peak
13,432'

Silver
Mountain
13,470'

San Joaquin Peak
13,446'

HIKES 67, 68, 70-73, 75, 76

Elevation: 8745 feet (Telluride), with vertical gains of 85 feet for San Miguel River Trail, 675 feet for Boomerang Trail, 1200 feet for Local's Loop

Distance: 4 miles one way, 8 miles round-trip; 1½ miles up, 3 miles round-trip; 18 miles round-trip **Loop**

Duration: 2 hours one way from Telluride Town Park (W) to the end of the Bike Path across from Society Drive at the W end of the Telluride valley, 4 hours round-trip; 25-minute bike ride up Boomerang Trail, 1 hour round-trip; 2 hours round-trip **Loop** for Local's Loop bike ride

Difficulty: Mix of easiest (valley floor walk), moderate (short but steep), and strenuous (steady grade, narrow, long)

TRAILHEAD

Telluride Town Park just E of downtown to the right (S) for the San Miguel River Trail (unless a summer festival has closed the parking lot to the public). Otherwise drive to the large, free parking area at the SW corner of town at the end of S Mahoney Drive for San Miguel River Trail or Boomerang Trail.

Local's Loop ride and the Bike Path begin at the N corner of Davis Street and Colorado Avenue (Main Street), heading W out of town.

NOTES

The San Miguel River Trail begins across from the intersection of East Colorado Avenue and Columbine Street, just E of Telluride Town Park. As an **Alt** day walk, you could continue E immediately on the Idarado Trail easily up the valley 1¾ miles on the right (S) side of the main road to the Pandora Mill. It's quite nice year-round (snowshoe in winter), wide and hilly but not steep.

Balloons rise over Telluride near the start of the summer season.

Avalanche on Ajax Peak in winter, 2013.

ROUTE

Going the other way (W), it's a lovely stroll to begin the San Miguel River Trail by Telluride Town Park. The trail turns left by the post office and continues W along the river. Cross a few bridges through town without elevation change and get to Mahoney Drive, the last paved road in town going N and S, a mile from Telluride Town Park. This is also the location of the free parking lot (just S of the river). Continue another mile along the left (S) of the river, and turn around near the Boomerang Trail to come back the same way. You could also **Loop** clockwise to the gas station N ½ mile on an access road, cross the highway, and follow the Bike Path a mile E to town.

If you are going up Boomerang Trail, it's the steep, wide road off to the left (S), opposite the little old bridge and access road over to the gas station. It is steeper and rockier, as you continue W ½ mile up to the ridge and road below a giant hotel. See hike 72 for the Jurassic Trail bike **Loop** or **Loop** up to the gondola on Ridge Trail 433, or return the same way, or **Loop** to the gas station and back to town.

For Local's Loop or the Bike Path from the beginning at the corner of Davis Street and Colorado Avenue, start on the paved trail W out of town immediately to the high point overlooking the valley ¼ mile from the TH. Remain on the right (N) side of CO-145 Spur until you go under it through a tunnel (2 miles from the TH). Say hello or ring your bell, as other bikers and pedestrians may be coming around the corner in there. Stay on the left side (S) of the highway past the airport road until the end around the corner S of Society Turn.

The road to the Lawson Hill neighborhood, the gas station, and the Galloping Goose Trail are across CO-145.

For Local's Loop, cross the highway and go right of the gas station on Society Drive more than ¼ mile to San Miguel River Drive and the cul-de-sac on the right (N). See the Galloping Goose Trail sign down at the end of the cul-de-sac. Ride the steeps from the parking area W next to the river ½ mile WSW crossing the little bridge, and continue 1 mile S along an old railroad grade into Illium. The trail is narrow for a time, with a steep drop-off, so be careful and mindful of others. When the trail meets the South Fork Road, turn right on it nearly 3 miles as it becomes paved through Illium (N, then W) by the gravel quarry and the police station. A steeper dirt road to the left (W) 50 feet below the intersection with the highway is your next path. The easier and less interesting **Opt** involves taking the highway more quickly ½ mile to Deep Creek FS Road 639. If you are taking the path from the steeper dirt road, be aware that it is narrow and sometimes rocky, and goes WNW ½ mile through trees along the N side of the river. You end up at the highway-maintenance igloo after a great ride.

Street sign to Imogene Pass.

Cross CO-145 to Deep Creek Road FS 639 (dirt), and follow it steadily 2½ miles NE up to the end and intersection. Go right on Last Dollar Road FS 638, cross the bridge immediately, and begin a steeper uphill climb more than 2 miles SE above the Telluride Regional Airport through a big, beautiful meadow. Continue left (SE) 2 miles steeply down the paved Airport Road, and go left on the Bike Path across from CO-145 Spur 2½ miles E through the valley to Telluride.

70   Lena Basin

Elevation: 12,520 feet, with 3720 feet vertical gain
Distance: 5 miles up, 10 miles round-trip
Duration: 2½–3½ hours up, 5–7 hours round-trip
Difficulty: Very challenging. Pretty long, bushwhacking

TRAILHEAD
See hike 60 for directions.

ROUTE
See hike 67, **Opt 2**, and hike the West Fork Trail in the Lower Basin to the four-way intersection and sign ("Wasatch Trail-Telluride Ski Area") 4 miles from the TH. Cross the little creek (E) opposite the Wasatch Connection Trail to the ski area, and go a few hundred feet up West Fork Trail steeply. Leave it as it levels out, and go right (SSW) on the narrow, slightly overgrown path to Lena Basin. The path almost disappears in a blanket of wildflowers, as you contour ½ mile more easily back to a flatter section of creek just above a very steep section that starts a mini-canyon through the rocks. Cross and follow the creek SSW on the W side much more steeply the last ½ mile to Lena Lake as the trail peters out through the rocky section nearest the creek. The route mellows in Lena Basin, as you pass the smaller lake first on the bushwhack to Lena Lake.

Go down the same way, or **Loop** with Gold Hill down the Coonskin Ridge to the gondola back to Telluride in a little less time and mileage. Traverse the distinct trail high and to the left (NNE) ½ mile while leaving Lena Basin to a grassy meadow and shelf SE of Gold Hill. The path goes steeply down E ½ mile to West Fork Trail/Wasatch Trail 508 or goes steeper 200 feet NW up to the saddle, then N a few hundred feet up to the nearby summit of Gold Hill (see hike 71).

Elevation: 12,748 feet, with vertical gains of 2223 feet from top of the gondola, 3948 feet from Bear Creek Trail

Distance: 3 miles from the gondola, 6 miles round-trip; 5 miles from Bear Creek Trail, 10 miles round-trip

Duration: 2 hours up, 3½ hours round-trip; 4 hours up, 6 hours round-trip

Difficulty: Mix of strenuous (fairly steep ridge hike up, route-finding, wide) and very challenging (long, steady grade)

TRAILHEAD

The free gondola at the bottom of S Oak Street in Telluride or Bear Creek Trail; see hike 60 for directions.

ROUTE

The main route from the top of the gondola will take you up the Coonskin Ridge SE and S on the See Forever ski trail. Walk ¼ mile (SE) from the gondola terminal past the Saint Sophia Nature Center on the main road to the base of the very steep, wide Coonskin Ridge. One of two **Opts** here is to leave the ski area road and climb very steeply SE up the bottom section of the wide ridge on the right (S) side up many convenient wooden steps (winter ski berm) to the semi-flats more than ¼ mile away. The longer, easier **Opt** would be to stay on the road to the right of the ridge and well below it, going S ¼ mile and left (N) opposite a ski company's snow-making pond. Leave the ski road to traverse up N on the trail a couple hundred yards through the woods to the main ridge, and go to the right (SE) up the wooden steps a couple hundred yards more to the semi-flats on the more pronounced trail.

When you reach the top of the first steep part, take the single track left across the center of the wide ski trail, and follow it on the N side of the (ski) trail to catch ski roads that go up the long ridge, sometimes leaving the ridge briefly. Don't take the first two roads left (E) from the high ridge, however, because

The doorway to Gold Hill and beyond.

West Dallas and Dallas Peaks from the Coonskin Ridge.

they go into West Drain (a ski area trail) and down. Take the third road, which is almost 1½ miles from the gondola, for easier walking than the ridgeline (Last Chance Catwalk sign is up the dirt road). Follow the road as it winds up gradually ½ mile back to the ridge, then hike directly S ½ mile under Lift 6; it's only 1 mile more, but much steeper at tree line where you finally climb S up to Gold Hill, going past Lifts 14 and 15. Stay on the narrow trail near the top. One little rocky, scree-filled outcrop ¼ mile N of the summit is easily navigated 30 feet up total and is the steepest part of the hike. See cairns and hike up the smaller scree path just left (E) of the crux on the ridge crest, then make your way to the ridge to finish without difficulty. From the peak area, the massive Bear Creek Canyon truly unveils itself all the way up to Wasatch Basin.

Return down the Coonskin Ridge, or take one of a few **Loops** down Bear Creek that will lengthen your day (without the gondola) and end near the start of the **Loop** in town. Lena Basin can be reached by going down Gold Hill to the S 300 feet, then down to the left (E) 200 feet from the saddle on a faint trail to the big shelf below. Stay high and to the right (S) ½ mile to get to Lena Basin, or simply go straight down E from the shelf to do a shorter **Loop** without Lena ½ mile down a pretty steep bushwhack path. You could also go a bit more easily back down N from the summit block area again, head right (SE) on Wasatch Connection Trail 200 feet below Lift 14, traverse a mile down to the four-way intersection high on the Wasatch West Fork Trail, and go left (N) down to Bear Creek. (See hike 67.)

72 Telluride Ski Area

Elevation: 10,565 feet, with vertical gain of 25 feet and loss of 1800 feet

Distance: 4 miles down Ridge Trail 433 to Telluride

Duration: 2 hours down Ridge Trail 433 to Boomerang Trail, San Miguel River Trail, and town; 30 minutes by bike

Difficulty: Moderate. Ridge Trail 433 down, steady, narrow

TRAILHEAD

The free gondola at the bottom of S Oak Street in Telluride or Bear Creek Trail; see hike 60 for directions.

NOTES

The top of the gondola, Station San Sophia, is a popular access point for bikers and hikers of various levels to many different places. It can even be a destination in itself for those wanting to just scout around and take pictures a few feet from the gondola. Best of all, the gondola is free!

ROUTE

Ridge Trail 433 (1½ miles to Boomerang Trail) and Scenic Overlook Trail (less than ¼ mile) begin on the left if you are coming out of the gondola building at Station San Sophia, as you descend steeply to the N on the Telluride side of the gondola station to begin. See the signs and go W up to begin both trails, as the Scenic Overlook Trail quickly ends at the bench on the short path to the right (W). Ridge Trail 433 continues WNW 100 feet up to arrive at the uneventful high point of Coonskin Mountain.

Bike or hike a clockwise **Loop** down the Ridge Trail 433 NW 1½ miles from the gondola to the Mountain Village, then right (E) ½ mile down Boomerang Trail, finishing with San Miguel River Trail 2 miles E back to the gondola. You could also extend the bike ride to Lawson Hill/Society Turn by going left (W) on the Jurassic Trail as Boomerang Trail goes steeply E to town. Ride it more than ½ mile down to the apartments and condos in Mountain Village Meadows, and bike the pavement ½ mile NW to where the road starts to go up again, leaving the Meadows. Ride the fairly flat trail ½ mile to Lawson Hill on the right (N) by going down when you reach the highway; or for a safer alternative, cross the road immediately to the trail past the gate. Go down through the tunnel momentarily and arrive at the Galloping Goose TH and

Most scenic commute.

intersection on Society Drive. Turn right (E) on Society Drive more than ¼ mile to the Bike Path across from CO-145. Finish easily 3 miles E up the valley on the paved Bike Path to Telluride.

Coming down Ridge Trail 433 from the gondola is the easiest way to Mountain Village or Telluride on a dirt and rock single track. Bike or hike a mile on and off the ridge crest NW down switchbacks in the coniferous and deciduous flora to the end (under the gondola) at a crossroads and sign. Go left (S) up 100 yards on Ridge Trail 433 to the sign on the right, and NW down to the Mountain Village core immediately, where you can take the gondola from Mountain Village back to Telluride. To continue to Boomerang Trail (½ mile), head right at the crossroads sign down paved Mountain Village Boulevard briefly and right onto a short single track after a big curve and Lookout Ridge Road. Go right onto the road below and right after the bridge (down a stone stairway if you are walking, and under a covered gazebo), then right at the big hotel onto Country Club Drive. Walk or ride around the hotel to the N, next to the golf course, and turn right (N) off the corner of Country Club Drive onto Boomerang Trail (E), or Jurassic Trail (W). Go right (E) at the bottom of the steeper Boomerang Trail (½ mile) onto San Miguel River Trail for 25 minutes (2 miles) of easier walking to the gondola station.

The wheelchair-accessible Nature Trail (closed to bikers) is less than ¼ mile long, wide, and smooth. Start and end at the top of the gondola. Look for signs, and be prepared for trails to change somewhat as the Forest Service finds suitable, legal, environmentally smart placement. One more trail, the O'Reilly/Ronbo/Wolverine Trail, might connect Mountain Village and Telluride, starting near the top of the Boomerang Trail. It would cross the ski area and use the Telluride Trail (ski run), possibly ending up on Bear Creek Trail near Camel's Garden Trail, if legal easement problems ever get settled.

For another bike ride, come down to Telluride (NE) directly under the gondola on the Telluride Trail. Some people see this and think it would make for a great hike, too. Wrong again, Bob! It is difficult enough as a 2-mile bike ride, with lots of loose gravel, ditches, pipes, and a super-steep pitch. Most hikes to town on the ski area are not so easygoing.

73 Palmyra Peak

Elevation: 13,319 feet, with 2160 feet vertical gain

Distance: 2 miles up, 4 miles round-trip

Duration: 1½ hours up, 2½–3 hours round-trip

Difficulty: Very challenging. Positively steep, scrambling, faintest trail, slight exposure

TRAILHEAD

Alta Lakes. From Telluride, head 3 miles W on CO-145 Spur, more than 3 miles S on CO-145 past Mountain Village and Sunshine Campground, and turn left (E) to bike or 2WD (in summer) 4 miles NE up Alta Lakes Road FS 632, passing the old ghost town of Alta. Skip the first left past the town of Alta, and drive S on the main road (½ mile to Alta Lakes), then SE past the last fork (to Gold King Basin), and NE (left) directly to Alta Lakes. Drive from Durango (103 miles, 2 hours) on US-160 W toward Cortez, right in Mancos on CO-184 W to the end, right through Dolores on CO-145 N, and right up ½ mile past the Ophir Loop onto Alta Lakes Road FS 632 (E). There is an outhouse.

ROUTE

Walk up the dirt road between the second and third beautiful high alpine lakes, which are worth spending quality time at. Walk W about 150–200 feet past the middle lake, looking for a path on the right (N) that goes up gently through trees to the grassy saddle between Bald Mountain and Palmyra Peak. A power line is a visible marker to follow up a couple hundred yards. Go right (SE) at the ridge crest toward Palmyra Peak up to the ski area, and follow the wide, steep ski run or the ski roads ½ mile up to Lift 12. Hike more steeply SE ½ mile up the

Purple Fringe in front of Palmyra Peak.

ridge on an easily seen trail over rocks; the trail disappears, and you must bushwhack and scramble up the super-steep, semi-grassy hill, aiming for a long rock rib slightly to the left (E) extending N from the peak. Climb single file 200 feet up the left on the right (W) side of the rock rib. For the last ¼ mile, cross 25 feet to the right (W) to a smaller rock rib and mini-shoulder, and grind SE about 75 feet up the steepest part of the slope, angling to the right (W) on the left (E) side of the peak. Once you are at the high ridge and little saddle, go around the summit 30 feet to the Lena Basin (S) side carefully. See the trail as it crosses big, flatter rocks that switchback N a few feet to the nearby tiny peak area. Uh oh, vertigo!

It's also possible, though not preferred, to climb to Palmyra Peak from Lena Lake by climbing WNW ½ mile and 800 feet up the right (N) side of the extremely steep, rocky, loose, wide gully extending SE from the summit. An **Alt** bushwhack lies a hundred yards N of the wide gully (from the top or bottom), and it's very steep over the grass and rock for the same distance. At the top, stay on the Lena Basin side. Catch the trail and switchbacks momentarily to the small standing area on top of this impressive peak.

74 Bald Mountain

Elevation: 11,868 feet, with 710 feet vertical gain

Distance: 1 mile up, 2 miles round-trip; little **Loop** around the summit

Duration: 1½ hours round-trip; little **Loop** around the summit

Difficulty: Moderate. Proper trail could be elusive, rocky

TRAILHEAD
Alta Lakes; see hike 73 for directions.

ROUTE
Walk up the dirt road between the second and third beautiful high alpine lakes, which are worth spending quality time at. Walk W about 150–200 feet past the middle lake, looking for a path on the right (N) that goes up gently through trees to the grassy saddle between Bald Mountain and Palmyra Peak. A power line is a visible marker to follow up a couple hundred yards. From the saddle, go left (NW) 100 feet to the huge Bald Mountain ski area sign in the woods under the power line. Hike to the right (NNW) and stay in the woods on a faint trail that ends in 150 feet or so, where the trees end. If you go counterclockwise, traverse right (N) at a big boulder in the clearing ¼ mile around the steep areas on the summit block, and proceed left 200 feet more easily, S up the ridge to the summit. Follow the ridge to complete a nice **Loop** down S, E, and SE near the trees again, going left (N) around the landmark boulder on the trail near the woods. Follow the ski area boundary rope, or take the trail down to the power line and clearing.

The steeper route going clockwise would be to follow the ski area boundary rope to the top of the trees and catch the trail by a big boulder in the clearing, going around it to the right (N). Then traverse left (W) 100 feet to more scree, and go right (N) 200 feet up the main ridge to the summit. It's steeper but more direct this way. During ski season, pass holders hike up and ski off the summit in all directions.

Elevation: 13,470 feet, with vertical gains of 4670 feet from Bear
Creek Trail, 2930-plus feet from the gondola

Distance: 5½ miles up, 11 miles round-trip; 4½ miles up, 9 miles
round-trip

Duration: 3½–5 hours up, 7–8 hours round-trip from either route

Difficulty: Very challenging. Route-finding from Lena Basin, very
steep, scree, scrambling

TRAILHEAD

The free gondola at the bottom of S Oak Street in Telluride or Bear Creek Trail;
see hike 60 for directions.

NOTES

See hikes 70 and 71, and get to Lena Basin from the Wasatch Trail or from a
traverse S of Gold Hill. The Gold Hill route makes use of the gondola and gets
you to Lena Basin in about the same amount of time as the Bear Creek Trail
route. You also get to do the extra summit and will have ridgetop views before
descending and continuing up to Lena Basin. And you can always hike a **Loop**
to Silver Mountain by connecting both of these routes to Lena Basin.

ROUTE

From Lena Lake, hike steeply a few hundred feet to the SSW to the top of the
basin through the scree and large rocks with no trail. Scramble 200 feet up the
right (W) side of a wide, rocky drainage gully to a fork where two big couloirs
come down N from Silver Mountain's summit. Go very steeply 50 feet or so
toward the wide gully on the left (E of the other gullies). Near the actual base of
that gully, leave the couloir routes and go hard to the left (E) on a 40-foot traverse to an opening in the outcrop and rock rib coming down N from the high
ridge. It will be much easier to climb from the N-facing shoulder rather than
continue up the super-steep couloirs. Traverse E from the gullies to the opening, and climb the 50-foot, thin chute, with better footing but a steep pitch to
the high shoulder. The brief chute quickly widens near the top of it, where you
see the little cairn and go to the right (S) up a wide, steep-sloping shoulder.
Hike over semi-stable, flat rock S 250 feet to the main ridge just E of the peak.
Once you are on the high ridge, walk to the right (W) and boulder easily over

moss-covered rock 150 feet to the summit and highest point on the ridge. On your way to the top, you will pass a "lightning rod" (steel pole) sticking out of the rocks on the ridge and realize that this may not be the best hangout when a storm is brewing! Return down the same route.

76 Silver Mountain Little or Big Ridge Loop

Elevation: 13,470 feet, with 4670-plus feet vertical gain

Distance: 10 miles round-trip **Loop** with Palmyra Peak; 13 miles round-trip **Loop** with Oscar's Peak

Duration: 8 hours round-trip **Loop**; 10 hours round-trip **Loop**

Difficulty: Expert-only. Little **Loop**: super-steep drop-offs, bushwhack, steep scree, heavy exposure. Longest **Loop**: Five to six summits, extreme day hiking, serious exposure; technical in one spot, but free climb possible, 30-foot rope to belay backpack necessary

TRAILHEAD
The free gondola at the bottom of S Oak Street in Telluride or Bear Creek Trail; see hike 60 for directions.

NOTES
Also see hikes 67, 68, 70, 71, and 75, and don't forget the camera with a fresh battery and memory card, because it's going to be a long day. For the big **Loop** over Oscar's Peak, look below and know that some climbers may wish to place protection near the Unnamed Peak just E of Silver Mountain. The little **Loop** starts and ends in Lena Basin and includes Palmyra Peak; it is much shorter than the big **Loop** but is not to be taken lightly.

ROUTE
For the little **Loop** ½ mile to Palmyra Peak from the top of Silver Mountain, descend NNE slowly and go slightly to the right (E) on the connecting high ridge when needed as a rule of thumb. It is very narrow, with much exposure and loose rock, so watch your footing. (If you slip off the bumpy ridge and fall to the W, your battered body/corpse will continue to fall nearly 2000 feet down to Alta Lakes. And if you fall to the E, the same unfortunate outcome will take

Wilson Peak, Silver Mountain, Unnamed Peak 13,463, and the major crux from the Big Ridge Loop.

you almost 800 feet down to Lena Lake.) About halfway across the ridge, it will be better to begin a slight traverse about 30 feet below the ridge crest to the right (E). Follow the extra-narrow but walkable ledges a few hundred feet N to the main crux. You will be just SE of the crux 150 feet before Palmyra Peak and must climb with care around a thin, E-facing couloir while still only about 30–40 feet below the ridgeline. Go directly to another thin, E-facing, rocky couloir through a small weakness. Climb W 35 feet up the gully itself easily back to the ridge at the notch, and walk N up the steep, narrow ramp from the ridge to better ground and the nearby peak. The only other option to going around the SE side of the notch is to down-climb from the ridge crest directly through the boulders. Unfortunately this ends at a 12-foot vertical wall with fairly insufficient holds and very loose rock. Also, you might not even land on the relative safety of the notch if you fell, so I don't recommend free climbing this.

To continue the **Loop** from Palmyra Peak, come down on the Lena Basin side slowly and steeply, and head to a larger saddle just NE of the peak. Once you are at the saddle, you can see the vague route down a giant ESE-facing couloir, which can be seen clearly from Lena Lake. Hike ½ mile down the supersteep, loose, rocky couloir to the lake. The huge gully is very steep and would be pretty difficult for anyone contemplating going to Palmyra Peak from Lena Basin in this direction. It's hard enough going down. An **Alt** bushwhack lies a hundred yards N of the wide gully (from the top or bottom), and it's very steep over the grass and rock for the same distance.

From Silver Mountain going in a counterclockwise direction, go E very briefly back to the saddle you ascended from a small N shoulder (and Lena Basin). Continue to the E along the high, wide ridge quite easily as the scree is flat and green ¼ mile to the top. Enjoy the scenery from this small summit (Unnamed Peak 13,463). One saving grace on this wonderfully long ridge is that the ups and downs lack a great deal of verticality between summits.

Begin toward the San Joaquin Ridge and summit (SE), as the "trail" instantly turns into the hardest part of the whole hike for the next ⅕ mile. Go one at a time, giving yourself some space as you stay in the middle of the ridge and boulder down good chunks at a time, already starting to face the mountain and most likely go backward. Taller folks will have it slightly easier, as hand- and footholds are far in between. As you stand firmly on top of the main crux boulder and tiny flat spot in the center of the ridge, you will have a couple of choices after you lower your pack to a small shelf 25 feet down to the right (S). You could go to the left (N) down the ultra-steep-sloping, sheer rock slab with a slight angle about 15 feet to a ledge below. The slab might be angled better for an ascent, but you can find a few holds where the boulder meets the steeper rock. From the ledge below, turn right (S) to the ridge crest to retrieve your pack and descend more easily. The other choice has you go to the right (Ophir side, S) from the top of the small flat spot on the crux boulder. Turn around, face the mountain, and move down a SE-facing crack very slowly for about 20 feet to a little shelf and flat area on the ridge. First see a tiny landing on the other side (S) of the crack almost halfway down, and make your way to the cubby (a few feet in diameter). Rest and find your holds from there to the shelf. See the best holds on the other side (N) of the crack from the cubby (left side if you are going down and right side, N, if you are going up). The rock is solid here and semi-loose to solid over most of the short and difficult ridge section. Go to the center of the rocky ridge immediately below the major crux, and cruise SE 150 feet down the gentler ridge section. Continue E on the main ridge directly over a bump to the saddle just to the W of San Joaquin Ridge (and summit at 13,446 feet). Boulder a couple hundred yards up to the peak, and go a few feet to the left (N) or straight (E) over a would-be obstacle directly below the top, over fairly stable scree. See the slender San Joaquin Ridge that heads to the N into Bear Creek from the summit.

Hike only ¼ mile down E and up to the next nearby high point at 13,450 feet (what locals call K-12). Work slightly to the left (Wasatch Trail side, N) or straight over the first section of ridge from San Joaquin Peak, as the route will become wider over semi-loose rock and scree. The summit of K-12's bark is worse than its bite. It is only a bit steeper as you go over flat but stable scree. Easily climb an 8-foot-long gully steeply on the ridgeline nearest the top. Move

Ophir Pass from Silver Mountain Big Ridge Loop.

down the connecting ridge from K-12 over bigger, bumpier rocks and scree more than ¼ mile to the semi-grassy saddle before (W of) the red rocks.

To hike to Oscar's Peak from its W ridge, go more than ¼ mile along the wide ridge crest and semi-stable red scree more steeply to the top, where there are a few summit markers. It looks pretty steep but is straightforward and not too difficult for tired legs climbing once more for the day. Leave the high ridge down a major shoulder NNE to the high saddle and the top of Wasatch Trail 508 at 13,060 feet. Hike over bigger, reddish rocks 20 feet left (W) of the shoulder itself down to the high saddle with Wasatch Mountain. Finish the **Loop** by going down to the left (NW) on Wasatch Trail 508 5 miles to Telluride.

TRAIL NOTES

....

....

....

....

....

....

....

CHAPTER 9

FAR SOUTH TELLURIDE (OPHIR–SILVERTON–DURANGO)

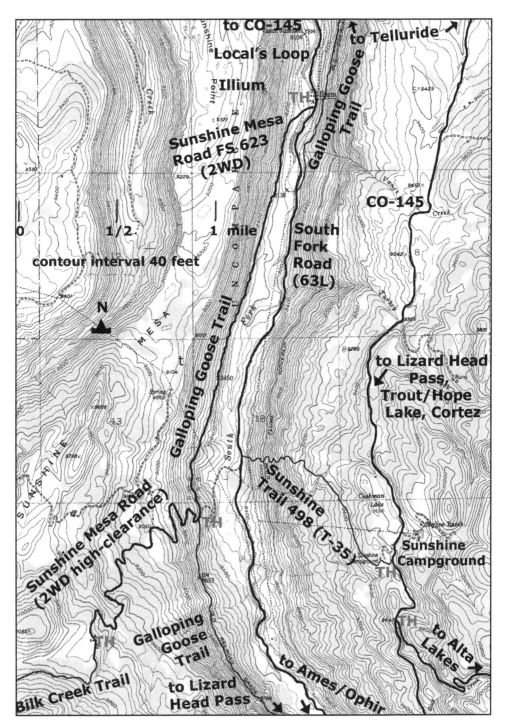

to CO-145

Local's Loop

Illium

to Telluride

Galloping Goose Trail

Sunshine Mesa Road FS 623 (2WD)

TH

CO-145

0   1/2   1 mile

South Fork Road (63L)

contour interval 40 feet

N

Galloping Goose Trail

to Lizard Head Pass, Trout/Hope Lake, Cortez

Sunshine Trail 498 (T-35)

Sunshine Mesa Road (2WD high-clearance)

TH

Sunshine Campground

TH

Galloping Goose Trail

TH

to Alta Lakes

Bilk Creek Trail

to Lizard Head Pass

to Ames/Ophir

HIKES 69, 77, 102

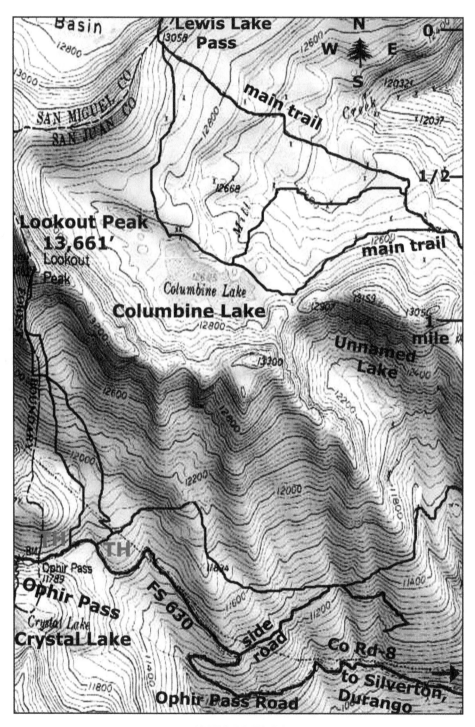

HIKES 56, 78-80

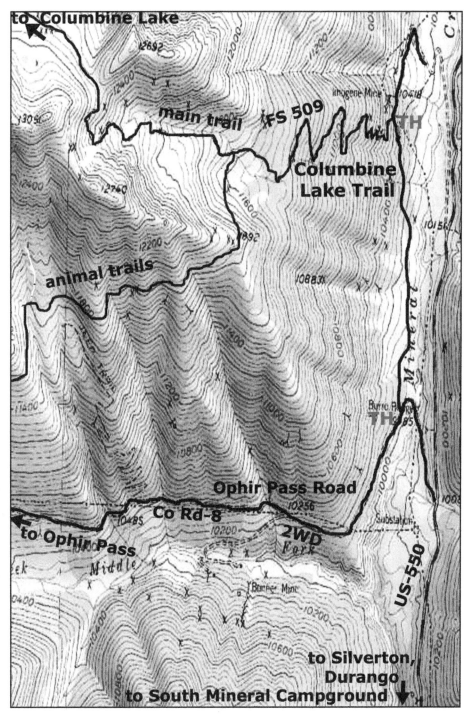

HIKES 78, 80

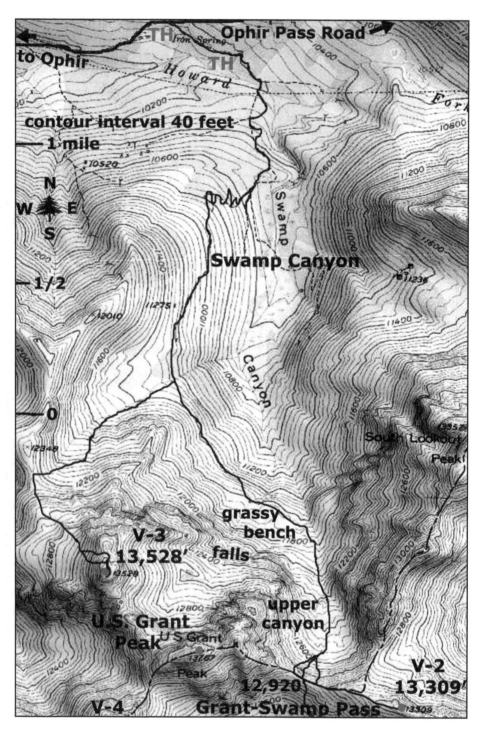

Ophir Pass Road

to Ophir

Iron Spring TH
TH

Howard

contour interval 40 feet

1 mile

N
W E
S

1/2

Swamp

Swamp Canyon

Canyon

Fork

South Lookout Peak

0

grassy
bench

V-3
13,528'   falls

upper
canyon

U.S. Grant
Peak   U S Grant

Peak

V-2
13,309'

V-4   12,920'
Grant-Swamp Pass

HIKES 81-83

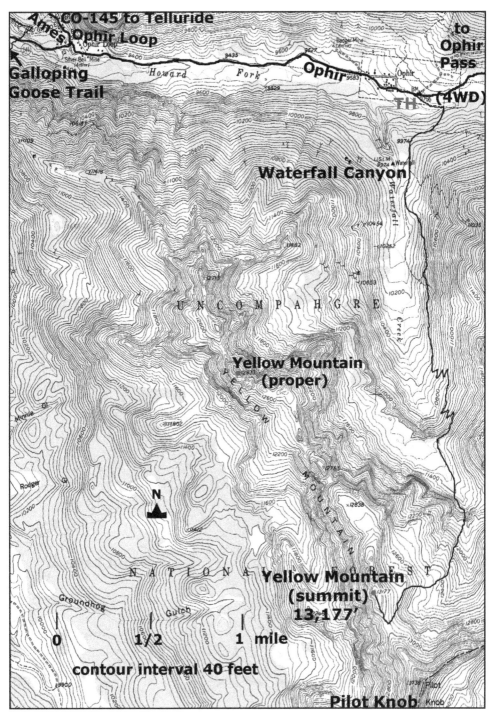

CO-145 to Telluride
Ophir Loop
Ames
Galloping
Goose Trail

Howard   Fork   Ophir

to
Ophir
Pass

TH (4WD)

Waterfall Canyon

UNCOMPAHGRE

Yellow Mountain
(proper)

Minnie Gl.

Rodger

N

NATIONA Yellow Mountain
(summit)
13,177'

Groundhog   Gulch

0   1/2   1 mile

contour interval 40 feet

Pilot Knob

HIKES 77, 84, 86

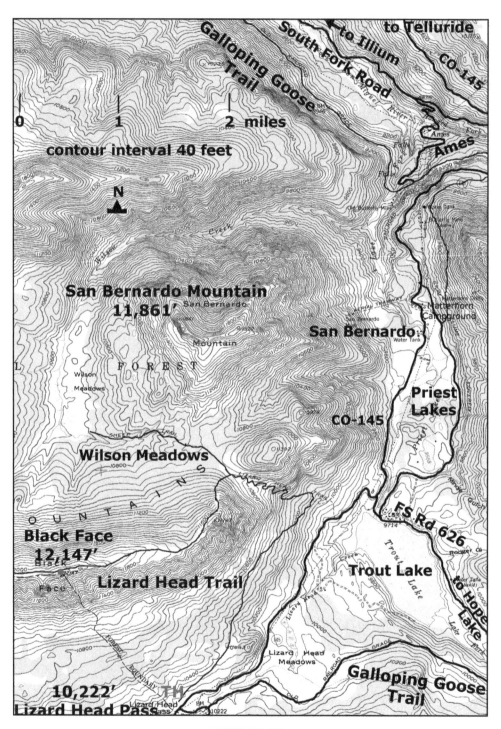

0   1   2 miles

contour interval 40 feet

N

Galloping Goose Trail

South Fork Road

to Tellurid

to Illium

CO-145

Ames

San Bernardo Mountain
11,861'

FOREST

San Bernardo

Priest Lakes

Wilson Meadows

CO-145

Matterhorn Campground

Water Tank

Black Face
12,147'

Lizard Head Trail

Trout Lake

FS Rd 626

to Hope Lake

10,222'
Lizard Head Pass

TH

Lizard Head Meadows

Galloping Goose Trail

HIKES 77, 101

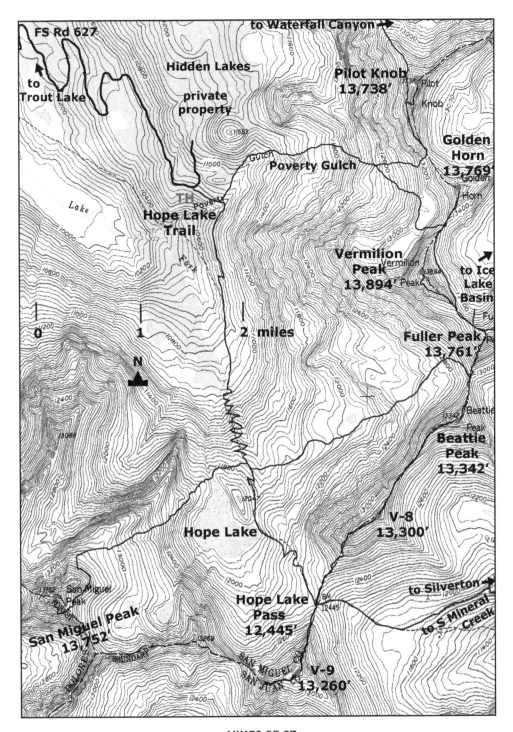

FS Rd 627

to Trout Lake

Hidden Lakes

private property

Poverty Gulch

to Waterfall Canyon →

Pilot Knob 13,738'

Golden Horn 13,769'

Lake

TH
Hope Lake Trail

Vermilion Peak 13,894'

to Ice Lake Basin

0   1   2 miles

N

Fuller Peak 13,761'

Beattie Peak 13,342'

V-8 13,300'

Hope Lake

San Miguel Peak 13,752

Hope Lake Pass 12,445'

to Silverton →

to S Mineral Creek

V-9 13,260'

HIKES 85-93

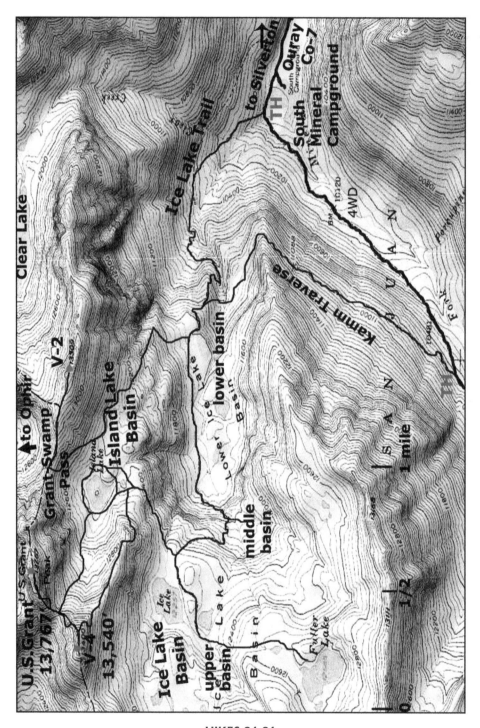

HIKES 94-96

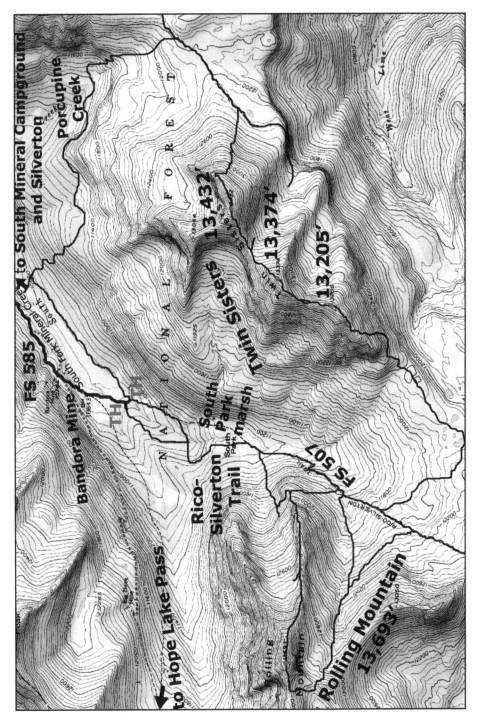

HIKES 97, 98

Elevation: 10,222 feet, with 2150 feet vertical gain from Illium (low point) to Lizard Head Pass

Distance: 21 miles one way biking from Telluride, 15 miles on CO-145 one way

Duration: 4 hours up biking, 1½ hours back to Telluride on the highway

Difficulty: Very challenging. Steady up to the top of the pass, very long, never too steep

TRAILHEAD

Begin at one of three spots, the first two being the Bike Path in Telluride and the official TH at Society Turn (3 miles W of Telluride on CO-145 Spur and ¼ mile onto Society Drive past the gas station on the right). The third, shorter, more popular option is to drive 5 miles W of town on CO-145 and less than 3 miles left (S) up South Fork Road (63L) through Illium. Turn right (W) at Camp Illium and across the river S up Sunshine Mesa Road FS 623 for 3 miles along the valley to the single track and parking on a switchback. This option saves 8½ miles from the Bike Path TH one way.

Good defense with spooky, catlike eyes!

NOTES

This route is for mountain biking only, not hiking. I have included it for its importance as a sort of rite of passage for local bikers.

ROUTE

This is a great bike ride all summer after the snow has melted up to Lizard Head Pass. Ride the Bike Path from downtown Telluride more than 3 miles W to Society Turn, and cross the road at Lawson Hill. Stay on Society Drive more than ¼ mile, turn right on San Miguel River Drive, and immediately look for the dirt cul-de-sac on the right (N). Galloping Goose Trail lies at the end of it. You will see Galloping Goose signs all the way to Trout Lake. Ride the steeps from the parking area W next to the river ½ mile WSW, crossing the little bridge, and continue 1 mile S along an old railroad grade into Illium. The trail is narrow for a time, with a steep drop-off, so be careful and mindful of others. When the trail meets South Fork Road in Illium, go right (N) on it ½ mile, and cross left (W) over the bridge at Camp Illium. Follow Sunshine Mesa Road FS 623 through the valley S 3 miles, and go straight (SE) 2 miles when the road starts up steeper switchbacks to the right (W).

Bike more steeply NE above Ames (12 miles from Bike Path TH, 3 miles from the Illium TH) to cross the highway in the tunnel going S. Continue up very briefly before the route gets really steep (S) going down to meet a dirt and gravel road (Old Butterfly Road) on a switchback. Descend Old Butterfly Road to meet the single track on the left (S), a few feet before the highway. Take it above CO-145 a mile more steeply above San Bernardo before coming down to the road that goes to Priest Lakes. This road is just above the Matterhorn camping area to the E (15 miles from the Bike Path TH). Take FS 628 road to the left (S) by Priest Lakes to enjoy a leisurely ride 6 miles more to Lizard Head Pass.

Turn left (E, then SE) on FS 626 along Trout Lake 2 miles. The road curves to the right (NW) and becomes FS 627, as you cross Lake Fork Creek and bike through thinning evergreens more than 2 miles in the direction of Black Face Mountain and to nearby Lizard Head Pass. Return the same way, or take the highway more quickly and using much caution. Many mountain bikers also do an opposite **Loop**, going S up CO-145 to Lizard Head Pass first, then down Galloping Goose Trail.

TRAIL NOTES

78   Ophir Pass to Crystal Lake

Elevation: 11,789 feet; 12,055 feet; with 266 feet vertical gain

Distance: ¼ mile up, ½ mile round-trip

Duration: 15–20 minutes up, 45 minutes round-trip

Difficulty: Moderate. Steep, rocky, extra short

TRAILHEAD

Ophir Pass. From Telluride, drive 3 miles W of town on CO-145 Spur, left (S) on CO-145 7 miles, and left (E) on FS 630 at Ophir Loop. Continue slowly 2 miles E through Ophir, and head up the left (N) side of the valley more steeply to tree line. The 4WD road gets narrow, rocky, and steep for a long straightaway (with one switchback near the top) 2 miles more to Ophir Pass (1 hour from Telluride). You'll hope that drivers coming down remember that uphill traffic has the right-of-way in Colorado, but use common sense to avoid head-to-head confrontations on the slender road. From the top of Ophir Pass, the going is much easier and wider 4 miles E in 2WD down to US-550. From Silverton, drive 5 miles N on US-550, then left (W) on Co Rd-8, staying on the main dirt road 4 miles up to Ophir Pass. Drive 53 miles from Durango on US-550 N, then 4 miles up Co Rd-8 in 2WD to the top of Ophir Pass (1½ hours).

NOTES

If you are hiking to the beautiful, blue Crystal Lake, look for the TH from the apex of Ophir Pass (no sign or restroom). Avoid looking for the lake in June; the pass is the first to open in the region, and 10- to 20-foot vertical walls of snow line the road while the lake is still covered and frozen. Try late July through October for the best driving and hiking in the area.

ROUTE

Look S up in the scree for the trail, which is slightly elusive, and a few feet right (W) of the center of the pass. It zigzags S steeply a hundred yards up the rocks, then more easily down and over to the nearby lake, where you should definitely hang out and let the dog take a dip in the chilly water. The scenery is stupendous!

79   Lookout Peak

Elevation: 13,661 feet, with 1872 feet vertical gain

Distance: 1 mile up, 2 miles round-trip

Duration: 1½–2 hours up, 3 hours round-trip

Difficulty: Very challenging. Super-steep but brief scrambling, loose rock

TRAILHEAD

See hike 78 for directions. Official TH is ²⁄₁₀ mile E of Ophir Pass (a few parking spots along a pullout next to the trail, no sign). However, down around the corner as the road continues to the right (SE), you'll see a steep driveway and parking lot on the left (N); this is an **Alt** TH, almost ½ mile E of Ophir Pass.

ROUTE

This **Alt** beginning to the official TH is less steep with a traverse, but includes bushwhacking on whatever animal trails are present. The main route is described below. From the unmarked parking lot E of Ophir Pass, go right (NE) 100 feet up the solid trail in the clearing to start, but get off the trail before it goes into the trees and switchback to the left (NW), as you stay on thin animal trails for the moment. Climb up about 200 feet and cross a scree field left (WNW) on the most prominent path. You are above the power lines and well E of the bump and a small lake that are N of Ophir Pass. Traverse and bushwhack upward 300 feet to the NW to the big, rocky basin (12,500 feet) SE of the summit. Cross the picturesque rocky area more easily, and go directly W to a low spot on the S ridge of Lookout Peak.

The main route from the pullout is hidden on the N side of the road to start, but becomes obvious after you walk through the brief wall of thick shrubs. Hike ¼ mile up the right (E) side of a steep drainage under power lines. Stay on the trail up the loose rock and grassier areas just to the right (E) of the small lake and bump N of the pass. Scramble steeply ¼ mile up a long rock rib more on the left (W) to the big, rocky basin.

Follow the grassy slope to the left (W) directly up to a lower section on the high ridge. Scramble 200 feet up the steep hillside and stay to the left (WSW), perhaps near the rocky areas for better footing. Once you are on the high ridge, continue N up the trail, which goes 10 feet to the right (E) of the ridge crest to start. Follow cairns 100 feet up steep-sloping, large rocks and boulders near and back to the ridge. Soon, another path will take you slightly to the right (E)

Ophir valley to the Wilsons from Lookout Peak.

again and 20 feet below the ridgeline for an easier, short stint but with some looser rock. Pass E-facing, red couloirs on your right (E), and make your way about 200 feet along the ridge to the super-steeps and an apparent obstruction at the summit block. From the very base, hike the thin trail to the right (NE) of the large rock outcrop, and go a few feet just to the right (E) of the actual ridge. Then turn left (N) 40 feet up a short, steep, rock- and dirt-filled gully to a short cliff band. The **Opt** to ascending the gully itself is to climb just left (W) from the bottom of the gully and find your way 40 feet up through the steep and larger boulders. Some cairns help, and it's easier and more fun than it looks from the bottom. This climb lasts only a few minutes, after which you contour to the right (E) on the trail 25 feet across the top of the gully under a short cliff. From there, look far down the S ridge and see the steep, grassy slopes and return route to the basin. See cairns up the next steep part. Climb some tough, larger ledges and rock shelves N for 30–40 feet, as you lift yourself up higher with every step over fairly solid rock.

Above the crux area, the hiking is a bit easier up smaller scree 75 feet to a narrow shoulder on the right (NE). Once you are on it, follow the shoulder, with some looser rock, 100 feet up to the left (N) to the very nearby summit. Columbine Lake is about 1000 feet down to the E and looks too blue to be real. The vista leaves you speechless and breathless—but mostly breathless.

Elevation: 12,685 feet, with 2485 feet vertical gain

Distance: 4 miles up, 8 miles round-trip

Duration: 2½ hours up, 5–6 hours round-trip

Difficulty: Strenuous. Some steep areas, trail-finding

TRAILHEAD

Bottom of Ophir Pass Road FS 630 8 miles NW of Silverton off of US-550 and N on US-550 from Durango 51 miles. From Telluride, take CO-145 W 16 miles, turn right onto CO-62 23 miles, and right onto US-550 S in Ridgway for 30 miles to Ophir Pass Road FS 630. (It is shorter to take Ophir Pass from Telluride, but this includes a mile or so of tougher 4WD terrain; see hike 78 for the 19-mile route.) Park just W of the bridge (near US-550) at the bottom of Ophir Pass Road FS 630 where it meets the slightly rougher 4WD road FS 820 going N, or drive it 1 mile to the official TH. Traverse the hillside above and W of US-550 to the semi-secret trail on the left (W) at 10,200 feet. There is room for a few vehicles along the road.

ROUTE

Hike more than a dozen steep switchbacks steadily W through the only trees 1½ miles up a solid path to begin. Continue ½ mile up the steep, grassy, small

basin E of the vast E-facing canyon belonging to Columbine Lake. The obvious steep above tree line goes W over a little saddle and into the huge canyon. T-11 is across the canyon and to the right (NE) of Lewis Lake Pass, with T-12 to the left (SW), and Lookout Peak is just to the W of and closest to Columbine Lake. Finish the last mile left (W, then SW) more easily on a traverse trail as it fades through some scree on the S side of the canyon down to the bright lake. Enjoy the 360-degree view before heading down.

Columbine Lake and
Lookout Peak.

81   Swamp Canyon to Grant-Swamp Pass

Elevation: 11,640 feet; 12,920 feet; with vertical gains of 1460 feet for the large, grassy bench under US Grant, 2740 feet for Grant-Swamp Pass

Distance: 2 miles up, 4 miles round-trip; 3 miles up, 6 miles round-trip

Duration: 2 hours up, 3 hours round-trip; 3 hours up, 4½–5 hours round-trip

Difficulty: Strenuous. Steep to very steep, scree, scramble to Grant-Swamp Pass

TRAILHEAD

From Telluride, drive left (S) at Society Turn on CO-145 7 miles and go left (E) on FS 630 at Ophir Loop. Continue slowly E through Ophir and head up the left (N) side of the valley more steeply. Thirteen miles and 25 minutes from Telluride, you leave the Ophir Pass 4WD road FS 630 and turn right at the second prominent dirt road past the first creek crossing over the road. Turn right (S) ⁷⁄₁₀ mile from the Ophir Pass sign in Ophir. Hundreds of aspens that were uprooted in this area by avalanches mark the TH in a semi-clearing next to the main road. Park and walk (best choice) or 4WD ²⁄₁₀ mile over the deeply rutted road to a big, green gate, where there are two parking spots at best.

ROUTE

Walk 200 feet past the gate blocking the road to a clearing, where you leave the road and walk S immediately past another green gate to go over Howard Fork Creek across a dilapidated double log bridge. Walk under the power lines to the obvious trail and dirt road, then go S up the wide old road, more steeply at times, for three switchbacks until it flattens out a bit (¼ mile from the creek). In about a hundred yards, you leave the road near the bottom of the canyon. Hike to the right (W) onto the trail, sometimes marked with cairns.

The path quickly becomes more distinct. Hike ½ mile steeply W up four switchbacks, the last two of which have some distance between them. Then go fairly steeply W up a small series of tight S-turns. The single track begins to contour high above the lower canyon and swamps, as you traverse more easily more than ½ mile across a steep, wildflower-covered, then skunk cabbage–covered, hillside. You can see V-3 and US Grant Peak up the canyon. Cross the creek coming from the NE-facing basin to the SW (V-3 route), and go left (S) to the

US Grant and V-3 from the Swamp Canyon Trail.

scree-covered slope. Follow the rocky trail and continue the traverse ½ mile to the SE over and up to a big, grassy bench overlooking the beautiful canyon. Hang out in this charming, large meadow where at least three cascading falls come down from US Grant's N slopes, and return the same way, or hike with more effort up to the high basin and Grant-Swamp Pass at nearly 13,000 feet.

To continue up, see the thinning scree trail to the left (E) of the flats on the bench just before the grass ends. There are many cairns on the very steep, pretty solid, but rocky path. Hike (S) to the high canyon slowly, as the route will be very steep for ½ mile. The path takes you up a semi-grassy rise with better walking to the super-steeps under Grant-Swamp Pass. Watch for constant rockslides, natural or not, and glissade down part of this sweet basin (above Swamp Canyon) in the early summer when snow is still present. The grass ends and you finally must scramble ¼ mile up the thin trail very steeply and loosely. Watch for cairns, and go left (S) up the path, which is left (E) of most of the rock ribs extending from Grant-Swamp Pass. Hug the left (E) side of a small rib nearest the saddle, and head directly to the pass. Or as another **Opt**, scale one of the rock ribs for some interesting, steeper climbing over slightly more solid rock than the paths. From the saddle and ridge, the view of Island Lake, Ice Lake Basin, and the Vermilion family is utterly incomparable. You are in the postcard!

82	V-2

Elevation: 13,309 feet, with 3129 feet vertical gain

Distance: 3½ miles up, 7 miles round-trip

Duration: 3½ hours up, 6 hours round-trip

Difficulty: Strenuous. Ultra-steep, scrambling, not long

TRAILHEAD

See hikes 81 and 94 for directions.

ROUTE

See hike 81, or hike 94 if you are starting closer to Silverton or Durango. From the saddle at 12,920 feet, go to the left (SE) ½ mile to the nearby summit over semi-solid to semi-loose rock. Immediately hike to the right (S), or climb straight over (more difficult) the steep bump on the ridgeline from the pass. Walk the wider, flatter ridge section a hundred yards. Then follow the trail to the right (S) of the ridge proper a few feet to continue fairly easily, though a little more steeply, up the summit block to the peak. From the peak you can see at least seven high alpine lakes and ponds, including the very large Clear Lake directly NE.

83	V-3

Elevation: 13,528 feet, with 3348 feet vertical gain

Distance: 3 miles up, 6 miles round-trip

Duration: 3 hours up, 5 hours round-trip

Difficulty: Very challenging. Loose scree, super-steep scrambling, brief exposure

TRAILHEAD

See hikes 81 for directions.

ROUTE

See hike 81. V-3 looks rugged, stunning, and steep when viewed from any angle or summit in this tremendous area in Southwest Colorado. At around an hour (1½ miles) from the TH, you arrive at a creek near tree line after a long traverse, where the trail to Grant-Swamp Pass continues to the left (SE) over the creek to the scree field. Cross the little stream, but leave the main trail and go to the

Tiny turquoise lake under V-3 toward Swamp Canyon.

right. Bushwhack SW ½ mile up the big, NE-facing, grassy basin, as you follow the creek up on its left (S) side next to the scree that comes down from the left (S). You are above tree line and should be able to see the path ahead of you, which goes more steeply SW 200 feet up a small, grassy rise just to the right (W) of the super-steeps near the end of the widest part of the basin.

Stay in the center of the narrowing, rockier basin by following a long slide path a few hundred feet. The rocks are small and solid on the bushwhack, as you ascend the meadow and begin to head to the left (S). Leave the slide path when it begins to get pretty steep, and go from left to right (going WSW) on a slanted bench in that upper part of the basin through the grass and rock. Walk more than 300 feet to the end of the shelf more easily, and continue SW very steeply straight up the rocks and hillside for about 200 feet to a low point in the wide saddle below the final ridge hike. It's 2½ hours and 2½ miles to this wide saddle from the TH, and it would be a great hike in its own right even if you went no farther.

Go left (SE) at the wide saddle ½ mile up V-3's steep, wide slope to the high ridge just N of the summit. Walk S to the end of the grass from the saddle, where it turns into loose talus and rocks with some cairns to help. You hike more than 100 feet up SSE by starting on a zigzag, left (N), then right (S) directly under larger boulders through the steeper scree. Walk briefly up the last small, semi-flat section through grass and between large boulders to the base of the super-steeps. See the wide gully to the high ridge straight up the slope and slightly left (N). Climb very steeply to the right (S) of the gully 50 feet to a nearby weakness,

Top: Close to the top of V-3 getting oh so dramatic! Bottom: Wide, scree-covered slope below the high ridge of V-3.

which is a steep and rock-filled, narrow couloir.

The wide gully route is actually much more difficult than the couloir, but here is the **Alt** route for that. The wide gully is ultra-steep and loose 150 feet up by any ascent. When you reach the small saddle of this difficult **Alt** route, you see that enormous boulders block the ridge. Go directly to the base of the biggest rock from thin ledges

Summit register from V-3.

near the saddle, and make your way to the left (E) off the ridgeline a few feet around the obstacles. Carefully traverse S about 100 feet past two consecutive, short couloirs E of the ridge, and climb the steep dirt and rocks W back to the ridge; or climb the super-steep rock wherever possible to the nearby high ridge, where it's a bit airy the last 100 feet S to the peak.

For the main route, carefully climb up to the positively steep, W-facing, narrow couloir, with very loose rock all around. Be mindful of others, giving a shout when rocks tumble, and keep in mind that you can scree-ski down this whole section from the bottom of the couloir later. Hike the couloir itself around 100 feet up, or climb the steep rock ledges just to the right (S), as you make your way to the high ridge crest.

Get a look around for the return route once you are on the ridge, and head right (S) to the top. Walk to the left (E) of the summit more easily but across a ledge, then back to the right (W, then N) for 30 feet. Hurray! See Waterfall Canyon to the W; Pilot Knob, Vermilion Peak, Golden Horn (camouflaged in front of Vermilion Peak), Fuller Peak, and Beattie Peak to the SW; and V-4 and US Grant to the S and SE. Return by either route, but the W-facing couloir before the bouldering will be the safest with the least exposure.

Elevation: 13,177 feet, with vertical gains of 1100 feet for the center of the canyon, 3517 feet for the summit

Distance: 3 miles up, 6 miles round-trip; 4 miles up, 8 miles round-trip

Duration: 2–3 hours up, 4 hours round-trip; 4 hours up, 6½ hours round-trip

Difficulty: Mix of strenuous (to steep areas near the middle falls) and very challenging (to the peak, scree, narrow path, scrambling, very steep, route-finding)

TRAILHEAD

From Telluride, drive left (S) at Society Turn on CO-145 7 miles and go left (E) on FS 630 at Ophir Loop a mile to the tiny but hard-core hamlet of Ophir, nestled between huge avalanche-prone mountains high in the San Juans. Pass the first set of historic homes to the nearby TH and road off to the right (S), and park to the side. A Ute memorial tablet is a trail marker.

ROUTE

Walk the side road down 200 feet SE, and cross Howard Fork Creek over the long wooden bridge (or downriver if the water is too high) and go up the road SW toward Waterfall Creek and Canyon. The road goes down in a couple hundred feet, up again, and then forks. The lower falls are 150 feet on the right (W) fork at 9974 feet. Head left (S) at the fork immediately up past the mining scraps and signage as the road narrows and turns into a small trail. Stay left (E) of the main creek the whole way up and right (E) of the creek if you are coming down. The route gets rockier, steeper, and skinnier, with lots of midsize to tall bushes almost 2 miles from the TH. At the end of the big lower canyon, huge cascading waterfalls flow W of the trail. You must ascend switchbacks almost a mile very steeply far left (E) of the falls to get above them before entering the next big basin.

As you pass large boulders to the S, you see the next pretty impressive cascading falls in the main creek. During wildflower season, you also end up bushwhacking ½ mile through an immense field of Rocky Mountain columbine, more commonly known as Colorado columbine, and other wildflowers to get to the trail up to the left (E) of the cliffs. Most people hang out in this area and return down to the TH, but by all means keep going higher. Several peaks are in sight, including, from left to right (E to SW), V-3, US Grant, V-4, and Pilot

Much water flows through Waterfall Canyon, not surprisingly!

Knob. As you proceed up the thin path, you see it continues SW on the other side (W) of the snowfield 75 feet (if it is still there) to above. Hike W up the second to the last pitch before the high saddle by going 200 feet up the rocks right (W) of the creek or farther right up the grassy shelves on a path. The trail changes from a brief, easygoing pitch in the highest basin to the grassy high drainage, which is much steeper ½ mile W up to the saddle between Pilot Knob and Yellow Mountain, with no solid trail to finish.

To the left (S) on the high ridge is the notorious Pilot Knob. This is the easiest route to that peak, which happens to be one of the most difficult hikes in this guide and not a big surprise if you're looking at it from the high ridge. Take a bazillion-times-easier walk to the right (N) 150 feet up to the highest of Yellow Mountain's pinnacles, this one being large and rounded on top. Go directly over the little bump to the summit. Definitely return the same way, as all other ways cliff out.

85   Hope Lake Trail 410

Elevation: 11,900 feet; 12,445 feet, with vertical gains of 1150 feet, 1700 feet

Distance: 3½ miles to Hope Lake, 7 miles round-trip; 4¼ miles to Hope Lake Pass, 8½ miles round-trip

Duration: 1½ hours up, 2½–3 hours round-trip; 2 hours up, 3–4 hours round-trip

Difficulty: Strenuous. Solid horse trail, steadily steep, wide

TRAILHEAD

Drive 3 miles W of Telluride on CO-145 Spur, then S 10 miles on CO-145 to Trout Lake. Go left (SE) 1½ miles on dirt road FS 626 past Trout Lake to FS 627 (2WD high-clearance), and take one of the immediate roads more steeply to the left (ESW) where a sign says "camping 7 days within 30 day period." The road goes up many turns 2½ miles to the TH and sign on a big switchback (no toilets). Easily drive CO-145 N from Rico, Dolores, Cortez (1½ hours), and Durango (2 hours, under 100 miles from US-160 W to CO-184 W to CO-145 N) to the Trout Lake Road (FS 626, 63A) on the right (SE), and follow FS 627 above for 15 minutes.

ROUTE

Walk SE up Hope Lake Trail 410 only ¼ mile to cross the creek at Poverty Gulch coming down from the ENE. Pilot Knob is up to the left (NE) at the very top of the gulch. Hike down two switchbacks on a 1-mile traverse S above the valley floor before coming down to cross multiple shallow creeks quite easily. Instead of crossing a slightly bigger creek (W) that splits above the trail, turn left (S) to hike more steeply up many switchbacks (about thirty-four actual turns, with many back to back for 1½ miles) to near tree line. Stay on the dirt and rockier trail going up or down without shortcutting. When you are above most of the trees and shrubs, it's just two more switchbacks and the last straightaway S ½ mile to Hope Lake (also called Lake Hope, a natural lake as opposed to man-made Trout Lake). Outstanding, indeed!

If you are motivated, walk left (E) of the lake by the sign that says "Hope Lake Trail–South Mineral Creek" as you dawdle up the solid, rocky horse path SE more than ½ mile to Hope Lake Pass at 12,445 feet in about 30 minutes from the lake.

86   Pilot Knob

Elevation: 13,738 feet, with vertical gains of 2988 feet from Hope Lake TH, 4078 feet from Waterfall Canyon TH

Distance: 2½ miles up, 5 miles round-trip; 4½ miles up, 9 miles round-trip; 7 miles round-trip **Loop** from Hope Lake TH to Waterfall Canyon TH in Ophir (arrange for a shuttle vehicle as THs are 6-plus miles apart)

Duration: 4-plus hours up, 6–8 hours round-trip for either route, **Loop** or not

Difficulty: Expert-only. Extremely steep, serious scrambling, punishing, sustained steeps from Poverty Gulch, high exposure, one or more Class 5 moves. Guide and climbing gear recommended but not mandatory except for a helmet

TRAILHEAD
See hike 84 or 85 for directions.

ROUTE

What's the shortest, steepest, hardest hike I can think of? Pilot Knob up Poverty Gulch. Walk SE up Hope Lake Trail 410 only ¼ mile to the creek at Poverty Gulch (coming down from ENE). Pilot Knob is up to the left (NE) at the very top of the gulch. The summit trail leaves the main trail and is 20 feet left (N) up from the Poverty Gulch water crossing. Follow it ½ mile up NE above the last of all plant and tree life, entering a world of rock and scree. Pilot Knob is directly above in front of you (ENE), and Golden Horn is to the right (ESE), with Vermilion Peak (SE) never too far out of sight. Hike more steeply ½ mile E up the rises and shoulders through semi-loose scree. You are now to the left (N) below the first shelf under Pilot Knob. Climb the fairly steep, grassy slope on its left (N) side ¼ mile, and as you probably guessed, there is no trail. From on top of this little shelf at about 12,400 feet, aim toward the red rocks slightly to the left (E) in the gulch and scramble the ultra-steep slope 1000 feet up in ½ mile, but to the right (S) of the bright red scree 30–40 feet on a right to left traverse NE up to the saddle between Golden Horn and Pilot Knob. Nearest the saddle, continue the slog NE to a small rock outcropping on the ridge. It takes about 2½ hours and less than 2 miles to reach the ridge from the TH.

Boulder N 100 feet to a position directly under the southernmost of Pilot Knob's huge chimneys that comprise the summit block. Go left (W) to contour ½ mile under Pilot Knob's W face, staying as high as possible on a super-thin trail. The first cairn is only a marker. The second cairn is much farther N and is the entrance to head E up the summit block. This traverse is surrounded by super-steep drop-offs, and the rock is semi-loose; watch your step and hand-holds, as you literally hug the cliff band that is part of the immense hoodoos that make up Pilot Knob.

At the second cairn, which is actually much closer to the Yellow Mountain side, the entrance to the high ridge on top of the summit block is gained from the "ramp" and by going nearly straight up 100 feet for the most precipitous part of the climb. The N peak is the highest point of the chimneys on Pilot Knob and is a very long ¼ mile away. Climb the rocky ramp E 10–15 feet, and immediately look to the left (N) and up for a small cairn. That route leads up a short, narrow chute you can take, or go just to the left (N) of the chute up broken rocks. Or forget the small cairn to the left from the ramp and climb straight up a steeper, wider gully that is directly in front of you (E). The least desirable route is the climb to the right (S) of the main gully and ramp up another short, super-steep chute. All choices from the ramp meet near the top and catch the exposed high ridge that is just wide enough to walk on.

Bouldering cautiously up to the left (N) on the exposed ridge to the summit brings you to the big "mushroom" rock and major crux of the day 75 feet S of the peak. That climbing rope could come in handy if you haven't used it yet, as protection is usually placed here. Work your way to the left (W) of the mushroom around the rock by going slowly down the steep-sloping, slickrock 25–30 feet, getting a bird's-eye view of exactly what you must deal with. You will have, at most, a couple of footholds at the base of the big rock on its W side. There is not much to hang on to, either, and snow or wet, icy rock could be a factor. Once you are around the big obstacle, the last little steep part N 60 feet to the peak is a walk up.

Hike down the same route with care, or try this **Loop**. After coming down from the peak, around the exposed mushroom rock and big boulder on the ridge, and (W) down from the ramp to the big cairn below the summit block, continue 150 feet along Pilot Knob's NNW ridge by staying as high as you can on the traverse N, hugging the knob toward Yellow Mountain. It's a much easier ¼ mile down the widening, scree-covered ridge NW to the saddle, where there is no other way down than by Waterfall Canyon to the right (E). See hike 84 for the descent.

87   Golden Horn

Elevation: 13,769 feet, with 3020 feet vertical gain

Distance: 2¼ miles up Poverty Gulch from Hope Lake TH, 4½ miles round-trip; 5½ miles up the large basin W of Fuller Peak from Hope Lake TH, 11 miles round-trip

Duration: 3 hours up, 5 hours round-trip; 5–6 hours up, 8–9 hours round-trip

Difficulty: Very challenging. Ultra-steep and loose, scrambling, extra peaks possible

TRAILHEAD

See hike 85 for directions.

NOTES

This jagged peak can be reached more easily from Fuller Peak by going around the E side of Vermilion Peak across a large shelf for ½ mile; see hike 89. Also see hike 86 for the much more demanding route directly up Poverty Gulch. And the routes could be connected for a difficult **Loop**.

ROUTE

From Poverty Gulch above the first little shelf at 12,400 feet, go right (SE) before you get too close to the red rocks high in the gulch (N). So you like loose scree? Head SE a few hundred feet to a whiter, super-steep section of rock, and hike 200 feet up it, perhaps on the left (N) side for better footing. Climb 50 feet more SE up to the nearby second shelf, and cross it 200 feet to the right (S) to catch the trail, which goes from right to left (E) up the steeper hillside 150 feet to the saddle between Golden Horn and Vermilion Peak.

Go left (NE) at the high saddle less than ¼ mile over a semi-loose, scree-filled trail up Golden Horn. Hike more steeply up broken rocks to the summit with the assistance of cairns. The left (W) and nearest high point is the summit.

From Fuller Peak, stay on the ridge a few hundred feet NW to the low point of the saddle with Vermilion Peak, and ignore the trail to the right (E) below the escarpment (to Fuller and Ice Lakes) near the ridge crest. For Golden Horn, go N off the high ridge and traverse down 30–40 feet to catch the shelf E of Vermilion Peak (under 13,500 feet) on a thin, steep path if any. Easily walk N to the end of the wide shelf and up to the saddle between Vermilion Peak and Golden Horn. Climb without any trouble less than ¼ mile NE steeply up larger rocks and scree to the slender summit.

Elevation: 13,894 feet, with 3144 feet vertical gain

Distance: 5 miles up, 10 miles round-trip

Duration: 4 hours up, 6 hours round-trip

Difficulty: Very challenging. Definitely steep, route-finding, scree, far
from tree line

TRAILHEAD

See hike 85 for directions.

ROUTE

See hike 89 for the description. From the Fuller Peak–Vermilion Peak saddle and
high ridge, Fuller Peak is so close by this route, you might as well walk
50 feet or so E easily to snatch another high thirteener! From Fuller Peak, descend
NW to continue to Vermilion Peak directly over the ridge rocks or slightly right
(E) to the saddle. Stay on the ridge and well-traveled path ¼ mile up, hiking by
obstacles to the left (S) where it's generally semi-loose and steep, with few cairns.
Climb NE 75 feet the last part of the wide couloir, which narrows at the top, and
turn left (NW) to go steeply up to the slender peak. Excellent! If you are standing
on Vermilion Peak, you are at the highest point in San Juan County.

Vermilion Peak on the way up to Fuller Peak.

89   Fuller Peak

Elevation: 13,761 feet, with 3011 feet vertical gain

Distance: 4½ miles up, 9 miles round-trip

Duration: 3½ hours up, 6 hours round-trip

Difficulty: Very challenging. Steep, loose talus, route-discovering

TRAILHEAD

See hike 85 for directions.

ROUTE

See hike 85. Leave the trail above most of the trees at about 11,700 feet 3 miles from the TH and just before the last two switchbacks before you reach Hope Lake. Leave the trail and head left (E) across the creek immediately. Bushwhack ¼ mile up the grass to where it meets the scree on the right (S) side of the big, treeless basin NE of Hope Lake. Continue ¼ mile NE up the easier grassy section to the left (N) of the scree. Walk around the marsh to the right (S), and go NE to the greenish, super-steep rock band 200 feet in front of you. Climb straight over the 40-foot-high rock band, maybe on the left (N) side of the doable section that is more to the right (S) in the basin, and look for cairns from there up to the saddle. When you are on top of the rock band, cross a little grass and catch the trail in the steep, loose scree up to the highest little rise. Stay on it ¼ mile NE to the end of the basin. Then scramble straight up (E, then SE), grabbing one of the trails for a few hundred feet going left to right to the saddle between Fuller and Beattie Peaks over steep scree.

Climb left (N) from the high saddle up an ultra-steep, loose, scree-filled slope on a trail that disappears several times as you travel NE, ascending more than 700 feet in about ¼ mile. At the top, you arrive at the Vermilion Peak–Fuller Peak saddle. Simply go right (E) 50 feet to Fuller Peak by staying on the ridge or a few feet to the left (N).

- **Bonus 1:** It's 30 minutes max to Vermilion Peak.
- **Bonus 2:** Golden Horn is about a mile NNW and easily accessible.

90	Beattie Peak

Elevation: 13,342 feet, with 2595 feet vertical gain (plus 300 feet if you add V-8)

Distance: 4¼ miles up, 8½ miles round-trip; 9 miles clockwise **Loop** with V-8

Duration: 3 hours up, 5 hours round-trip; 6–7 hours round-trip clockwise **Loop** with V-8

Difficulty: Very challenging. Much scree, steeper, **Loop** has airy ridge section

TRAILHEAD

See hike 85 for directions.

ROUTE

See hikes 85 and 89, and hike to the saddle between Fuller Peak and Beattie Peak in hike 89. Go right (SSW) on the high ridge up more stable scree on a faint trail opposite Fuller Peak, which is much steeper. Stay on or near the wide ridge ¼ mile to the nearby summit.

• **Bonus:** Hike the connecting ultra-thin ridge more than ½ mile SW to V-8 to complete a semi-difficult **Loop**. You cannot be afraid of heights or lack confidence to walk this somewhat exposed section. With wind it can even be scary. Be focused. Stay in the center of the skinny ridge from Beattie Peak over loose rocks going SW. It's possible to go straight over the farthest notch, which is around 200 feet E of V-8. Or you could go around on the Trout Lake side (N) more easily and get right back to the super-narrow ridge, following it up much more steeply, with looser rocks to the peak.

To complete the clockwise **Loop**, go to the left (S) of a couple small boulders, as you come down the V-8 ridge ½ mile SW to Hope Lake Pass. When it starts to get steeper and splits in 200 feet or so, hike the shoulder down to the left (SW) to the pass and saddle between V-8 and V-9. Close to the bottom of the ridge, pick up the trail near larger rocks on the left (S) and scramble directly down to Hope Lake Pass. The trail is on the other side of the saddle next to a big cairn. Follow the horse path down more easily to the right (N) more than ½ mile to Hope Lake. It's only an hour down from there.

Elevation: 13,300 feet, with 2550 feet vertical gain
Distance: Almost 5 miles up, 10 miles round-trip
Duration: 3 hours up, 4½–5 hours round-trip
Difficulty: Very challenging. Pretty steep, loose, faint path

TRAILHEAD

See hike 85 for directions.

ROUTE

See hike 85 to Hope Lake Pass, and walk to the left (N) to the base of the shoulder. Slightly to the right (S) at the bottom of a little gully is a rock wall someone has built. Scramble straight up very steeply ¼ mile over pretty loose scree on the disappearing trail up the SW shoulder. A cairn might be there at about 13,000 feet, where you head to the right (NE) 200 feet on V-8's lovely high ridge. Go a few feet to the right (S) of the only two little rock obstacles on the high ridge to attain the peak of V-8 (also known as Point 13,300).

V-8 and Beattie Peak under Vermilion Peak from V-9.

Elevation: 13,260 feet, with 2510 feet vertical gain

Distance: 5 miles up, 10 miles round-trip

Duration: 3½ hours up, 6 hours round-trip

Difficulty: Very challenging. Some exposure near the peak and its twin peak to the W

Grizzly Peak from V-9.

TRAILHEAD

See hikes 85 and 94 for directions.

ROUTE

See hike 85 to Hope Lake Pass. It is 1 hour more (½ mile) to the summit from this saddle between V-8 and V-9, where the routes from South Mineral Creek and Silverton/Durango converge. See hike 94 for the route description.

Start by going to the right (SSW) of Hope Lake Pass, and hike 10 feet to the right (W) of a long rock rib coming down the ridge's left side. Go 400 feet up steeply in the rock and scree to the thinner ridge above the rib. Climb the semi-exposed ridge a few hundred feet, and hike to the right (W), left (E), right again, and left again of the obstacles, with a very short left to right in the middle. It sounds confusing but isn't too tough—just don't be in a hurry. On your very last left (E) off the ridge crest, you will pass a small cave just below the peak. See Rolling Mountain down the connecting ridge SE from the summit marker (cairn). Also see Twin Sisters to the E and the stunning Vermilion family to the NNE.

• **Bonus:** Carefully walk over to the W peak and back in 30 minutes (less than ½ mile) by hiking on or just left (S) of the narrow ridge. The terrain is semi-loose and rocky, with some really steep drop-offs, but this interesting jaunt is worth it.

93   San Miguel Peak

Elevation: 13,752 feet, with 3000 feet vertical gain
Distance: 4 miles up, 8 miles round-trip
Duration: 3 ½ hours up, 5½–6 hours round-trip
Difficulty: Very challenging. Route-locating, bouldering, steeper

TRAILHEAD
See hike 85 for directions.

ROUTE
See hike 85 and leave the trail above most of the trees at about 11,700 feet, 3 miles from the TH. Look for a thin trail to the right (W) off the main trail, or find it by bushwhacking about 100 yards above a steel silo lower in the scree. Traverse a hundred yards over to the uppermost N part of the lake, where it is dammed, and cross over the dam itself. Hike steeply on the left (SW) up to the grassy slope, with San Miguel Peak straight in front of you. To the right is San Miguel Peak's cliffed-out, super-steep, scree-filled NE ridge. Stay to the left (S) of it for almost a mile SW with no distinct trail, as you bushwhack up big, stable rocks steeply, and head for the peak's NE ridge at a big break in the cliffy area above small ponds SE that feed into Hope Lake. Locate a cairn near the base of the super-steep section of high ridge ¼ mile NE of the peak. This should direct you around the summit block to the left (SE) 150 feet. Find the trail up a steep segment. More cairns help keep you on a descending traverse for a few hundred feet while you cross the wide, SE-facing, rocky gully that goes up to a big notch. Once you are on the other side, climb steeply 100 feet up the huge boulders to the right (N) and the nearby summit. The peak is SW of the notch and low summit. You'll see a marker.

San Miguel Peak
above Lake Hope.

Elevation: 12,257 feet, with vertical gains of 2407 feet for Ice Lake,
1607 feet from an **Alt** TH 2 miles past South Mineral Campground

Distance: 3–4 miles up, 6–8 miles round-trip from all routes

Duration: 2½–3 hours up, 5–6 hours round-trip from all routes

Difficulty: Strenuous. Steep in places, long day above tree line,
popular trails

TRAILHEAD

South Mineral Campground (9850 feet) or almost 2 miles farther to a quiet (but 1 mile longer) **Alt** TH. Drive 43 miles N of Durango and 2 miles W of Silverton on US-550, and go left (W) on the dirt road Ouray Co-7 (FS 585) 4 miles. From Telluride, take CO-145 W 16 miles, turn right onto CO-62 23 miles, and right onto US-550 S in Ridgway for 33 miles to Ouray Co-7 (FS 585) on the right (W). (It is shorter to take Ophir Pass from Telluride, with tougher 4WD terrain; see hike 78 for the 19-mile route, where you go right [S] at the bottom of Ophir Pass Road FS 679 on US-550 S 2½ miles to Ouray Co-7 [FS 585] on the right [W].) Take Ouray Co-7 from US-550 near Silverton for about 4 miles W to South Mineral Campground. There is ample camping, wildlife, traffic, and parking along this lower valley. Most people start the hike from the main campground, parking, and restroom. From there, walk to the TH, which is just a few feet before the corner on the road where FS 585 crosses Clear Creek and turns SW to follow South Mineral Creek. One cheating **Opt** is to 4WD Co Road-12 NW ½ mile E of South Mineral Campground less than a mile up to the first switch-back toward Clear Lake, park on the corner, and take the obvious traverse path ¼ mile to meet the main trail.

NOTES

For those who wish to leave the crowds behind for more primitive camping and hiking (Twin Sisters, Rolling Mountain), FS Road 585 continues (4WD recommended) another 2½ miles until it ends. From South Mineral Campground, a small wooden sign on the corner of the road before Clear Creek says "Rico-Silverton Trail 2½ miles." A side road on the right (N) just past the Bandora Mine turns into a trail that contours gently SW and W almost 2 miles up to Hope Lake Pass (see hike 92). The **Alt** TH is about halfway up the high valley, 1½ miles SW up from South Mineral Campground, and begins on the right (N) side of the road, which is very bumpy but not especially steep, with only a

Great reflections from Ice Lakes.

couple parking spots at the rock fire pit, bushes, and trail switching back to the NE. This is also known as the Kamm Traverse, named for Ulrich Kamm, a long-distance runner who rediscovered the trail in 1993, putting it back on the map (though which map is anyone's guess, as this trail remains fairly unused).

ROUTE

For the Kamm Traverse (2 miles long), walk the trail to the NE above the high valley with a steady, easy grade and a fair amount of overgrowth near the thin path, as you contour the steep, grassy, wildflower-covered slope a mile. Behind you (S) lie the Twin Sisters, and above the trail and grassy hillside (N) are a couple of little cliff bands. Walk around the corner less than ¼ mile through the trees (NW), where everything is green and lush, and small streams try to take over the barely visible trail. Notice a black rock band above you and to the left (W). Hike down ¼ mile and continue the traverse down more steeply to a decent-sized creek crossing. Many fallen trees cross the creek bed, as well as a crude log bridge to hike over going N. Once you have crossed the water, go 30 feet up steeply N to get out of the creek bed, and walk to the left (NW) to stay on the path. Climb up the steepest part of the trail for 200 yards nearly straight up N through the woods. The saving grace here is the trail's tackiness. Soft yet firm dirt and wood chips make the short ascent quite bearable to the main trail and intersection, where you'll find a small cairn but no signs. Continue a couple hundred yards up through the semi-clearing and switchback below a rock band, and walk more easily into Lower Ice Lake Basin. A side path right is very steep as it fades and bypasses the beautiful Ice Lakes area to go 1½ miles directly and very steeply N, then NW to Island Lake and Grant-Swamp Pass.

For the main route next to South Mineral Campground, walk FS 585 about 100 feet W to the trail on the right (N) just before you reach the creek and corner. Ice Lake Trail 505 is steep because there are fewer switchbacks ½ mile through the evergreens to begin. Then follow switchbacks W and continue on a traverse through a big clearing with V-2 visible to the NW. There are more switchbacks up through the clearing, as you hike back into the woods and fairly steeply up to Lower Ice Lake Basin before it levels out for ½ mile, even going down a few feet. See the small, brown Lower Ice Lake to the left (S). It is at least 1½ hours (2 miles) from the official TH to the end (farthest W) of the huge lower basin, where water can be seen ripping down from several places in the cliff band surrounding the basin. Go W to the end of the lower basin on the right (N) side quite easily, crossing creeks. Hike ½ mile steeply SW, then W up the rock band to exit the basin, entering a very small midbasin. Continue to follow the trail ¼ mile to the right (N) on a brief traverse steadily to the upper basin. When you arrive at the mouth of the upper basin, where it opens up and flattens out, a trail appears to the right, going to the NE across the creek. That is the trail to the **Bonus**, Island Lake.

Walk more easily by wildflowers a couple hundred yards to Ice Lake, which is one among many lakes in this remarkably pristine area. The mountains, from left to right (NW to NE in a reflection of Ice Lake as well), are Fuller Peak, Vermilion Peak, Golden Horn, and Pilot Knob, with V-4 between Ice Lake and Island Lake Basins. They all set the scene for a perfect backdrop, as you noticeably stand in the very dramatic, special San Juan National Forest. Continue W up the trail to the left (S) of the fairly large Ice Lake, and walk to the right (N) of the nearby smaller second lake. See the path through the grass to the left of the little falls, and hike S up to Fuller Lake. It's about 25 minutes (more than ½ mile) to Fuller Lake from Ice Lake if you wish.

• **Bonus** to Island Lake: As you exit the upper basin by the creek just below (E of) Ice Lake, see the thin trail at the foot of V-4's SE ridge (directly in front of you, N) that goes to the left (N) ½ mile up to Island Lake at 12,400 feet. Be careful on the steep slope as you traverse around to the mouth of Island Lake Basin over a loose, narrow, rocky trail from the main creek crossing. The walking is more level in the basin itself, as you pass wildflowers and a small pond to Island Lake. Here you see how this lake got its name, but you may be more blown away by how exceptionally picturesque it is with its bright viridian color! From Island Lake, notice the super-steep path down from Grant-Swamp Pass to the N on the other side of the basin. To the W and deep in the high basin above Island Lake is the route to the saddle between US Grant Peak and V-4.

95	V-4

Elevation: 13,540 feet, with 3690 feet vertical gain

Distance: 4¼ miles up from either route (SE or NE ridges), 9 miles round-trip

Duration: 3–4 hours up from either route (SE or NE ridges), 5–6 hours round-trip

Difficulty: Very challenging. Super-steep, route-finding, bush-whacking, scree

TRAILHEAD

See hike 94 for directions.

ROUTE

See hike 94 and the **Bonus**. V-4 is a total bushwhack on both ridges (SE or NE) with no distinct trail. The NE ridge route from the saddle with US Grant Peak would be somewhat easier and is described below. For the SE ridge route, leave the trail before you can see Island Lake in Island Lake Basin (just W of the little pond), and climb W a few hundred feet up the steep, grassy slope to the base of the SE ridge of V-4. This part is not hard.

Climb W steeply directly over the first obstacle to the bottom of the more defined high ridge, where you can see all the lakes and mountaintops in the area. Hike the superb ridge for almost ½ mile to the WNW without any difficulty to the main crux and very steep section. Go hard to the left (W) on a traverse for about 200 feet total once you reach the base of the very steep section and couloirs on the ridge crest. The rock and scree are more stable than they look, as you cross a narrow gully 100 feet to the left (W) and then hug the bottom of rock ribs (on your right, N) for 100 feet more. Climb very steeply 10 feet or so to the right (N) after the ribs and rise 30 feet above the outcrop. Then make your way to the right (NE) 150 feet to the ridgeline for better walking. Follow it steeply a hundred feet, and boulder the last pitch without difficulty to the nearby peak. About 25 feet E of the summit, hike up a wide, 20-foot-long, E-facing gully, barely left (S) of the ridge, with ease.

From the lean standing area on top, the mountain drops off for thousands of feet in all directions, and a little vertigo might set in. Return by the same route, or **Loop** to US Grant Peak or the saddle (13,220 feet) between V-4 and US Grant Peak and descend very steeply to Island Lake. For all routes, go back to the main SE ridge where it is wider at a flat spot just below the summit of V-4.

From V-4 to V-3 and US Grant Peak.

For the NE ridge or **Loop**, go right (E) almost immediately a few feet around the first large rock outcropping and obstacle. It's steep and loose through larger scree, as you hike briefly and directly back to the ridgeline.

At the second big blockage and gendarmes, you may wish to leave the ridge for over 200 feet as you hike very steeply to the left (W), meeting it again near the saddle. Go through the large scree and rocks down, hugging the steep-sloping rib on your right (N) for 150 feet. Contour N and then right (NE) when possible below the rock rib to scramble NE over loose rocks to the ridge and low saddle. Continue NE to US Grant Peak or save it.

To go from the high saddle between these dramatic peaks to Island Lake, descend ESE several hundred feet into the upper basin. Bushwhack the open drainages several hundred feet farther down to the grassy areas for better footing and an easier grade. Go 100 feet to the bigger boulders near the creek, and hike to the right (W) as you hug the large, steep-sloping, partially green boulders at their base. Then follow the little creek 150 feet down to Island Lake, and head S to the right (E) of the lake to catch the solid trail.

96   US Grant Peak

Elevation: 13,767 feet, with 3917 feet vertical gain

Distance: 4½ miles up, 9 miles round-trip

Duration: 4 hours up, 6–7 hours round-trip

Difficulty: Very challenging. Slight crux, steep, busy, solid trail, scrambling, drop-offs

TRAILHEAD

See hike 94 for directions.

ROUTE

See hike 94 and the **Bonus,** and the end of hike 95 for the description. It's only 30 minutes (¼ mile) from the high saddle (13,220 feet) to the top of US Grant Peak. Hike to the right (NNE) once you are on the ridge and boulder up the trail immediately. Stay to the right (E) of the couloirs and spires on the ridge that are facing Waterfall Canyon. Hint: see the cairns and don't get sucked into a steep couloir on the Island Lake side (E) when you come down from US Grant, as you should stay closer to the ridge proper. Go through the stone pillar gateway directly to the main crux on the ridge only a few hundred feet from the saddle. Choose from at least three **Opts** next to each other, where you must climb very steeply about 12 feet up the rock band in the middle of the ridge to a shelf. There are plenty of solid hand- and footholds. The route on the left (W) of the ridge center has a small, flat ledge, halfway up, and might be the best choice. Contour the narrowing ledge to the right (E) of the cliff for about 60–70 feet, and be careful as you encounter looser rock and steep terrain. The first opening to the left (N) in the cliff band reveals a super-steep, S-facing, 20- to 30-foot-wide gully with green, semisolid rock that you must ascend nearly 100 feet back to the high ridge. It's very manageable up the ledges as the gully widens near the top. Finish with some easier bouldering ENE 200 feet to the peak. The summits of V-2, V-3, and V-4 surround US Grant Peak, but this high thirteener tops them all!

Elevation: 13,374 feet; 13,432 feet; with 2782-plus feet vertical gain

Distance: 4½ miles up, 7½–8 miles round-trip **Loop**

Duration: 4 hours up, 6 hours round-trip **Loop**

Difficulty: Very challenging. Long, steep, difficult **Loop** with ups and downs

TRAILHEAD

See hike 94 for directions.

ROUTE

The difficult, high-clearance FS 585 road ends at the creek in the flats. Cross South Fork Mineral Creek immediately (over that convenient log, perhaps) for Rico-Silverton Trail 507, and don't look for informative signs anywhere in this area. Walk ¼ mile SSW, as you cross two smaller creeks close together and then the main one again going W. It's 10 minutes and ¼ mile more S through the woods to the bottom of the very damp South Park and canyon. Follow the trail up the right (W) side of the canyon fairly effortlessly, with a few steeper turns thrown in. Bushwhack to the left (SE) off of the Rico-Silverton Trail before it ends at the Colorado Trail on the crest of the flat ridge (1½ miles from the TH). The main trail gradually bends to the right (SW) in the canyon at about 12,000

Looking at the route up Twin Sisters.

Hoodoos on Twin Sisters.

feet and beyond a creek crossing and the last of the bushes. After the creek, leave the trail and hike left (SE) through the wildflowers, grass, and embedded rock. You will arrive shortly (½ mile) and without difficultly at the wide ridge on top of South Park. Continue more than ½ mile to the left (E, then NE); stay near the middle of the fat rise as you pass several small ponds, and pass little rolling hills just W of the Colorado Trail on the way (NE) to the steep SW ridge of Twin Sisters. The pyramid-shaped (from this angle) summits are up the ridge.

The going will become steeper over the scree, as you walk just to the right (E) 50 feet of a mini cliff band on the bottom of the rugged ridge. Climb the slope straight up NE 100 feet to the base of the steepest part and the only real crux section of the hike. Leave the vertical rock blocking the ridge, and traverse hard to the right (E) for 100 feet or less along the obstacle. Pass the rocky gullies to a steep, grassy, wide gully, and climb the S-facing opening to the left (N) very steeply up through the stable grass and rock. The 500-foot-long gully narrows up higher. Boulder and hug a small rock rib on its right (E) side without trouble, but with some looser, larger scree to the nearby high ridge.

Follow the adequately wide ridge over semi-loose scree. The first nearby high point is at 13,205 feet and is not actually one of the Twin Sisters, so continue NE 100 feet down as the trail thins to a small obstacle. Barely go to the left (N) at the little saddle to contour up steeply 30 feet and directly back to the ridge. The slightly more difficult little alternative has you go straight over the ridge from the saddle. No worries either way. It's fairly stable 250 feet up to the low summit of Twin Sisters (W) and then down over bigger rocks a couple hundred yards NE to the main saddle between the peaks. For Twin Sisters (E) peak almost 500 feet up from the grassy saddle, hike the ridge to the ENE steadily and steeply. Obstacles are easily navigable, as you traverse to the right (E) over looser scree on the thin trail. Hike next to the steeper rock outcropping on the ridge, and go back to the ridge crest near the summit. Return by the same route, or continue a counterclockwise **Loop**, knowing that there will be steeper ups and downs either way.

Stay on the NE ridge for 200 feet longer before you exit and go hard to the right (S) for about 40–50 feet on a thin trail that leaves the rocky ridge. The steep, grassy ledges appear left down the E shoulder to a grassy valley with a small pond below. Follow the super-steep E shoulder 800 feet through the grass and scree down the fading path. The scramble becomes a scree-ski to the bottom, where you arrive in the middle of the grassy valley left (N) of a small pond. See the path ½ mile on the other side of the valley coming down from a small saddle to the NE, and bushwhack to it. Follow the trail down N steeply 40 feet, and hike over flatter terrain 150 feet N on the right (E) side of a very marshy area. Walk N down another steep, short cliffy section, and wind down on the trail to the left (E) through a meadow, where you cross Porcupine Creek less than a mile from the high valley.

Begin a mile-long traverse W through the woods, hiking up and down rises, steeply at times, and across creeks and drainages. First hike through a semi-clearing, where you see huge boulders in a scree field on the left (S). The route travels upward for about 10 minutes, then levels for a short time. Head down through the super-green forest, quite lush and dreamy for Colorado. Climb 75 feet up steeply next to a huge talus pile on the maintained trail (it seems more suited for horses, but even then it would be difficult). No more ups after this part of the traverse, thankfully. Next, descend a series of steep S-turns NW more than ½ mile down the trail on soft ground. Get to a clearing in the trees, and continue steeply down on the rocky trail to the bottom of the slope and the big valley belonging to South Fork Mineral Creek. Take the thin path to the left (SW) just before you would leave the trees for the open valley, and skirt the forest ½ mile in the flats, as you pass the Bandora Mine (on the other side of the valley) to the TH at the end of the road. The path dissipates in a swampy section near the creek crossing at the end of the hike. I hope you weren't planning to keep your feet dry on this hike! Both routes on the **Loop** to the peak are very wet at their bottom portions.

98 Rolling Mountain

Elevation: 13,693 feet, with 3043 feet vertical gain

Distance: 3 miles up, 6 miles round-trip **Loop**

Duration: 3½ hours up, 5–6 hours round-trip **Loop**

Difficulty: Mix of expert-only (from the E ridge, climbing gear not mandatory) and very challenging (from other routes including the SE basin, bushwhacking, super-steep, much scree)

TRAILHEAD

See hike 94 for directions.

ROUTE

The difficult, high-clearance FS 585 road ends at the creek in the flats. Cross South Fork Mineral Creek immediately (over that convenient log, perhaps) for Rico-Silverton Trail 507, and don't look for informative signs anywhere in this area. Walk ¼ mile SSW, as you cross two smaller creeks close together and then the main one again going W. It's 10 minutes and ¼ mile more S through the woods to the bottom of the very damp South Park and canyon.

The E ridge route and SE basin route are both very difficult. For the counterclockwise **Loop** up the E ridge, there are two ways to the bottom of the high ridge proper. You could go W to ascend the E basin for more than ¼ mile a few hundred feet after entering the clearing in South Park, and scramble 200 feet to the left (S) up the right (W) side of the wide rock rib and sloping boulders to the E ridge proper. Or you could go ¼ mile past the E basin on the Rico-Silverton Trail, and traverse the loose scree field N ¼ mile steeply to the E ridge proper.

You will have three successive climbing sections immediately in front of you on the lower, main E ridge; none of them are technical, but all are very steep to free climb up around 200 feet. Stay in the middle of the ridge for the first, most challenging part of the hike, as you need to ascend the sheer rock directly in front of you. You only climb 10 feet or so up each little cliff band, and there are quite a few choices up the tough area. The second little problem has you you hike up a precipitous area while still near the bottom of the E ridge. Move slowly, testing all hand- and footholds carefully, as loose rock dominates the area. The third section is the easiest, so to speak. Climb a few feet to the left (S) or right (N) of what would be the ridge crest for the best way up. Boulder up with better footing once you are above the demanding bottom portion, and follow the red, yellow, then red scree ½ mile up the ridge. There is some pretty fun

Rolling Mountain and a pond from the top of South Park.

bouldering, and the rock is fairly stable on the high ridge. You will encounter a little exposure near the steep summit block.

If you continue the **Loop** down to the SE basin, it would behoove you to follow the ridge 200 feet to the W to the small saddle with Rolling Mountain's lower summit. The hike down the S ridge proper is nearly vertical. Avoid the ultra-steep, tight couloirs directly on the ridge by going 30–40 feet to the right (W) of them, as you scramble S down the steep, loose rocks and scree trails from the saddle 300 feet through the miniscule basin SW of the peak. Hike to the left (SE) of the little snowfield in the tiny basin to a larger saddle. You will be a few feet to the left (N) of the bump on the saddle SW of the summit and at the very top of the SE basin at about 13,180 feet. Go left (ESE) into the large SE basin, and immediately hike to the right (SE) 30 feet down a wide ramp in the rocks and scree to the highest grassy areas. Avoid other animal paths that traverse in the scree to the SE to another ridge and shoulder of Rolling Mountain, and go directly (ESE) ½ mile down the open basin on the steep slopes to the snow pile on the creek. Cross the creek to the right (SE) over unmelted snow (above a super-steep area), and follow whatever paths you find. Hike the scree path from the grass before coming down to cross the creek again, and traverse to the right (SE) down a more gradual slope ½ mile to the Rico-Silverton trail. From the main trail, turn left (NE) for the easy way down. Walk a mile down soggy South Park to finish.

CHAPTER 10

FAR SOUTHWEST TELLURIDE (RICO–CORTEZ–DURANGO)

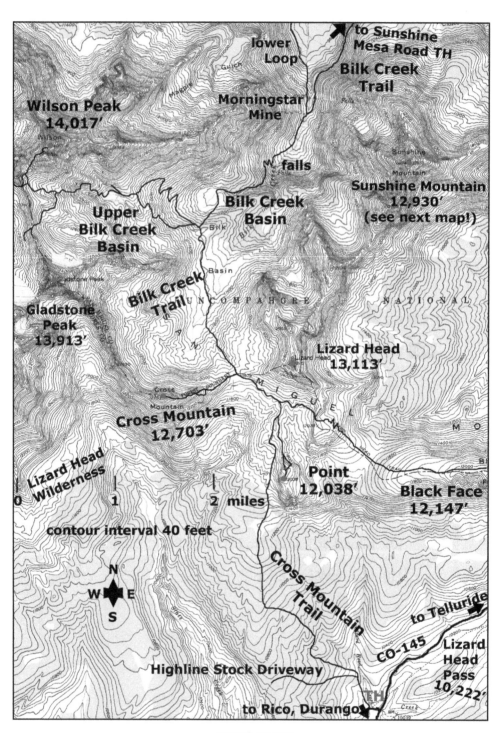

to Sunshine
Mesa Road TH

lower
Loop

Bilk Creek
Trail

Morningstar
Mine

Wilson Peak
14,017'

falls

Bilk Creek
Basin

Sunshine Mountain
12,930'
(see next map!)

Upper
Bilk Creek
Basin

Bilk Creek
Trail

UNCOMPAHGRE

NATIONAL

Gladstone
Peak
13,913'

Lizard Head
13,113'

MIGUEL

MO

Cross Mountain
12,703'

Lizard Head
Wilderness

Point
12,038'

Black Face
12,147'

0   1   2 miles

contour interval 40 feet

N
W   E
S

Cross Mountain
Trail

to Telluride

CO-145

Lizard
Head
Pass
10,222'

Highline Stock Driveway

TH

to Rico, Durango

HIKES 99-103

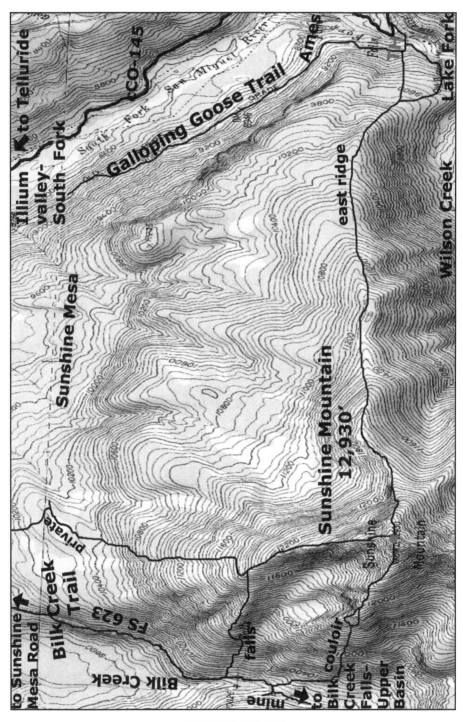

HIKES 77, 102, 104

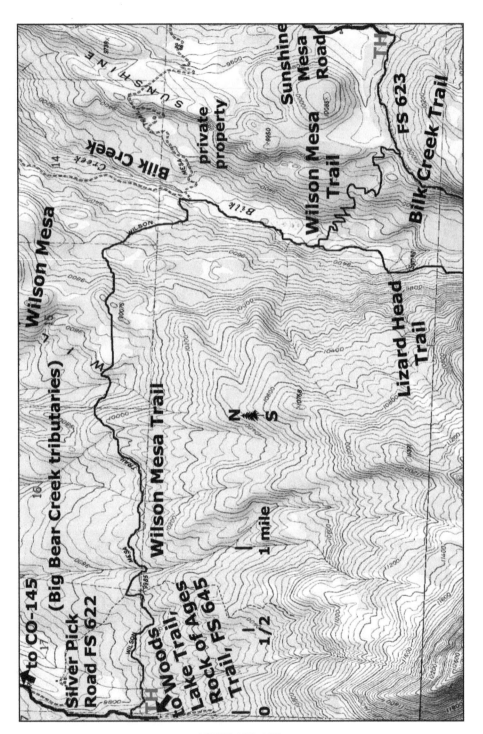

HIKES 102, 105

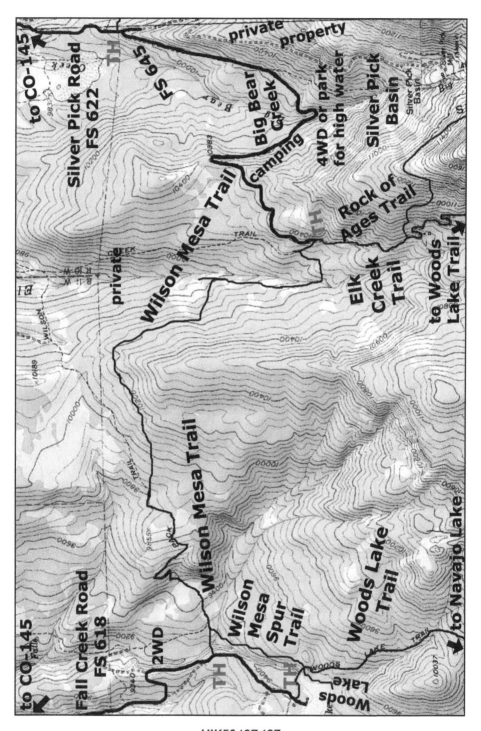

to CO-145

Silver Pick Road FS 622

FS 645

TH

private property

Big Bear Creek

camping

4WD or park for high water

Silver Pick Basin

Silver Pick Basin

Rock of Ages Trail

TH

Wilson Mesa Trail

TRAIL

private

Elk Creek Trail

to Woods Lake Trail

to CO-145
Falls

Fall Creek Road FS 618

Wilson Mesa Trail

2WD

PICK
TRAIL

TH

Wilson Mesa Spur Trail

Woods Lake Trail

to Navajo Lake

LAKE TRAIL

WOODS

TH

Woods Lake

HIKES 103-107

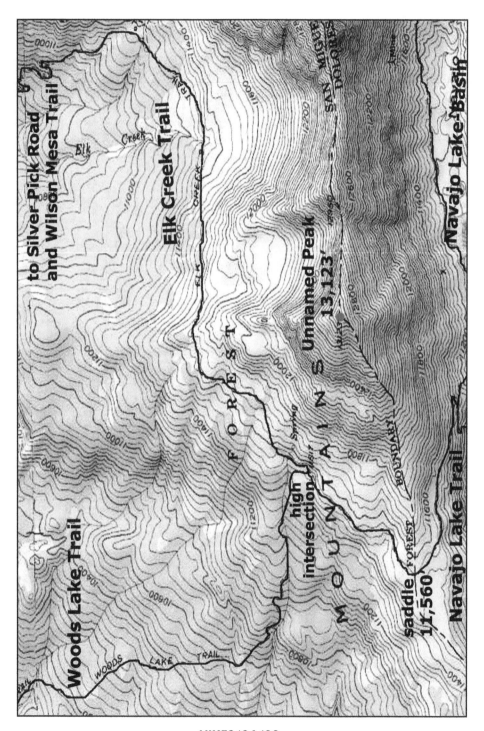

HIKES 106-108

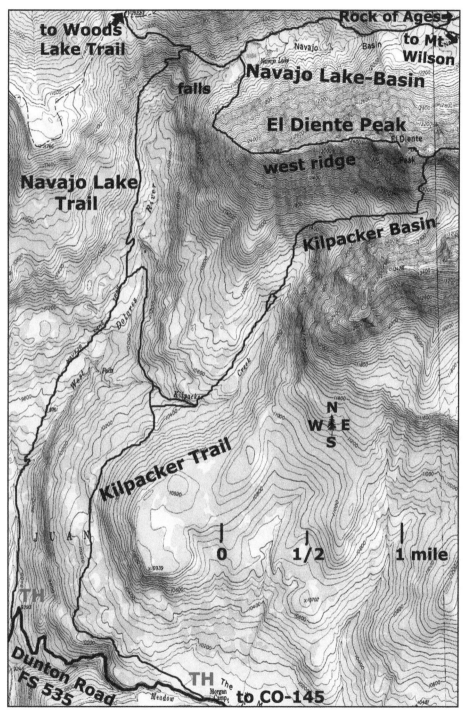

to Woods
Lake Trail

Rock of Ages→

to Mt.
Wilson

falls

Navajo Lake-Basin

El Diente Peak

Navajo Lake
Trail

west ridge

Kilpacker Basin

River

Dolores

West Fork

Kilpacker Creek

Kilpacker Trail

N
W E
S

0   1/2   1 mile

JUAN

TH

Dunton Road
FS 535

TH   The
Morgan
Camp

Meadow

to CO-145

HIKES 106, 108-110

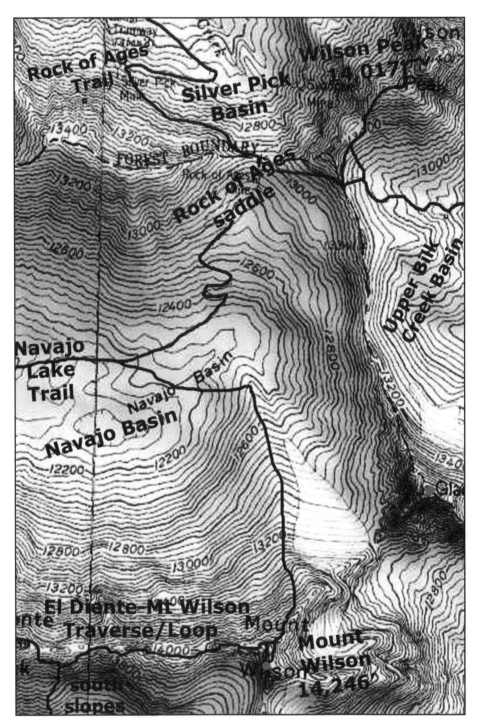

HIKES 102, 103, 108-110

99 Cross Mountain Trail to Point 12,038

Elevation: 12,100 feet, with 2060 feet vertical gain

Distance: 3½ miles up, 8 miles round-trip with Point 12,038

Duration: 1½ hours up, 3 hours round-trip with Point 12,038

Difficulty: Strenuous. Nice grade, simplest walk to spectacular view

TRAILHEAD

Lizard Head Pass. Drive 3 miles W of Telluride on CO-145 Spur, then S 14 miles on CO-145 just SW of Lizard Head Pass to FS 424 road and Cross Mountain TH off to the right (N). Park on the near side of the stream, and walk over the footbridge or drive across the water to the nearby sign. Drive 11 miles from Rico or 94 miles (more than 1½ hours) from Durango, taking US-160 W to Mancos and going right on CO-184 W 17 miles, then right on CO-145 almost 49 miles to the TH on the left (N) 2 miles before (W of) the top of Lizard Head Pass.

ROUTE

Walk up the left (W) option of two paths from the sign 100 feet, and take the narrow horse trail to the right (E) of the next fork and sign ("Groundhog Stock Trail"). Continue NW, then N up through an old evergreen forest more than 2 miles to near tree line. Go ½ mile up around the corner (NE) above the trees, and see the trail in front of you traversing the steeper slope. Hike N another mile to the end and intersection under Lizard Head Peak.

• **Bonus:** Hike to the bump, Point 12,038, S of the intersection under Lizard Head without difficulty. Turn left (E) 200 feet down (S) on Cross Mountain Trail from the intersection. Flat rocks and a narrow path mark this TH on the E side of the trail. If you can find the path, bring the family on this one, as it's only ½ mile and 10 minutes more to the top. Walk left (E) of the little bump to the obvious little ridge trail, and go left (SE) directly under the short cliff band 75 feet (an **Alt** scramble is directly up and down the 40-foot-high rock obstacle on the ridge crest). Once you are around it, hike more steeply to the right (SW) 35 feet up the loose, black pebbles to the ridge. There is no trail from here to the marker on top, but the grassy, wide summit is only a hundred yards or so away. I don't care what they say: it may not be much compared to the surrounding behemoths, but you're undeniably on top of something!

Elevation: 12,703 feet, with 2665 feet vertical gain
Distance: 4½ miles up, 9 miles round-trip
Duration: 2–3 hours up, 4–5 hours round-trip
Difficulty: Very challenging. Steep scramble, scree, drop-offs

TRAILHEAD
Lizard Head Pass; see hike 99 for directions.

ROUTE
See hike 99 for the description. Directly below Lizard Head at the end of Cross Mountain Trail, go left (NW) at the intersection on Lizard Head Trail 505 toward the Wilsons. Walk ½ mile NW down easily to the saddle between Lizard Head and Cross Mountain, leaving the trail at the second post by heading left (W). Hike ¼ mile ESE up to a position below the steepest section on the E ridge of Cross Mountain, and stop at a cairn to the left (S). This is the easiest of three routes to the high ridge. Take the path left (S) of the main ridge about 100 feet, traversing over to a small shoulder extending S. Scramble steeply 150 feet WNW up the scree or a few feet to the left (W) of the shoulder to the main ridge.

The second route begins at the steepest part below the crux, as you follow the white rock band on narrow, broken ledges carefully around to the left (S) 60 feet. In a few minutes you see cairns that go steeply to the right (N) up the fairly stable rocks 75 feet to the main ridge. The most difficult, direct route is to climb 35 feet straight up the extra-tight, steep chute at the bottom of the steeps and crux directly on the ridgeline. Only thinner hikers can make this work up the solid rock (going down the chute would be even harder). When possible, get out and up to the left (S), then immediately back to the right (N) for more solid

footing. You will gain the slightly wider ridge in a few feet going WSW. Once you are on the narrow high ridge, it's an easier walk up W a couple hundred yards over loose talus to the peak.

Lizard Head from Cross Mountain Trail.

101   Lizard Head Trail 409 to Black Face

Elevation: 12,147 feet, with vertical gains of 1887 feet, 2100 feet **Loop**

Distance: 3¾ miles to Black Face, 7½ miles round-trip; 9 miles round-trip **Loop**

Duration: 2½ hours up, 4 hours round-trip **Loop** or not

Difficulty: Strenuous. Steep parts, horse trail, popular

TRAILHEAD

Lizard Head Pass; see hike 99 for directions. For Black Face, start almost 2 miles E of Cross Mountain TH to the top of Lizard Head Pass and the Lizard Head TH on the N side of CO-145 (15 miles from Telluride). For the clockwise **Loop**, leave a bicycle at the Lizard Head TH just W of the outhouse, drive to the Cross Mountain TH, and ride (or walk) downhill 2 miles to your vehicle after the hike.

ROUTE

See hike 99 for the first part of a great clockwise **Loop**. From the end of Cross Mountain Trail, continue right (E) at the intersection under Lizard Head Peak. It's an easy traverse on Lizard Head Trail 409 for ½ mile, then down steeply SE ¼ mile to a big meadow and low point on the ridge. Begin ascending a couple hundred feet through the trees ESE, and stay on the trail more than ½ mile steadily up to the high point of Black Face (visible from CO-145). Reverse directions below to finish the clockwise **Loop**.

For Lizard Head Trail 409 to Black Face from Lizard Head Pass, go NE from the parking area and outhouse on the official trail 1½ miles, traversing down through aspens across from Trout Lake easily, then abruptly up the very steep horse trail for a mile and along thirteen switchbacks to the NW. Wilson Meadows Trail continues NW. Go left (WSW) 1 mile more up through trees on the main trail to the Black Face ridge and summit.

Bilk Creek Trail 408

Elevation: 10,150 feet, with vertical gain of 400 feet (Morningstar Mine); 10,750 feet, with vertical gain of 1000 feet (Upper Bilk Creek Falls); 12,200 feet, with vertical gain of 2440 feet (Upper Bilk Creek Basin)

Distance: 3 miles one way, 6 miles round-trip; 4 miles up, 8 miles round-trip; 5 miles up, 10 miles round-trip

Duration: 1 hour one way, 2 hours round-trip; 1½ hours up, 3–4 hours round-trip **Loop**; 3 hours up, 5–6 hours round-trip **Loop**

Difficulty: Mix of moderate (easy, wide horse trail) and strenuous (steeper, longer to Upper Bilk Creek Basin)

TRAILHEAD

Gate at the top of Sunshine Mesa Road FS 623. Drive 5 miles W of Telluride on CO-145 and less than 3 miles left (S) up South Fork Road (63L) through Illium. Go right (W) at Camp Illium and across the river up Sunshine Mesa Road FS 623 (63J) for 3 miles S along the valley, then steeply a mile (2WD high-clearance) up switchbacks to Wilson Mesa, Lizard Head, and Bilk Creek trails between and past two old buildings (rough road and a plethora of no-trespassing signs on both sides) near the gate.

ROUTE

A sign at the TH and gate says "Wilson Mesa 421, Bilk Creek and Lizard Head 2 miles and Silver Pick Road 4 miles." After almost a mile of easy walking on Bilk Creek Trail 408 (FS 623), the narrower Wilson Mesa Trail 421 goes down to the right (WNW), and the main trail continues 2 miles to Bilk Creek and the Morningstar Mine vestiges. Be careful crossing the creek, and walk to the left (SSW) to stay on the trail to the falls and Upper Bilk Creek Basin. Go back the same way, or hike ½ mile farther up the creek to the falls. You can also **Loop** to Wilson Mesa Trail 421 and back up to the TH without the falls (or Bilk Creek Basin) by going right (N) instead of left once you are on the W side of the creek next to the mine.

To visit the falls, head left (SSW) past the Lizard Head Trail 505 sign, between the old miners' cabin and the old truck trailer along the creek, and proceed ½ mile up steeply to the attractive set of waterfalls. To pass both falls to Upper Bilk Creek Basin, continue ½ mile SW on the solid trail above the switch-

Upper Bilk Creek Basin to Lizard Head.

backs to an intersection and a post on the left (E). Going left (S) takes you to Cross Mountain Trail in 2 miles near Lizard Head Pass. Turn right (W) at the juncture on a wide trail that zigzags easily ½ mile WNW up to a small lake in gorgeous Upper Bilk Creek Basin. To hike to the little cabin at the top of the basin, or to reach Wilson Peak or Navajo Basin, bushwhack more steeply W past the little lake to catch the thin trail to the left (S), right (N) of the stream, 75 feet through grass a few hundred feet up to the top of Upper Bilk Creek Basin. Wonderful rock patterns and a superb view make this an exceptional (and somehow overlooked) destination. The saddle between Wilson and Gladstone Peaks is W from the cabin and slightly to the right up a steep, 300-foot, rocky scramble.

Once you are back at Morningstar Mine, cross the water to take the easy road NE down to the TH in 45 minutes (3 miles), or take the **Loop** going down left (W) of the main creek N, remembering there will be an uphill section to finish. For this, stay on the W side of the creek and pass the sign where it's 1½ hours (3½ miles) to the TH by this route. Hike 30 minutes (1 mile) easily N down to the first open meadow, posts, and creek. Continue ½ mile N to the intersection with Wilson Mesa Trail 421 and a sign that says "Sunshine Mesa 3–Silver Pick Road 5." Go right (E) a couple minutes, over the creek, and steeply more than 1½ miles ESE up to the main trail by staying on the most worn, obvious path, avoiding private property. Turn left (E) on FS 623 for almost a mile to finish on the flat trail.

Elevation: 14,017 feet, with 3667 feet vertical gain

Distance: 4 miles up, 8 miles round-trip

Duration: 3½ hours up, 5–7 hours round-trip

Difficulty: Very challenging. Steeper, last pitch can be hazardous if ice lingers, scrambling

TRAILHEAD

The most popular, shortest route from Rock of Ages Trail 429 is 9 miles W of Telluride on CO-145 (6 miles E of CO-62/Placerville), then S in a 2WD high-clearance vehicle and possibly into 4WD up Silver Pick Road FS 622 4 miles toward Silver Pick Basin to a three-way fork. Take the middle road slightly right (SW) 2½ miles more, then turn right (W) on FS 645 past the parking lot and **Opt** TH (restroom) for Wilson Mesa Trail 421. Drive more easily 2¼ miles to the TH, crossing Big Bear Creek at 1 mile if the water isn't too high. Wilson Mesa Trail 421 shares this section of road, so be mindful of hikers, bikers, and folks camping along the traverse.

ROUTE

For the famed SW ridge route where most routes meet near the saddle between Gladstone and Wilson Peaks, start S ½ mile up from your vehicle and FS 645 on the shared part with Elk Creek Trail 407. Just before (N of) the switchbacks on Elk Creek Trail 407, turn left (E) onto Rock of Ages Trail 429, and hike more than ½ mile up and around a shoulder and more SE up the right side of Silver Pick Basin. Follow the obvious trail and signage a mile S, then roads by old mining debris, avoiding private property to the E as the old closed trail converges. Hike the right (W) side of the basin another mile on a final traverse SE to the Rock of Ages saddle at 13,020 feet. See the continuation of the trail that goes SSW a mile steeply down to Navajo Basin or the other way on a traverse ¼ mile E to the Gladstone Peak–Wilson Peak saddle around an impassible obstacle on the high ridge. Walk E to the saddle, where you meet the scramble route coming from Upper Bilk Creek Basin for the SW ridge route.

From the saddle, go right (N) up the side of Wilson Peak on an ascending traverse well below the high ridge. You can see the route S of the ridgeline through the scree. Start E of cliffs and follow the cairns up broken, slickrocks ½ mile to the high ridge proper at nearly 13,500 feet. It's loose and steep but looks more difficult from afar. Follow the ridge NE a few hundred feet to the

Hikers navigate
the steep gullies
to Wilson Peak.

13,900-foot bump that almost no one who has done any research mistakes for the actual peak. Descend very steeply about 50 feet from the left (N) side of the ridge. Go one at a time, watching for falling rock and scree. Next, scramble immediately and very steeply to the right (E) 75 feet up the narrow, rocky chute, just left (N) of the actual ridge, with good holds all around. Continue more easily on the ridge crest a hundred feet NE to the unexpectedly large peak area.

TRAIL NOTES

....
....
....
....
....
....
....

104   Sunshine Mountain

Elevation: 12,930 feet, with 4000 feet vertical gain

Distance: 3 miles up, 6 miles round-trip

Duration: 3½–4 hours up, 6–7 hours round-trip

Difficulty: Very challenging. Scramble, very steep, loose scree, peaceful

TRAILHEAD

From Telluride, drive 3 miles W of town on CO-145 Spur, then left (S) on CO-145 7 miles to Ophir Loop. Turn sharply to the right (W) opposite the road to Ophir, continue NW down FS 625 for almost 1 mile, take a hard left (SE) onto Ames Road, and follow it a mile to the tiny, historic town of Ames. Turn left (S) after the first big curve onto the first steep dirt road, and park up at the corner (4WD maybe), or below the switchback in a rocky clearing on the left (E) side of the road. Or it may be best to park below the fairly steep road and simply walk 5–10 minutes (½ mile) up to the TH, where you'll see a sign at a turn for Galloping Goose Trail.

NOTES

There are at least six options up Sunshine Mountain's highly exceptional shoulders and ridges, but only the shortest, easiest one is described here. This mountain is a lot of fun to climb, even though most people seem to be more attracted to the neighboring fourteeners in the San Miguel Range. The summit is not to be confused with the fourteener Sunshine Peak near Lake City, or Telluride's other distant cousin in the San Juans, also called Sunshine Mountain, closer to Capital City, at 13,321 feet.

ROUTE

Walk to the right (W) past the signage on the road corner onto the Galloping Goose Trail, and head SW down ¼ mile and across the bridge over Lake Fork Creek. Up on the very first big turn 50 feet past the creek, leave the main trail that goes N to follow a much steeper path to the left (SW) a couple hundred feet. Within moments that path fades, and you bushwhack ½ mile across other animal trails to keep going uphill W on the most distinct path that goes directly up through the thinning forest. A hundred yards below the high ridge, go slightly left (WSW) to get to the ridge more quickly than by following the slope up. Gain it now or gain it later! Stay on the thin, steep, high ridge NW for a while

The author is glad to be on Sunshine Mountain and not Lizard Head.

(2 miles to summit), as you walk among thicker trees; on occasion you must go to the right (N) of the ridge crest slightly without any trouble. Hint: keep the smaller, dual-peaked San Bernardo Mountain in sight (nearby to the S, directly across from Wilson Creek) for most of the ridge walk. It's 2½ hours from the high-clearance dirt road and parking to tree line. Follow the rocky, grassy hill on or very near the E ridge itself, as the route is obvious over more level terrain before the summit block.

About 500 feet below the peak you will get to a more difficult section on the scree-covered, steep ridgeline; there is a narrow, loose gully on the right (N) that you can climb, but it would be safer to climb the wide, brief rock rib 10 feet to the left (S) of the gully. Go directly WNW up the bigger, more solid rocks closer to the ridge crest for 25 feet or so to the top of the super-steep section. Approach the peak 25–30 feet from left (S) of the ridge for 200 feet up the trail to the nearby high ridgetop and summit.

Elevation: 10,430 feet, with vertical gains of 670 feet from Sunshine Mesa TH, 530 feet from Silver Pick TH, 1030 feet from Woods Lake TH

Distance: Around 7 miles from Sunshine Mesa TH to Silver Pick TH; 6 miles from Silver Pick TH to Woods Lake TH

Duration: At least 3 hours from Sunshine Mesa TH to Silver Pick Road, 6 hours round-trip; 2½ hours from Silver Pick Road TH to Woods Lake TH

Difficulty: Strenuous (long traverse, some steeper walking or biking) or moderate if you are only going one way from Silver Pick Road TH to Woods Lake TH (Fall Creek Road FS 618)

TRAILHEAD

Choose from three options: the TH described in hike 102, the **Opt** TH described in hike 103 (Silver Pick Road), or drive to Woods Lake 14 miles W of Telluride (2 miles SE of Placerville) on CO-145 and almost 9 miles S up Fall Creek Road FS 618/621 with decent signage. This third option involves a high-clearance 2WD road with decent signage and a washboard effect to finish the last mile on FS 621; an **Alt** TH is ½ mile before (N) of Woods Lake.

NOTES

If you take this marvelously lengthy trail from E to W, start from Sunshine Mesa down to the Bilk Creek drainage, and then go up to Wilson Mesa under Wilson Peak. You eventually traverse past Silver Pick Road FS 622, Big Bear Creek (on FS 645), and Elk Creek. The route ends at two different THs within ½ mile of each other at Woods Lake.

Arrange a shuttle vehicle if you need to, or return the same way whenever you wish on Wilson Mesa Trail 421, or from Silver Pick Road FS 622. Motorcycles, bikes, horses, and hikers are allowed on most of the trail, so be alert, but don't assume it will ever be overcrowded. The solid trail rolls through the woods and never leaves tree line on the long traverse.

ROUTE

The TH on Sunshine Mesa is also the TH for Bilk Creek Trail 408 and Lizard Head Trail 409. Walk almost a mile on the wide, old road FS 623 to the sign for

Wilson Mesa Trail 421 on the right (WNW). Take this down steeper turns on the solid trail for 1½ miles, and cross Bilk Creek over the log bridge. Go right (N) at the intersection and signs when you get to the flats over the water, and parallel the creek on its left (W) side through a big valley for a mile. Look back up the large clearing to the S to see Sunshine Mountain and Lizard Head. Hike away from the creek and up the trail to the left (W) at a sign and intersection, as the going becomes steeper back into the woods.

It's ¾ mile from Bilk Creek up to a wonderful, small lake in the woods, with excellent reflections of Wilson Peak and the aspens. Head right (N) around the lake on the trail, and hike a couple hundred feet through a very small clearing in the woods. When that closes up, you arrive at an orange gate and wooden fence with barbed wire. Go through the gate (leaving it how you found it) to the wide trail on the other side. Continue up directly to a pretty large meadow and clearing. Follow the wooden posts and trail W down through the pasture, trying not to trip over the cows in this broad area (4½ miles from Sunshine Mesa TH, 2½ miles to Silver Pick Road). Now cross one of many streams and creeks. In 200 feet you will find two more little water crossings. The trail is more level as you hike W up and down minimally, with more aspens starting to mix with the evergreens. About ½ mile past the last water crossing, pass over the next stream and hike down a bit and through an old wooden fence. It's a mile from that last stream to the next one, which is in a thin drainage; it might be the second to the last creek crossing before Silver Pick Road FS 622 depending on the flow and time of year. The trail rolls on as you continue to the W through the tight woods and ascend through a small clearing. Cross the final arm of Big Bear Creek, and head up slightly ¼ mile to Silver Pick Road FS 622. Return the same way to Sunshine Mesa for an excellent day hike or press on.

Cross Silver Pick Road FS 622/TH and restroom to the sign and wide path for Elk Creek Trail 407 and Wilson Mesa Trail 421 to Woods Lake. Wilson Mesa Trail 421 shares this road grade, FS 645, with Elk Creek Trail 407. Drivers can park on Silver Pick Road FS 622 or the TH for Rock of Ages Trail 429 at the end of FS 645 more than 2 miles W, as you ascend the road steadily and cross Big Bear Creek (if not too high) at the halfway point.

From Rock of Ages TH, see the sign pointing to the left (S) for Elk Creek Trail 407 and to the right (W) for Wilson Mesa Trail 421 and Woods Lake Road (3½ miles). Go right (NW) and down 200 feet on the thin trail, and ignore a side trail (N) as the route is steeper 300 feet to the creek. Cross Elk Creek where possible and walk for a mile in the flats N. Pass through little clearings and back across a small waterway, which you follow on its right (E) side. A sign on a tree to the right (E) of the irrigation ditch indicates that you must go left (W) to

Wilson Peak and fall-tinted aspens reflected perfectly from the Wilson Mesa Trail.

the steep trail on the other side of the water again. (The trail that continues along the ditch is on private property.) Hike up steeply W a couple hundred feet, and contour NW, then W a mile around a ridge while you are still in the woods. Then it's all downhill (1½ miles) to Fall Creek Road FS 618/621. Continue down bigger meadows, aspen groves, and switchbacks, as the going is sometimes fairly steep on the narrowing trail. See a sign down in a large clearing. A spur trail will take you to the left (SSW) across the clearing ¾ mile up to Woods Lake, where it's ¼ mile to the TH and large parking area. You can also go to the main road in a hundred yards or so if you continue on the trail W instead of taking the spur at the sign. Walk to the left (SSW) ½ mile up the road to the parking lot below Woods Lake if you didn't park on the road next to the **Alt** TH.

TRAIL NOTES

Elevation: 11,560 feet, with 2160 feet vertical gain

Distance: 4 miles up, 8 miles round-trip; 13 miles round-trip **Loop**

Duration: 2 hours up, 3–4 hours round-trip; 5–7 hours round-trip **Loop**

Difficulty: Strenuous. **Loop** or not, steep, wide horse trail, easy traverse near tree line, long **Loop**

TRAILHEAD

Woods Lake 14 miles W of Telluride (2 miles SE of Placerville) on CO-145 and almost 9 miles S up Fall Creek Road FS 618/621. This involves a high-clearance 2WD road with decent signage and a washboard effect to finish the last mile on FS 621. You'll find restrooms and a large parking area.

ROUTE

The parking lot is before Woods Lake, and the trail is less than 100 feet past the main parking area on the left (E) side of the road. Saunter on this easily past the lake (E side, noting the reflection of Dolores Peak), and go into the trees directly to a four-way intersection and sign. From here, Lone Cone Trail 426 goes 2 miles right (W). The Wilson Mesa spur trail goes ¾ mile down to the left (N), and Elk Creek Trail 407 (Woods Lake Trail 406, too) goes S straight up the sometimes soggy path.

El Diente Peak from Woods Lake Trail.

Hike up Woods Lake Trail 406 from the four-way intersection at Woods Lake, leaving the aspens behind as you continue through evergreens. The path is wide to start, muddy depending on the season, and okay for horses, though bikes and motorcycles are not allowed as the trail lies within the Lizard Head Wilderness Area. Cross several small creeks and two separate log bridges going ESE. It takes about 1½ hours (2½ miles) to get to a vertically challenged cabin near an arm of Muddy Creek, with steep switchbacks below and above the cabin. Then it's ½ mile E to tree line, a meadow, and the high three-way intersection and sign.

Elk Creek Trail 407 goes to the left (NE), and Woods Lake Trail 406 continues another ¾ mile to the right (SW) more easily to a wide saddle at 11,560 feet between Dolores Peak to the W and an unnamed thirteener up the steep ridge to the E. From the saddle you will have stunning views of Navajo Basin, Gladstone Peak, Mount Wilson, and El Diente Peak's colossal W ridge. It's another mile on the connecting trail SE down to Navajo Lake (not visible). Go to the lake, or return down Woods Lake Trail 406, or **Loop** counterclockwise with Elk Creek Trail 407 and Wilson Mesa Trail 421 to Woods Lake. See hike 107 to continue the **Loop**.

TRAIL NOTES

....
....
....
....
....
....
....

107   Elk Creek Trail 407

Elevation: 11,730 feet, with 2330 feet vertical gain

Distance: 3½ miles up, 7 miles round-trip; 11½–13 miles round-trip counterclockwise **Loop** from Woods Lake

Duration: 2 hours up, 3 hours round-trip, 5–7 hours round-trip **Loop**

Difficulty: Strenuous. Steeper near the Elk Creek drainage, some scree, hunters in season, long **Loop**

TRAILHEAD

See hike 103 or 106 for directions.

ROUTE

You can pick up the trail from the top of Woods Lake Trail 406 at the three-way intersection, or from the official Rock of Ages/Elk Creek/Wilson Mesa TH near Silver Pick Road FS 622. From the sign, three-way intersection, and high point of both trails, continue to the left (NE) on Elk Creek Trail 407, as you contour steadily near tree line ½ mile through and around big talus fields. See Little Cone to the NW. The Elk Creek Trail is narrow, but posts and cairns help keep you on the traverse another 1½ miles E, as you cross several streams with some steep but brief up and down action. There are great views of Wilson Peak in front of you to the E, behind the long, gnarly ridge that separates Silver Pick Basin from Elk Creek Basin (closer). When you get to the signs, one crooked old one says "Big Bear Creek 3; Silver Pick Rd 4." Avoid any other paths, and follow the trail down to the left (NE) semi-steeply into a few trees for ¼ mile. Cross a branch of Elk Creek to the E into the clearing, and walk 75 feet up to a little sign on a scree-covered road. Walk a mile more easily with some steeper parts N down on the wide trail into the woods to the Rock of Ages TH and intersection with Wilson Mesa Trail 421. Silver Pick Road FS 622 is more than 2 miles to the right (E) on FS 645 from the signs, and the **Loop** continues down to the left (NW) on Wilson Mesa Trail 421. See hike 105 for the details back to Woods Lake. Enjoy!

Fall-tinted Little Cone from Elk Creek Trail.

108   Navajo Lake Trail 635

Elevation: 11,154 feet, with 1815 feet vertical gain

Distance: 5 miles up, 10 miles round-trip; 1-plus mile more to the high basin and 3 miles to Rock of Ages saddle from Navajo Lake

Duration: 2 hours up, 4 hours round-trip

Difficulty: Strenuous. Steeper above and below Navajo Lake, solid trails, some traffic, much talus

TRAILHEAD

Drive 3 miles W of Telluride on CO-145 Spur, 12 miles S on CO-145 to Lizard Head Pass, and 5 miles more SW to the Dunton Road FS 535 turnoff on the right (N, then SW). From Durango, go 27 miles on US-160 W to Mancos, right 17 miles on CO-184 W, and right 44 miles on CO-145 N. From Cortez, drive 56 miles N on CO-145. From Dunton Road FS 535, 2WD 5 miles up the dirt road and continue almost 2 miles past Kilpacker TH (N). Go W down a steeper section of Dunton Road FS 535 with a washboard effect, and to the right (N) into the large parking lot by the sign next to the creek. No restrooms at either TH.

ROUTE

No bikes, motorcycles, or hovercrafts are allowed on the trails here as they fall within the Lizard Head Wilderness Area. From the sign at the N end of the parking lot, leisurely walk the wide Navajo Lake Trail 635 on the right (E) side of the West Dolores River for 1 mile. Go past the first bridge (Groundhog Trail) to the second, superbly built wooden bridge. Cross the river W and hike up steeper turns for ¼ mile to big, open, rolling meadows. Walk a mile NE by the multitudes of skunk cabbages (nature's toilet paper, if they are in season) and hike up the gradual slope. Notice a small waterfall through the trees just before you enter another set of pines. You quickly enter another big clearing with patches of high, green flora. Walk ½ mile NNE through the huge meadow and up to the little Kilpacker Trail sign and intersection.

Continue ½ mile N into the woods on Navajo Lake Trail 635 and up a couple steeper turns. It's about 45 minutes (1 mile) N to the next clearing from the Kilpacker Trail sign, as you follow nice terrain on a steady incline. Immediately into the high meadow, you see the little falls coming out of Navajo Basin to the right (E). The path gets decidedly steeper for ½ mile, as you climb the final switchbacks to a sign ("Woods Lake 4 miles, Navajo Lake ¾ mile") and intersection. This is above the cliff band and waterfall protecting Navajo Basin. Stay

Navajo Basin/Lake to Dolores Peak.

on the main trail, as you descend 10–15 minutes and cross large scree fields en route to the beautiful lake. Meander, check out the reflections, and return down or continue on the trail through the scree up the left (N) side of the basin. Hike through much scree steeply to the top of the high basin (12,200 feet) in Navajo, where many people climb to the right (S) to get to Mount Wilson (see hike 110 for more upper basin details), or to the left (N) for Wilson Peak (see hike 103).

TRAIL NOTES

....

....

....

....

....

....

....

Elevation: 14,159 feet, with 4150 feet vertical gain

Distance: 6 miles up, 12 miles round-trip with W ridge **Loop** or not; 3½ miles one way, 7 miles round-trip Kilpacker Trail 203

Duration: 5 hours up, 7–8 hours round-trip; 1½ hours one way, 3 hours round-trip

Difficulty: Mix of very challenging (from Kilpacker Basin, super-steep, endless scree, solid trail, definite exposure—ice axe and crampons if early or late in the season, helmet advised), expert-only (from all other routes, super-steep bouldering, sustained exposure), and moderate (Kilpacker Trail 203 one way and back or a counter-clockwise little **Loop** with Navajo Lake Trail 635, nice slopes, big meadows, steep for a short time, creek crossings)

TRAILHEAD

See hike 108 to locate the Kilpacker TH, following the ¼-mile side road to a small grove of trees in a big clearing on the right (N) of Dunton Road FS 535.

NOTES

El Diente Peak is actually visible to the NE across the big meadow from Kilpacker TH, unless of course you begin this hike in the dark of early morning, as many people do. El Diente translates to "the tooth," but it is much more than that (tooth of what exactly?)!

ROUTE

Walk the easiest part of the day 2½ miles on Kilpacker Trail 203, as you start off in the flats and go NW through huge, rolling meadows. You actually lose a bit of elevation on the walk N, then NE into trees and to the Kilpacker spur trail going E ("El Diente Peak route" sign). This trail is a few hundred feet before you would cross Kilpacker Creek, and people sometimes miss this sign when there is still snow on the trail. If you miss the trail, you can go down to nearby Kilpacker Creek and follow the attractive creek and narrow path S of the creek ½ mile up E to meet the other trail.

To stay on Kilpacker Trail 203 to the end (1½ miles) and continue with a **Loop** (3 miles to Navajo Lake TH) or not, take the main trail from Kilpacker Creek NW and traverse steeply down to the West Dolores River. Climb a couple hundred yards SW up from the West Dolores River in the clearing, and hike down to the left (SSW) on Navajo Lake Trail 635 more easily to finish a counter-clockwise **Loop**.

To continue up Kilpacker Creek to Kilpacker Basin and El Diente Peak, go ½ mile up the spur trail somewhat more steeply to the creek crossing. Go N over Kilpacker Creek wherever possible, and walk to the NE up the obvious trail 1 mile along a big meadow. See Kilpacker Falls far up the valley (NE), and go to the lower falls in the same direction, which you can hear but cannot yet see.

Keep on the main path and route through the meadow and stay left (N) at two forks. The second fork is in a small clearing, where you go to the left (N) on the main trail and hike very steeply a few hundred feet above and left (N) of the lower falls. A more difficult choice is to go straight at the small clearing and fork ¼ mile to the base of the lower falls to get a closer look. They are quite nice actually, but from there you'll have to scramble to the left (W) of the falls up the very steep ledges and broken rock for about 25–30 feet to get back to the main trail directly above. Stay on the main trail, which is far to the left (W) of the upper falls, ¼ mile through the semi-loose talus. A big cairn next to the low flora marks the beginning of the long scree hike. Look for the trail up the middle of a small rise after you do a short traverse 100 feet to the right (E). The trail is extremely steep but solid for 100 yards, as you climb to the left (NNE) up the tiny rise and go through the last of the shrubs and trees. Continue to the right ½ mile on the trail with better walking NE, then E up broken-pottery scree world (not as hard or tedious as some would have you believe).

Traverse the smaller middle basin ¼ mile E around the corner to the upper basin, where you follow the flats a few hundred feet more E. See cairns and a solid but slippery path to the left (N) up the super-steeps SE of El Diente's monster summit block. Climb the ultra-steep trail and S slopes, and go a few feet to the right (E) of the first mini-cliff band 75 feet up the steep, brown, scree-covered slope. Then go N a couple hundred feet up lighter rock to the much bigger second cliff band. The talus turns into a bouldering path, as you hike directly to the cliff band and go to the left (W) at its base to contour 200 feet a bit more easily until the cliff ends. Turn sharply to the right (NE), and climb the major rock rib steeply 200 feet up larger rock and ledges on its left (W) side.

See cairns straight up the wide, boulder-filled gully to the left (NNW) of the long rock rib that will take you to the rock towers above known as the Organ Pipes. Technically the Organ Pipes are just to the W and E on the high ridge crest, but from this angle the pipes stretch to the S and to the intersection with the Mount Wilson traverse. Call it how you see it. Scramble the gully

Close to the ridge near El Diente Peak.

steeply N another 250 feet to the intersection and the traverse route (100 feet below the high ridge) that goes to either Mount Wilson or El Diente Peak.

Go left (W) on the rocky trail to El Diente once you are directly under the Organ Pipes. The slope is very steep, but the bouldering on the wide path and traverse is okay and fun. Cairns lead you 250 feet to a steep, fairly well-traveled gully (75 feet or so long) SE of the peak. It's at least 15 minutes (¼ mile) more to the peak from the notch at the top of the gully where you will have your first taste of the high ridge. Here you have glorious views within the Wilsons and are surrounded by ultra-steep slopes. Cairns direct you to the N and the other side of the narrow ridge crest. Take the path 50 feet down to a tiny saddle and semi-crux. You will be near the top and E of the last 25–30 feet of a long, narrow, snow- and ice-filled couloir that faces Navajo Basin. Climb 30 feet to the top of the couloir by going barely to the left of the snow and ice in the couloir itself up semi-stable rock S to the nearby high ridge. Don't even pretend to cross the icy gully without proper equipment, or you will be sorry and very sad! Some fairly exposed bouldering with better footing is all that separates you from your goal 150 feet away. (Can I get a hell yeah?)

The demanding traverse to Mount Wilson is more than 2 hours long. Return the same way carefully, or try the vastly more difficult **Loops** going in

El Diente's infamous west ridge.

both directions on the high ridge. For the Class 4 W ridge route from the grandiose summit of El Diente, go W only 150 feet before your first major crux. It seems there are just enough cairns on the W ridge to entice you into going a little farther. Your first move is to go 25 feet right (N) of the ridge crown just before it cliffs out in all directions. Very carefully, down-climb a short section (30–40 feet) and go directly back to the ridge crest, keeping it in sight the whole way. You will have to turn around and face the slope, as the rock is exceedingly steep and slick down a few ledges, which get smaller closer to the ridge. Check your holds and make no mistakes.

Immediately following the crux is the knife's edge on the ridgeline. Walk the highly exposed area W for 50 feet, then barely go to the left (S) when possible and scramble along very steep rocks back to the ridge proper and the next obstacle. Go left (S) down the steep gully 15 feet or so. You are around yellowish rock as you contour to the right (W) and back to the ridgeline in 35 feet with loose rock everywhere. Hike immediately between the next yellow towers, barely left (S) of the ridge proper, and go N back to the nearby high ridge immediately by climbing up steep rock. Another huge, yellow rock tower appears S when you arrive at a tiny high point on the ridge. From there, the main ridge will be more obvious and with better walking down to a 13,082-foot bump. See

Kilpacker Falls.

and take the little ramp that goes 30 feet down the left (S) side a few feet off the ridge and more easily back to the ridge crest. Then climb 10 feet or so up a very short, steep part just to the right (N) of the ridge from a small saddle. Go directly to the ridgetop above the rock, and continue without any difficulty for ½ mile while still only ½ mile from the summit.

Follow cairns to the left (S) around the 13,082-foot high point on the ridge for the best descent. One super-steep spot near the high point makes you think you might be lost, but it is actually not bad. Move down the steep, tight gully for 25 feet to a flat spot, and go to the right (NW) on the more solid trail. Contour around and just under the high point, and hike up a few feet to the actual ridge again. Stay on the ridge 200 feet more where it breaks into a NW shoulder route and a S shoulder route. Continue NW down the steep shoulder ½ mile until near the end, where it begins to cliff out. Traverse to the right (N) on a faint path (if any) through the scree just above the cliffs and gullies 150 feet to a low spot on the steep slope. Then hike through the loose rock 200 feet hard to the right (NE) to a sizable weakness in the cliff. Go left (N) and down the wider slope very steeply 100 feet, then traverse a steep line to the right (NE) on the most prominent scree path 250 feet down to tree line at the W end of Navajo Lake. (Also see hike 108.)

Elevation: 14,246 feet, with vertical gains of 4946 feet from Navajo Lake TH, 4146 feet from Kilpacker TH, plus 400 feet from Dolores River back to Kilpacker Trail 203 (arrange shuttle vehicle between THs)

Distance: 7–8 miles up, 16 miles round-trip **Loop** or not

Duration: 6–7 hours up, 10–13 hours round-trip **Loop** or not

Difficulty: Expert-only. Highly exposed, very long **Loop**, tons of scree, scrambling. Ropes not mandatory, helmets recommended, Class 4

TRAILHEAD

See hike 108 to locate the Kilpacker TH, following the ¼-mile side road to a small grove of trees in a big clearing on the right (N) of Dunton Road FS 535 for the high ridge traverse route and **Loop** from El Diente Peak. See hike 108 for Navajo Lake TH, and see hike 103 (Rock of Ages TH) for Mount Wilson alone.

ROUTE

Take the most direct route to this peak from Navajo Basin by following Navajo Lake Trail 635 and reversing the description below. To complete Mount Wilson **Loop** counterclockwise, start at Kilpacker TH and climb to the Organ Pipes under El Diente Peak (see hike 109). **Bonus:** traverse to the left (W) and hike up to El Diente Peak in less than 30 minutes from the Organ Pipes.

Contour to the right (E) to go to Mount Wilson, and follow cairns ENE 150 feet to the nearby high ridge and intersection with the mostly dangerous N slopes route. The more popular cairned route drops 200 feet to the right (S) and traverses 150 feet under the Organ Pipes on the ridge, then regains the ridge just as steeply going N. This long drop is not necessary. You'll have bigger fish to fry along the ridge, so let's not make mountains out of molehills (so to speak!). Go either way, but the more stimulating **Opt** has you stay on the ridgeline past the first nearby little section of towers easily 100 feet or so before you go just to the left (N) directly to a notch in the center and below the huge towers blocking the ridge. There is a convenient little opening in the rock to slip through from the left (N) to the right (S) side. Now leave the ridgetop, and go right (S) to scramble the semi-loose but very feasible, wide, steep gully for 60–70 feet. Go left (E) around the base of the huge rock obstacle extending from the ridge, and

The high ridge from El Diente makes you wonder whether this was the right hike!

pick up the cairned main route. Traverse for 30 feet before you have more choices. Stay on the solid traverse path 100 feet and head N up to the ridge steeply 20 feet or so, or try this **Opt**: Go directly to the high ridge by ascending very steeply just to the right (E) of the large towers you just traversed under and N up a short (30–35 feet), semi-loose, thin gully directly to the ridge crest. Routes meet and you walk over the thin ridge somewhat more easily a couple hundred feet E up to a small high point (14,100 feet).

The ridge is slender as you boulder down 150 feet in the center down the larger rocks to the next saddle (13,980 feet) and a major crux (¼ mile from peak, ½ mile from start of traverse route). Once you are at the saddle, face the sheer wall directly on the ridge crest. A few feet to the left (N) is a technical route. Climb up ultra-steep ledges 100 feet NE by starting only 6 feet down to the right (S) of the actual ridge. See a large cairn on the rock ledge near the bottom, and follow more cairns up to the ridge proper with solid hand- and footholds.

The rock on the entire hike and climb is surprisingly solid considering the pitch, altitude, and location within the usually loose San Juans. If you are on top of this crux area and are coming from Mount Wilson, go slightly to the left (SW) before the technical climb directly on the ridge crest at the W end of the razor's edge. Carefully walk the wafer-thin ridge 75 feet to the E; it is 2 feet wide or less, with about as much exposure as you can imagine, shearing away for thousands of feet on both sides of you! Walk 50 feet more easily to rock columns in the middle of the 14,000-plus-foot saddle, where you hike right (S) and

The high ridge from Mount Wilson to El Diente Peak.

traverse 150 feet to the E well below the ridgeline on the barely visible trail. At the end of the easy grade, climb up a W-facing, rocky gully 50–60 feet to a small notch and saddle just N of Mount Wilson's summit. From the notch, the long traverse route meets the N slopes route from Navajo Basin, and you finally get to see what all the hoopla is about. There is no easy way up the steep, rocky summit block, last major crux, and final 60–75 feet.

For those not thrilled with extreme exposure, the **Opt** route to the left (E) of the high ridge crest may be preferred, but it is more slippery than the ridge. About 20 feet down NE from the traverse route intersection, go right (E) from the saddle (left of ridge proper if facing the peak) and find your way very steeply S up the loose, rocky ledges. There are a few traverses that work well to the top. Or follow the exceedingly narrow ridge over 60 feet S up to the summit. Pass over some tough spots with more solid rock, including the most difficult part of the high ridge: a giant chockstone as big as a small car. This big boulder, split by cracks, is best approached by going directly over the lowest part. Pull yourself up the first crack (best for taller folks, or carefully use a spotter). To the right of the chockstone is a technical move, and to the left is a doable but fairly difficult move around the rock.

The peak is quite attainable once you are on top of the major obstacle. How's the weather on this peak, the highest in Dolores County, Lizard Head Wilderness, and San Miguel Mountains? It's also the second highest peak in the San Juans and the sixteenth highest peak in the state—no big deal.

The Organ Pipes near the high ridge.

Altitudinous, indeed! Relish the moment, but I'm sure you are already thinking about the return down either route to the little notch you were just on to the N. Unless you have arranged to be picked up by helicopter, I'm afraid you will need to hoof it down a long way before you are near tree line again!

For the **Loop** into Navajo Basin, say good-bye to Kilpacker Basin, the airy traverse route and summit, and descend to the left (N) once you are safely back to the notch on the high ridge N of the peak. See cairns in the scree, and traverse 75 feet across the top of a very steep gully, usually filled with snow, just left (W) of the N ridge. Go 150 feet in the direction of Gladstone Peak (NE) to another small notch in the high ridge. Hike left (N) away from the ridgeline as the ridge turns into a shoulder going N into Navajo Basin. Go steeply more than ½ mile N down the rocky, cairned path over the widening, rocky, grassy shoulder. What remains of the Navajo Glacier is just to the right (E) of the shoulder. The footing is better as you boulder down through the larger rock, but on a steeper slope. Follow cairns a few hundred feet to a solid trail at the top of the grassy areas on the N-facing shoulder, and move down the grassy bottom of the shoulder a few hundred feet more NW. Cross the creek bed over flat rocks, and head W directly to the main trail going up (NE) to Rock of Ages Saddle or down a mile W to Navajo Lake. Walk more easily to the giant cairn in the middle of the high basin, and follow the trail next to it. Enjoy the wildflowers, lake, and views down the grassy basin, with some embedded rocks and boulders becoming more prevalent. Return up the very steep hillside toward Rock of Ages TH, or finish up past big cairn columns, moving through scree fields on the right (N) side of the basin. The rock trail comes down before the lake and turns to dirt as the flora surrounds you. Unequivocally momentous! Many Thanks!

Acknowledgments

Thanks to ChartTiff Enhanced Geographic Data, Norwood Ranger District, KOTO radio, Telluride Mountain Club (especially Tor Anderson), Andrew Sawyer, Mary Beth Mueller-Tukman, Jon Tukman, Dawn Burgess, David Emery, Christopher Shields, Bill Burgess, Erin Leveroni, Michelle Montague, Rob Huber, Neil Matthews, Tim Young, Patrick Ray, Glenn Oren, Michael Schoo, and editor Mindy Fitch.

Index

CPSIA information can be obtained at www.ICGtesting.com
Printed in the USA
BVOW10s1804050913

330370BV00003B/3/P